Cinema i

1896 - 1931

Cinema in Leicester
1896 - 1931

David R. Williams

Foreword by Sir John Plumb

Heart of Albion Press

Contents

Cinema in Leicester 1896-1931
David R. Williams

ISBN 1 872883 20 6

Cover design by David Taylor

Printed in England by
D.A.R. Printing (0664) 424785

Heart of Albion Press
2 Cross Hill Close, Wymeswold,
Loughborough, LE12 6UJ

Acknowledgements

Many people have contributed to the successful conclusion of the research for this book. In particular, I would like to thank Sir John Plumb for gracing the book with a genuine foreword; the staff of the following organisations: Bishop Street Reference Library, Leicester, both in the 1950s and the 1990s; Durham City Reference Library; British Library, Colindale; Sheffield Polytechnic Art and Design Library; Mitchell Library, Glasgow; Leicestershire Records Office; British Film Institute Library; Steve England of the *Leicester Mercury* archives; Dr John Florance of Radio Leicester; Miriam Gill for her researches into cinema buildings in Leicester; Brian Hornsey for unselfish contribution of his own research; Mervyn Gould for his valuable information on Loughborough cinemas; John Barnes of the Museum of Cinematography, St Ives; John Wilkinson, National Secretary of the Cinematograph Exhibitors' Association; S.C. Scott of Fara Estates; J. Moore of the Moore/Scarborough circuit; J. and H. Moorhouse of the H.D. Moorhouse circuit; C.E. John Aston; Bernard Bates; Carl Jennings, David Robinson and Philip Hall for their valuable assistance with photographs; Brian Johnson for checking the text and pointing out some anomalies; Rob Foxon; G. Henshaw; J. Leader; Mrs Godby; Mrs L. Hall; I. Patterson; W. Shenton; Mrs F. Tomlinson; R.N. Trubshaw for enhancing the text with valuable observations and for guiding the book through publication; and Rosemary Williams for her support and her assistance in the research over the last thirty-five years.

Foreword

Sir John Plumb FBA

When I was nine or maybe ten, I looked forward with intense excitement to Saturday afternoons when I and my friends would hurry, as fast as one of our mothers would allow, to the Olympia Cinema. Once we were in the queue, she disappeared. We pushed and shoved with impatience and surged through the doors as soon as they opened. I believe it cost sixpence, and then there was two pence for the okey - a rather chewy ice cream served in greaseproof paper.

We roared with laughter as comic followed comic but really what we were waiting for was Tom Mix or Pearl White, in an interminable serial which always left us at a moment of high drama - Pearl strapped to a railway line, about to be sliced to bits by a large bellowing train, or Tom Mix galloping towards an impenetrable rock face pursued by howling Red Indians keen on his scalp. Next week, the train would be diverted to another track, and the indomitable Mix outwitted the Indians by pressing an unobtrusive knob which made the rock face part like the waters of the Red Sea. Mix vanished. Participation was total and we came out drained of emotion, to be collected by mother and duly returned home speechless and absorbed. Little did we or our parents realise that we were participating in one of the greatest revolutions of the twentieth century. By 1919, film had ceased to be a novel excitement; mine was the first generation to absorb it into our culture as a natural part of the world.

David Williams brings these early years of Leicester's cinemas vividly alive. His scholarship is profound and no scholar of film history will need to do this work again. It is all here - a valuable contribution not only to the history of film but also to the social history of the world.

At the same time that film was developing and becoming ever more technically adroit, so was the wireless: a little behind film perhaps, but growing dramatically. As one grew out of the

Saturday matinee, many boys and girls took to the crystal set and the headphones. In the end, of course, these techniques fused and television was born. From 1920 to 1980, the evolution of communication was profound; it reached for the stars and captured them.

The ease with which men, women and children accepted these techniques stems from our biological nature, although this is rarely stressed. The human eye, unlike that of most mammals, can register colour in all its exquisite variety. Furthermore, the human eye was designed to catch and follow movement so that even the most adroit camouflages in nature might be detected by the hunter's sharp eye. Human eyes were designed for a colourful, moving world. Reading, on the other hand, was never natural to man - it was hard to learn, and required patience and strict discipline for the eye to move along a straight line for hours at a time unrelieved by colour (although the value of illustration in books was quickly realised).

The twentieth century has witnessed a massive explosion of colour and movement in its culture - and so the early history of film when written with the perception and scholarship of David Williams has become of far greater importance than simply stirring the nostalgia of men and women of my age - immensely pleasurable though that is.

John Plumb
Christ's College, Cambridge
December 1992

Chapter One
The Beginnings

Like so many great industries, cinema had a humble beginning. The desire to make pictures move had manifested itself in the numerous optical toys of the Victorian era, in the huge dioramas of Poole and Dyson, and in the photographic motion studies of Muybridge and Marey. Whoever invented the original moving picture device, it is indisputable that the first public cinematograph performance was given by the Lumière Brothers in the Grand Café of the Boulevard des Capucines in Paris on December 28th 1895.[1]

The first British performance at which the public paid for admittance was given by Monsieur Felicien Trewey, representative of the Lumière Brothers, at the Marlborough Hall of the Polytechnic in Regent Street on February 20th 1896.[2] Such was the secrecy of the device that the projector was hidden behind an all encircling screen. Admission was one shilling (5p).[3]

The cinematograph was not a Lumière monopoly, however, because on the same day Robert W. Paul was giving a private performance of his Theatrograph at the Finsbury Technical College.[4] This rivalry continued later when the Lumière show was exhibited in the smoking lounge of the Empire Music Hall, Leicester Square on March 9th

A poster for the 1896 Paris Lumiere shows.
Courtesy of National Film Archive.

1896 and the R.W. Paul show was produced as a counter-attraction at the neighbouring Alhambra Music Hall a fortnight later.[5]

The First Leicester Cinematograph Performance

The move from Leicester Square to Leicester took about six months. The first documentary evidence for this is a playbill for the Empire Theatre, Wharf Street, for the week beginning November 9th 1896.[6] This announced the 'Animatoscope', with a footnote that it was 'the first appearance of this marvellous show in Leicester'. The Animatoscope was a projector manufactured by John Ottway and Sons of St John's Road, Clerkenwell, London, and it resembled Paul's Theatrograph in many respects.[7]

The programme included amongst its items 'Waves Dashing Over Dover Pier', 'The Emperor of Germany Reviewing his Troops', 'Yarmouth Fishing Boats in Full Sail' and 'Niagara Falls'. These films were all about 80 feet in length. Their projection time depended very much upon the hand-turning of the projector, but standard times are usually calculated on the scale of one foot per second, or sixty feet per minute.

There is no indication to suggest which showman was in charge of the performance, but he must have bought his films from R.W. Paul and Birt Acres, since all the ones mentioned were in either the Paul or Acres film lists.[8]

The next 'living picture' display in Leicester was, in fact, R. W. Paul's own Theatrograph, which he himself introduced. The performance took the place of the usual trans-formation scene at the Royal Opera House pantomime,

AMUSEMENTS.

ROYAL OPERA HOUSE SILVER-STREET.
Sole Lessee & Manager, Major J. A. Winstanley.
TO-NIGHT and Every Evening will be produced on a Scale of Magnificence never before attempted in Leicester. MAJOR WINSTANLEY'S FOURTH PANTOMIME entitled
"THE FORTY THIEVES."
Powerful Company, Full Chorus and Grand Corps de Ballet.
THE MARVELLOUS ANIMATOGRAPHE
Costly and Magnificent Dresses New and Splendid Scenery and Effects
The Pantomime produced by Mr. W. H. Hall, and under the Personal Supervision of Major Winstanley.
MORNING PERFORMANCES, Saturday December 26, and every Saturday at 2 o'clock:- Children half-price to all matinees and Friday evenings only.
Doors open at 7 o'clock, overture at 7.5. Early door. Silver street at 5.30. Carriages at 10-15. Saturdays half-an hour earlier.

The *Leicester Daily Post* advertisement for December 24th 1896.

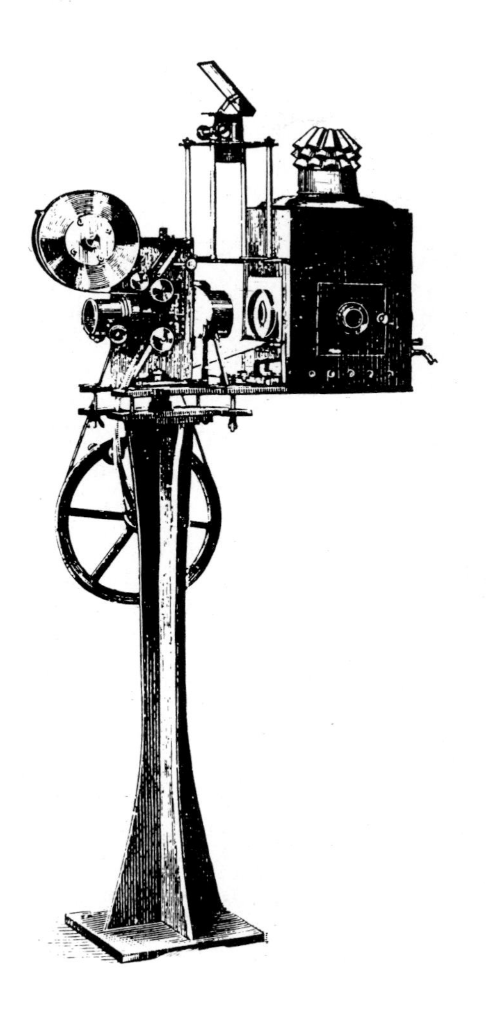

Ottway's Animatoscope of 1896.
A machine similar to this was used at the Empire during the week of November 9th 1896.
Courtesy of Barnes Museum of Cinematography.

The Forty Thieves, which opened on December 24th 1896.[9]

'By some ingenious contrivance,' wrote the *Daily Post* theatre critic, 'it shows animated photographs; and scenes such as Blackfriars Bridge, the arrest of a bookmaker, Conjuring, Brighton Beach, the Derby of 1896, and sea-bathing are displayed, so to speak, to the very life'.[10] 'For five or ten minutes, attention is rivetted by the startling disclosures of this machine.'[11] The sea-bathing item was shot near Lisbon by H.W. Short on his Iberian tour for Paul in the summer of 1896. Also included in the programme, a correspondent to the *Leicester Mercury* recalled in 1924, was 'A Sea Cave near Lisbon'. The letters editor prints this quotation from his review of the programme that he says he wrote 28 years earlier: 'The Animatograph brings astonishment to those who have seen nothing like it before. The view of the cave on the coast of Gallacia showing the waves rolling into a beautiful cave splashing up on the rocks and receding in a mass of foam, is simply wonderful.' The same show was given at Loughborough in the play 'Muldoon's Picnic' in January 1897.[12]

In the first week of February there was a change of programme at the Royal Opera House in Leicester. Amongst the new films reported were 'The March Past of the Gordon Highlanders' and 'The Turn Out of the Fire Brigade', both of which were 'vigourously cheered'. The *Leicester Daily Mercury* indicated also that two local views had been added: 'A scene showing the Clock Tower, and a photograph showing the removal of snow from the Market Place after the recent storm. The latter is very succesful indeed, as good an example of photography as the march of the Gordon Highlanders, or the starting of the Fire Brigade.'[13] The fire brigade depicted was that of Newcastle-upon-Tyne filmed in October or November 1896.[14]

The Tivoli kept up with other houses of entertainment by 'securing Dr Birteno's Cinematograph' on January 18th.[15] However, the programme of live items on the Monday evening was so long that the film had to be omitted. After a fortnight's run, the pictures were due to come off, but the non-appearance of a variety artiste, Ada Fawn, caused them to be retained for another six nights. The content of the programme is not described by the theatre columnist, but he does offer a word of criticism. 'The pictures were spoiled to a certain extent by the excessive vibrations that seem to be the fault, more or less, with all

Still from a film thought to be R.W. Paul's 'The Arrest of a Pickpocket' which was shown in the Opera House programme in December 1896.
Courtesy of Science Museum. Crown copyright.

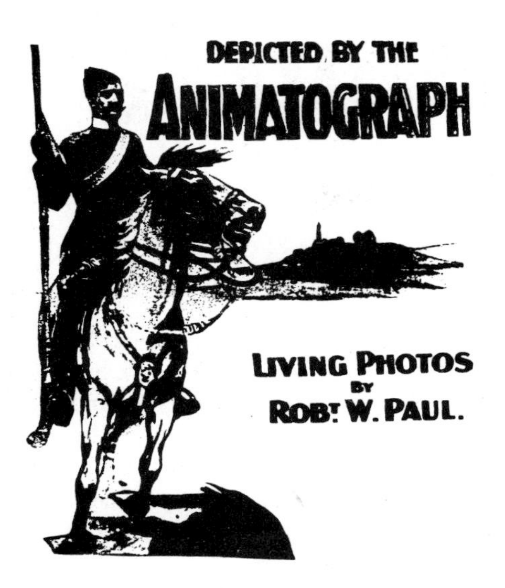

animatographs'.[16] An advertisement in *The Era* magazine of January 30th 1897 lists the programme as 'a motor car race, operatives leaving a Lancashire mill, the sea washing over the rocks at Blackpool, and a military church parade.'

Film performances came to be called 'the flicks' because early film projectors had no cut-off shutters to disguise the intermittent movement of the film strip. Even when shutters were fitted, a showing speed of 16 or 18 frames per second was not really fast enough to eradicate flicker. Hand-cranked cameras could also add to the flickering pictures by giving variable exposures to successive frames.

In March 1897 the Floral Hall was the venue for the Leicester Jubilee Commemoration Exhibition. The hall had originally been built in 1876 as a skating rink, but it had been fitted up by the management to accommodate circus performances and exhibitions. It had a floor space measuring 212 by 83 feet. The Jubilee Exhibition included all the latest novelties, and amongst them were the Theatrograph and a number of Edison Kinetoscopes.

The Kinetoscope was not entirely new to Leicester. A shop displaying

Top: Early R.W. Paul advertisement.
Courtesy National Film Archive.

Bottom: The Tivoli.
Drawing by author from a photograph.

MOVING PHOTOGRAPHS.

MESSRS. JOHNSTON & WORMALD'S

THEATROGRAPH

(R. W. Paul's Patent).

Read the following Press Notices we have received:

SCARBOROUGH POST—

"The Theatrograph is in charge of Messrs. Johnston and Wormald, of London, whose manipulation of this wonderful invention is to be commended."

HUDDERSFIELD ADVERTISER—

"At Mr. Rowley's Empire this week one will see the most marvellous of modern inventions, the Theatrograph: a treat to the young and old, and a puzzle for us all."

We have received excellent notices from the following papers:

SCARBOROUGH GAZETTE
JEDBURGH POST
SCARBOROUGH ADVERTISER
BERWICKSHIRE ADVERTISER
JEDBURGH NEWS
SELKIRK NEWS
DURHAM ADVERTISER
DALKEITH ADVERTISER
&c., &c., &c.

The Public Ponder in a Queer, Quizzical, Quandary, over these wonderful and amusing animated photos.

HOW IS IT DONE?

COME AND SEE FOR YOURSELVES!

"A heavily-laden passenger train is seen approaching Calais Station, followed by the hurry and bustle of a busy railway platform. Porters hurry about, helping the alighting passengers with their luggage."

"Another most realistic picture shows H.R.H. Prince of Wales's horse, Persimmon, winning the 1896 Derby, with the *finale* of an excited, surging crowd flooding Epsom Downs after the conclusion of the race."

Selections from the following subjects will be shown at each Exhibition, viz.:

Gordon Highlanders leaving their Barracks.
SS. Columbia at Rothesay Pier.
Calais Railway Station.
Blackfriars' Bridge, London.
Father Playing with his Children.
Chirgwin, the White-eyed Kaffir.
Bank Holiday Scene, Hampstead Heath.
The Prince's Derby.
Gardener Burning Weeds.
Children Playing on Sea Shore.
Moonlight Scene on Brighton Beach.
Chirgwin Impersonating a Scotchman.
Rough Sea at Ramsgate.
Engineers' Workshop.
Cave Scene on Atlantic Coast.
Bathers, South of Spain.
Devant Conjuring.
Street Scene, Westminster, London.
Travesty from Trilby.
Etc., etc., etc.

MOVING PHOTOGRAPHS.

Frequent Exhibitions daily of the Theatrograph in an annexe of the Commemoration Exhibition.

ENTRANCE NEAR THE WORKING DAIRY.

MOVING PHOTOGRAPHS.

ADMISSION—

Afternoons = = = = = = 6d.
Evenings = = = = = = = = 3d.

A page from the catalogue for the Jubilee Exhibition held at the Floral Hall 1897.

several linked with cylinder phonographs had been opened at 31, Gallowtree Gate sometime in 1895. This continuous-loop moving picture device, showing 50 feet of 35mm film, was given its first British demonstration in London in Oxford Street on October 17th 1894. Spectators could each look through the eyepiece to view three scenes for sixpence. The experience would have lasted about two minutes, but the thrill of observing that Carmencita, the Spanish beauty, towards the end of her dance 'gives the least little bit of a kick, which raises her silken draperies, so that her well turned ankles peep out', may have made it all worthwhile! [17]

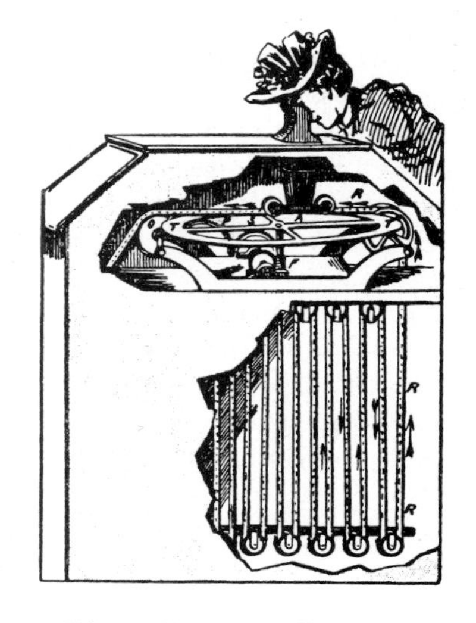

Edison's Kinetoscope Viewer.

The Theatrograph was advertised as belonging to Messrs Johnston and Wormald using R.W. Paul's patent. Some of the films included had been shown in Leicester before at the Royal Opera House pantomime, but others were new. A selection of scenes was shown at each demonstration. Most of the films were R.W. Paul productions, but 'Travesty from Trilby' was an Edison production originally made for the Kinetoscope, and 'Gardener Burning Weeds' was produced by French pioneer film-maker Georges Méliès.

Later the same year, the Floral Hall staged a 'High Class Minstrels Show' which included 'Herr A. Rosenberg's Jubileeographe or Animated Pictures with all the latest improvements.'[18] The critic reported that the scenes of the Royal Diamond Jubilee Procession were of 'conspicuous clearness, and without the

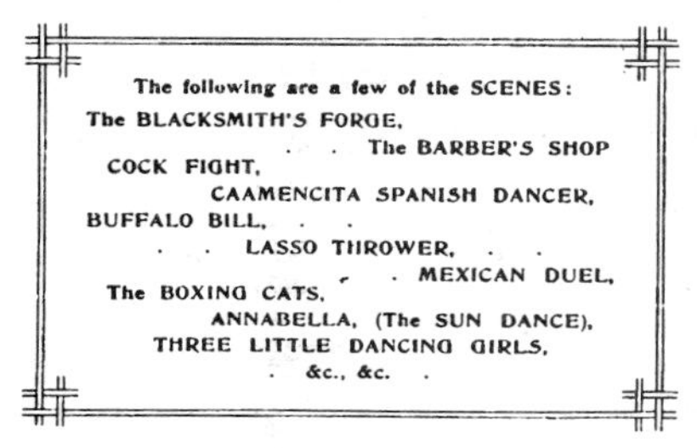

The following are a few of the SCENES:
The BLACKSMITH'S FORGE,
. . The BARBER'S SHOP
COCK FIGHT,
CAAMENCITA SPANISH DANCER,
BUFFALO BILL, . .
. . LASSO THROWER, . .
. MEXICAN DUEL,
The BOXING CATS,
ANNABELLA, (The SUN DANCE),
THREE LITTLE DANCING GIRLS,
. &c., &c. .

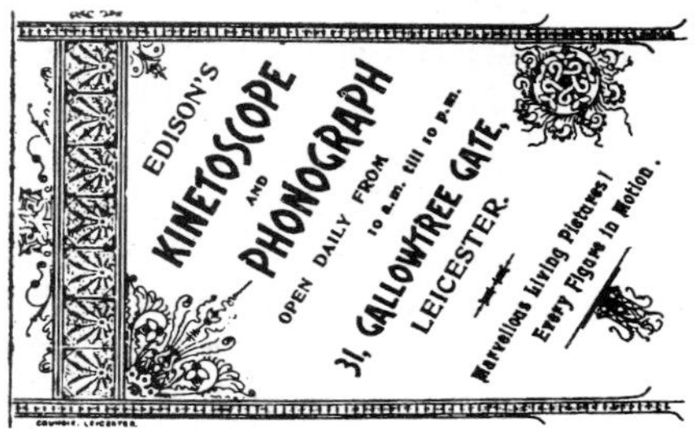

Courtesy Leicestershire Record Office.

unpleasant noises and vibration attendant on some of its kind.'

This particular device, as John Barnes' brilliant research demonstrates, was the invention of Newcastle engineer William Routledge, patented under the name of Kineoptograph in 1896. Augustus Rosenberg and William McDonald were responsible for its commercial exploitation[19], and the name 'Jubileeograph' was simply a commercial reference to Queen Victoria's Diamond Jubilee celebrations.

ROYAL OPERA HOUSE,
SILVER STREET, LEICESTER.

Proprietor & Manager .. .. Lieut.-Col. J. A. WINSTANLEY.

Lieut.-Col. J. A. WINSTANLEY'S
FIFTH LEICESTER PANTOMIME,
ENTITLED—
Robinson Crusoe
WILL BE PRODUCED
MONDAY, DECEMBER 27th, 1897.
(Written expressly for this Theatre by FRED LOCKE.)

TO BE FOLLOWED BY
Mr. W. R. PAUL'S
ANIMATOGRAPH,
From the Alhambra Theatre, London.

TO CONCLUDE WITH
THE HARLEQUINADE,
Iuvented and arranged by Mr. R. Ernest Liston.
ENTITLED:
"THE CLOWN'S NIGHT OUT."
Scene—A QUIET APARTMENT ON FROG ISLAND.

From a ninety-page booklet for the 1897 pantomime.
Courtesy Barnes Museum of Cinematography.

In the 1897 pantomime *Robinson Crusoe* at the Royal Opera House, the Theatrograph was once more included in the attractions. The film performance took place after the pantomime and before the traditional Harlequinade. 'The machine is no novelty in Leicester,' said the reviewer, 'but with a constant supply of up-to-date pictures, it is always interesting.'[20] The titles included 'Scenes from the Geisha' and pictures of the Queen's Jubilee already seen at the Floral Hall. There were also some local scenes: 'The First Meet in the Present Season of the Quorn Hunt

Rosenberg's Cinematograph of 1896. A similar machine was used at the Floral Hall in 1897. *Courtesy of Barnes Museum of Cinematography.*

at Kirkby Gate and at Gartrie Hill', 'Some Scenes in Granby Street', and 'The Clock Tower, Leicester'. A scene of snow clearing in the Market Place, Leicester, a pantomime rehearsal, and London Road shot in February 1897 are included amongst the films in Paul's catalogue. These were taken the year before when Paul himself was in Leicester with his Theatrograph.[21] 'Lumière's Magnificent Animated Photographs of the Queen's Jubilee Procession' were shown at the Theatre Royal in January 1898 after a musical comedy called 'Morocco Bound'.[22]

Professor Barron's Beograph

In the first week of January 1898 a machine described on the playbill as 'Professor Barron's Beograph' shared top billing with 'the important and welcome return of one of Leicester's favourites, Mr Charles Chaplin.' The name of Professor Barron does not appear singly in John Barnes' *The rise of the cinema in Britain*, but there are references to the Barron brothers, who were theatrical showmen during 1897 and 1898. They used an Edison Projecting Kinetoscope, but no doubt hit upon the name Beograph and the slogan 'Life-size pictures' because this was how 'The American Biograph' was being advertised.

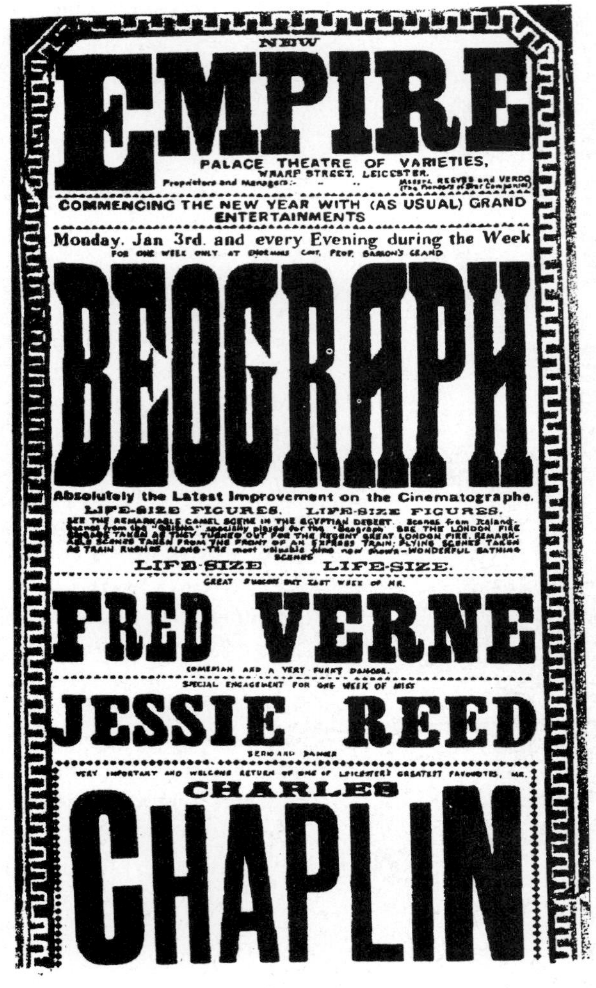

Part of a playbill for The New Empire Palace of Varieties for the week of January 3rd 1898. *Courtesy David Robinson Collection.*

The content of the programme is described on the poster and it is possible to construe the origins of some of the titles. 'The Remarkable Camel Scene in the Egyptian Desert' could be one of several of the 40 feet scenes shot by H.W. Short in Egypt in March and April 1897 for R.W. Paul. 'The Geisha', described as 'specially played for the Beograph', is listed in R.W. Paul's 1897 catalogue as 'specially played for the Animatographe'. 'The London Fire Brigade Taken as they Turned Out for the Recent London Fire' could be any one of a number of catalogued fire brigade scenes. The reference to a 'recent' London fire is almost certainly a piece of timely showmanship. 'Bathing Scenes' were also pretty common fare in film catalogues; they added the human touch to the ubiquitous 'Rough Seas at . . .'. Scenes taken from the front of railway engines were known as 'Phantom Rides'. They were very popular and, with no more details, this item on the programme is very difficult to identify.

The existence of the poster is important, too, because it makes references to 'films' rather than 'animated photographs' or 'pictures'. The term was not used in newspaper reviews in Leicester until 1901.

The Cinematograph and the Showmen

Throughout the next few years the basic pattern of cinematograph shows was very similar. Each year there would be the May Fair run by an enterprising showman, Pat Collins, who was noted for his Electric Theatre Booths. The Opera House did not include a film show in its 1898 pantomime, but it was possible to see films at the Pavilion and the Floral Hall in Belgrave Gate and the Temperance Hall in Granby Street, at various times in the year.

The projector still had no special name, just as it had no special home. The Brightograph appeared in the Bright Lights Show,[23] the Edisonograph was at the Floral Hall,[24] and the Vitagraph at the

Two frames from an American Biograph 70mm film (shown actual size). *Courtesy Barnes Museum of Cinematography.*

Tivoli.[25] In April 1898, the American Biograph was introduced to Leicester.[26] This name became synonymous with film projectors for some years. It was announced as 'The Perfection of Animated Photography', and it suitably impressed the *Daily Post* critic who wrote, 'It is an American invention, for which it is claimed with good grounds, that it is an elaboration and perfection of the 'living photographs' with which we have now become familiar. The pictures are life-size and there is little of the unpleasant and trying jarring that spoils other machines.'[27] The American Biograph used 70mm film, which was taken and projected at 40 frames per second.[28]

The show at the Floral Hall was so well-received that it was retained for a further week with two performances an evening, a novelty in Leicester. 'In the present instance', wrote the reviewer, 'the first house which extends from 6.30 to nearly 8 o'clock is ostensibly for the purpose of offering the children an opportunity of seeing what is without doubt one of the most wonderful inventions of the day, and the enthusiasm and unstifled joy with which the youngsters last evening received the various pictures was a genuine tribute to the sterling qualities of the entertainment presented.'

Though the clarity and steadiness of the pictures may have been improved, the programme content was much the same as before. For example, it contained 'Pillow Fight', 'Pussy's Bath' and 'A Hard Wash' as the comedy part, and 'Niagara Falls', 'The Gordon Highlanders Marching to Camp', and 'The Turn out of an American Fire Brigade' as part of the interest section. In all 22 items were exhibited.[29] The programme was almost identical to that shown at the Palace Theatre, London in March 1897.[30] The film show was contained within a good quality variety performance, and it was thus not the only attraction.

G. West and Son's 'Our Navy' programme at the Floral Hall on April 18th,

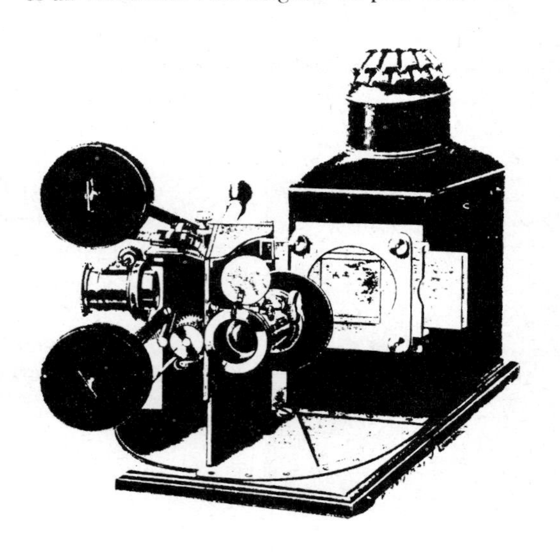

The Wrench Cinematograph of 1898 which projected slides and films.
Courtesy Barnes Museum of Cinematography.

1899 could stand on its own. This firm had long established itself in the field of marine still photography, and the animated photographs shot by Alfred J. West were also of outstanding quality. The *Daily Post* reporter enthused about the programme.

> 'These illustrations furnish not only a most interesting entertainment, but afford an excellent opportunity for the general public to learn something about our coastal defences, and Jack Tar's life afloat and ashore. Captain Edwards, R.N. enhances the value of the pictures by his remarks on the various slides shown. Amongst the most keenly appreciated of the photographs were 'March around the quarter deck of H.M.S. Crescent', 'Dancing the Hornpipe', and the excellent photographs of the Turbinia both on and off the boat. The photographs taken from the stern of the Turbinia, showing the water whirling away in the wake in beautiful curves are of great beauty, whilst the pictures of the boat steaming at 35 knots give a vivid impression of tremendous speed. This unique entertainment undoubtedly has a great future in it.' [31]

More Music Halls and More Bioscopes

During the first eighteen months of the new century, there was a three-fold increase in Leicester's music halls. The Tivoli, which had been closed down for almost a year, after an alleged unsavoury performance, re-opened on Monday Oct 1st 1900, with a strong variety bill, the last item of which was the Vitagraph.[32] The Vitagraphe, with and without an 'e', was the machine patented by Clément and Gilmer of Paris and first introduced into England in 1896.[33] By May 1901 this had been replaced by the Wrenchograph.[34] The firm of J. Wrench and Son produced a series of reliable and popular projectors from the middle of 1896. It continued in the film business until 1925.[35]

In April 1901 the Royal Empire, Wharf Street, also re-opened with variety and cinematograph pictures[36] and, in June 1901, the Palace Theatre of Varieties, 'one of the most commodious in the provinces',[37] opened on part of the site of the Floral Hall. The Palace was designed by Frank Matcham and built by George Duxbury at a cost of £50,000. The evening's performance closed with an exhibition of Bioscope pictures which were referred to in the newspaper reports as 'Gibbon's Bio-tableaux'. The 'Anglo-American Bio-Tableaux' was the trade name of Walter Gibbons. The son of the manager of Messrs J. Neve and Sons, nail manufacturers of Wolverhampton, he used an improved Urban Bioscope in his shows. In previous years, he had also exhibited his films at the Empire, Leicester. He later became the owner of the Holborn Empire.[38]

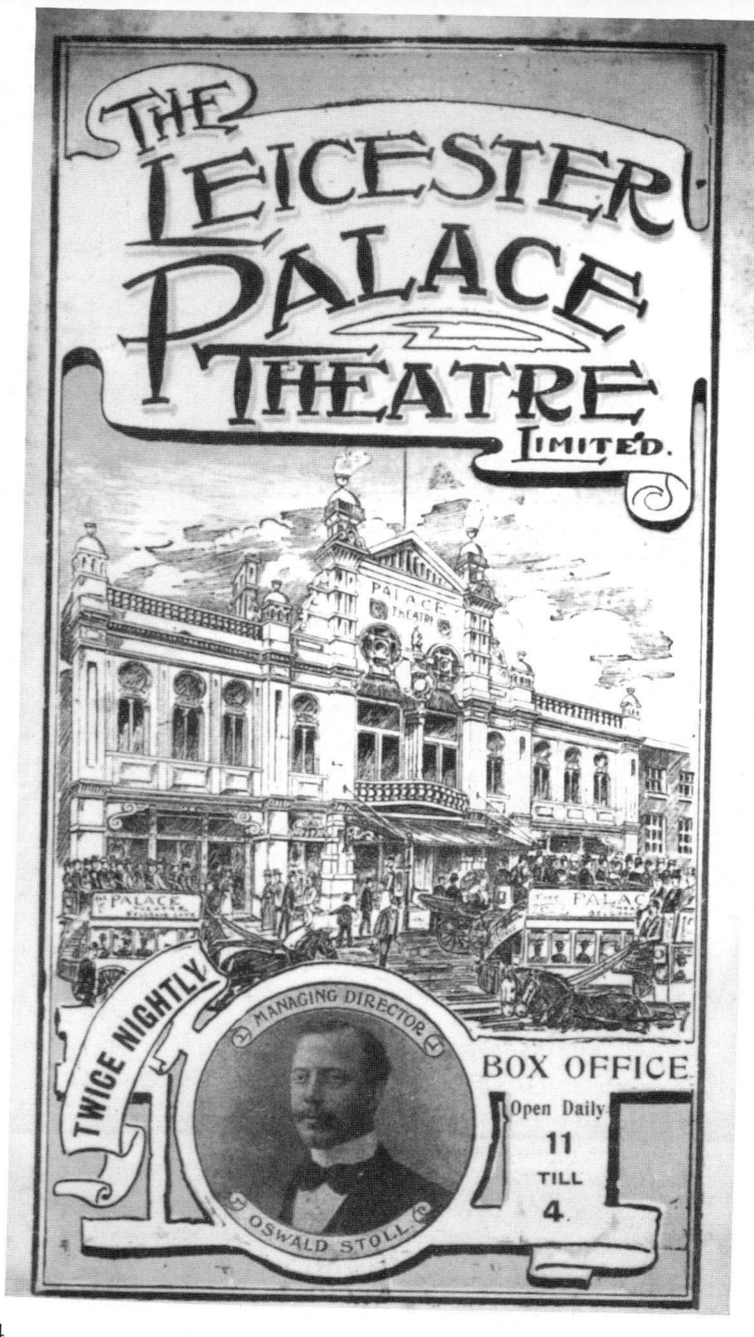
THE
LEICESTER
PALACE
THEATRE
LIMITED.
PALACE THEATRE
PALACE
THE PALACE
TWICE NIGHTLY
MANAGING DIRECTOR
OSWALD STOLL
BOX OFFICE
Open Daily
11
TILL
4.

Left: The front cover of the Palace programme for September 2nd 1900. *Courtesy David Robinson Collection.*
Above: The Leicester Palace as shown on a postcard. *Author's collection.*

With Poole's 'Myriorama and Living Pictures', and Dyson's 'Diorama and Gypsy Choir' occasionally at the Temperance Hall, the three houses of Variety and the May Fair, Leicester was now well supplied with opportunities for seeing 'this wonderful invention'. The American Bioscope even topped the bill at the Palace in August 1901, when the programme of films (and this was the first use of the word in a Leicester report) included the 'Landing of Major-General Baden Powell at Southampton, and the return of the Leicester Volunteers'.[39] The American Bioscope was introduced into Britain in September 1897. It was a 35mm machine for which it was claimed 'Freedom from flicker' and 'Absolute steadiness'.[40]

The content of the programme began to change a little at this time, and the topical pictures were now evenly balanced with comedies and the beginnings of story films. Such titles as 'The Children's Dream of Pantomime',[41] 'Red Riding Hood (an animated pantomime in 12 scenes)'[42] and 'Bluebeard'[43] appear. This

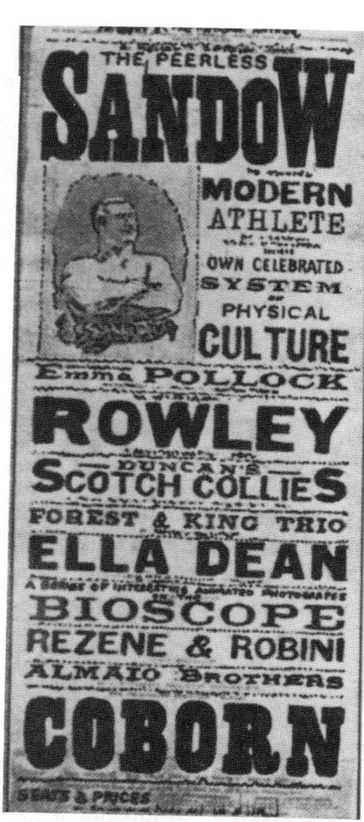

THE PEERLESS

SANDOW

MODERN
ATHLETE

OWN CELEBRATED
SYSTEM
PHYSICAL
CULTURE

Emma POLLOCK

ROWLEY

DUNCAN'S
SCOTCH COLLIES

FOREST & KING TRIO

ELLA DEAN

A SERIES OF INTERESTING ANIMATED PHOTOGRAPHS

BIOSCOPE

REZENE & ROBINI

ALMAIO BROTHERS

COBORN

SEATS & PRICES

Above: The interior of the Palace as shown in the programme for September 2nd 1900. *Courtesy David Robinson Collection.*

Left: The opening programme at the Leicester Palace as advertised in the *Leicester Mercury.*

Below: Posters for the 'New' Empire and the Tivoli on a High Street building Monday November 13th 1898. The 'Bio-Tableaux' was top of the bill. *Courtesy Leicestershire Records Office.*

The 'Universe', a machine similar to the 'American', as advertised in *Kinematograph Weekly*.

latter film may have been the one produced by Charles Urban's Warwick Trading Company showing a comedy scene from Dan Leno's production at the Drury Lane Theatre.[44] It was made by the Brighton pioneer producer and cameraman, G.A. Smith.

Topical Films

The topicality of actuality films was improving. At the Palace in March, 1902, the Football International between Wales and Scotland was shown as six week-old news,[45] but the next week pictures of the 'Launch of H.M.S. Queen' were only 10 days old.[46] These may be regarded as extremes, however, and the average age of the news items was about three weeks.

The first Coronation since the invention of the cinematograph was bound to cause a stir in the affairs of both the film producer and the film exhibitor. Pre-advertising was used for the first time in connection with this, but no-one could have foreseen the sudden illness of King Edward which caused everything to be postponed. Instead of showing the coronation film as advertised, there were pictures of 'The Splendid but Futile Preparations'.[47]

Many fake films were passed off as the real thing. Of such a type was the film described as 'An Attack on a Mission Station in China and the Rescue by British Bluejackets'.[48] This 230 foot four-scene film made by James Williamson was shot in the garden of 'Ivy Lodge', an about-to-be-demolished house in Hove in January 1901. Mrs Florence Williamson played the missionary's wife.[49]

George Méliès, the French magician and film-maker became a skilled hand at faked actuality, and it was his Coronation re-construction that was shown soon after the actual coronation of King Edward VII. There was no intention here of duping the audience (supposing it had been possible) for the announcement read, 'Owing to the light in the Abbey not admitting of the taking of Animated Photographs of the crowning of the Sovereigns, and to afford an idea of this impressive ceremony as enacted on August 9th in Westminster Abbey, there has been produced at great expense, a representation of the crowning of the King in 10 scenes.'[50] The film was 330 feet long and its making was supervised by G.A. Smith.[51]

The very long film was an exception. Many films were still as short as 90 or 100 feet (approximately 90 seconds), and it was possible for the Bioscope section of the Palace programme to be quite brief whilst containing 30 film items.[52] A film about the ascent of Mont Blanc of 300 feet (5 minutes)[53] and one of the Durbar at Delhi of 240 feet (4 minutes)[54] were considered to be long enough for special mention.

Still from a fake newsreel. Entitled 'British Bluejackets Save a China Mission' - but shot in Hove by J. Williamson. *Courtesy National Film Archive.*

By 1903 the topical films had become even more topical. When the walking season was in full swing, several films of local events were presented at the earliest opportunity. For example, the Wheatsheaf Walk, which took place on Saturday July 25th, was shown at the Palace on July 27th. The topicality of distant actualities was improving, too. The Gordon Bennett Cup Motor Car Race which took place in Ireland on July 1st was shown in Leicester on July 7th.[55]

An 'Improved R.W. Paul Projector' of 1902 as advertised in *The Bioscope*.

A great advance in cinematography was evident at the Temperance Hall in October 1903. 'Jasper Redfern's World Renowned Animated and Singing Pictures and Grand Vaudeville Entertainment' included in its programme an item entitled 'The Unseen World', taken by means of the Urban-Duncan Micro-Bioscope which 'magnified the subject 2,200,000 to 76,000,000 times'. The films were from 50 to 150 feet in length with titles such as 'The Fresh-water Hydra', and 'The circulation of Blood in a Frog's Foot'.[56] The film 'Cheese Mites' was presented as a comedy with a diner surprised by the life on his piece of cheese.[57] The programme also included a 'spectacular reproduction in 15 scenes of the rise and fall of Napoleon', and the orchestra provided 'some most acceptable selections' to accompany the films. The 'Singing' aspect of the programme was not described by the reviewer.

Jasper Redfern began a new career as a cinematograph entrepreneur in 1896 in Chesterfield. He had been an optician and instrument dealer in Sheffield prior to this, and his film shows at Central Hall were so popular that he expanded his enterprise into a touring company. Some of the films in his repertoire were produced by the Sheffield Photo Company.[58]

Still from 'The Great Train Robbery', 1903. *Courtesy National Film Archive.*

Topping the Bill at the Palace on April 5th 1904 was the film 'Robbing the Mail'. The reviewer's description reveals that this is really 'The Great Train Robbery', Edwin S. Porter's 1903 landmark film. 'Prominent among other items is a remarkable representation of an American train robbery on the bioscope. This must be one of the longest films on record, as it takes a considerable time to present all the incidents of the holding up of the train by the thieves, the robbery of the passengers and the pursuit and capture of the robbers.'[59]

Waller Jeffs' First Visit to Leicester

The first Leicester visit of the showman Waller Jeffs took place in December 1904. This pioneer exhibitor had, for some years, been showing films at the Curzon Hall, Birmingham and he was now touring Midland towns with his 'New Century Pictures'. Jeffs had formed this company in 1902-3 with Sydney Carter of Bradford.[60] The programme at the Temperance Hall was described by the reviewer as 'an entertainment of living pictures which surpasses in quality anything of its kind ever seen in Leicester', but its content was little out of the ordinary with the usual topicals, travelogues and comedies. 'Colour in animated photography,' the reviewer also claimed, 'is a novelty never before seen in

TEMPERANCE HALL, LEICESTER
FOR ONE WEEK ONLY, Opening Dec. 12,
FIRST VISIT OF
MR. WALLER JEFFS'
NEW CENTURY PICTURES.
10,000 LIFE MOTION PHOTOS 10,000
From the Curzon Hall, Birmingham
A TOUR THROUGH ITALY IN COLOUR PHOTOGRAPHY.
GREAT MILITARY TOURNAMENT
THE HULL FISHING FLEET,
BEFORE AND AFTER THE TRAGEDY.
MRS. BROWN OFF FOR THE HOLIDAYS.
LATEST PICTURES WAR IN THE FAR EAST
Every Evening at 8, doors open 7.30
Admission 2s. 6d., 1s. 6d., 1s., 6d., and 3d.
Reserved Seats booked at J. Herbert Marshall's Music Galleries.

Top: Caricature of Waller Jeffs from a 1911 issue of *The Bioscope.*

Bottom: Facsimile of advertisement in *Leicester Mercury* of December 10th 1904.

Leicester, but it is demonstrated with great success in the photographic opera, 'William Tell'.[61] Perhaps it had been a different reviewer who reported that the Palace had shown 'The Condemnation of Faust' in colour in April 1904.[62]

The hand-colouring of films had been practised from their beginnings. Indeed, *The British Journal of Photography* in September 1896 was able to declare that 'the colouring of pictures is almost a matter of course now.' Such colouring was carried out by a team of painters, usually women. Using a powerful magnifying glass and a fine brush, each girl applied her designated colour to the several hundred feet of film before passing it on to the next person in the team.[63] Dyes already existed for the colouring of photographic lantern slides. The Pathé Film Company were about to revolutionize hand-colouring with their Stencil process, which was able to produce multiple prints in six colours from stencils cut from black and white positives by an ingenious pantograph.

The Temperance Hall was fast becoming the home of travelling film shows with the annual visits of Waller Jeffs, Poole, and Dyson. It had been opened in September 1853 and its wide auditorium obviously enabled large audiences

Above: The Temperance Hall *circa* 1906. A Kodak exhibition is the main event at the time this postcard was photographed. *Author's collection.*
Below: Facsimile of *Leicester Mercury* advertisement of September 11th 1905.

to view the screen unhindered by pillars. There is no indication in reports as to the location of the projector, but the configuration of the hall suggests that a position in the balcony would have been the most suitable for isolated convenience and length of throw.

TEMPERANCE HALL, - THREE WEEKS ONLY
TONIGHT, MONDAY, SEPT 11.
THE NORTH AMERICAN
LIFE MOTION PICTURES PRESENTS

L'ENTENTE CORDIALE
British and French Fleets at Brest and Portsmouth

SWITZERLAND and CANADA

LOUIS XIV
LIVING LEICESTER.
RUSSO-JAPANESE WAR
SMART VAUDEVILLE COMPANY
MILES AND MILES OF PICTURES
LEICESTER IMPERIAL PRIZE BAND
Nightly at 8. Doors Open 7.30 Early Door 3d. extra. Matinees, Wednesdays, Thursdays, and Saturdays at 3.
Prices 2s., 1s., 6d., and 3d. Children halfprice except back seats.

In 1905 yet another travelling show appeared: the North American Life Motion Pictures. Prices of admission were 2 shillings (10p), 1/6d ($7^1/_2$p), and 3d (1p). Children could get in for half-price but not on the back seats. The musical accompaniment was provided by the Leicester Imperial Prize Band. Surprisingly, the first performance of this three week engagement was 'filled to overflowing'.[64] The programme looked very ordinary with such items as 'The Turn out of

'Rescued by Rover'. *Courtesy National Film Archive.*

the Metropolitan Fire Brigade' and 'The Entente Cordiale' interspersed with turns by a comedian and interval selections by the band. But two Sheffield Photo Co. comedy items, 'Two Young Scamps' (150 feet) and 'An Eccentric Burglary' (400 feet), were brand-new releases, and a weekly change of programme could have been a factor in favour of the popularity of the presentation.

Another new release was featured at the Palace on November 27th 1905. 'Rescued by Rover' has achieved fame as a 'milestone' film in the history of British film production. The *Daily Post* reviewer seemed quick to spot the innovations: 'a charming subject, absolutely new in conception and realization and one of the best incidents ever recorded by the Bioscope.'[65] His 'original' comment was, in fact, a word-for-word copy of the opening statement of the publicity material that accompanied the film.[66]

The film was so popular that Cecil Hepworth sold 395 prints. Because the original negative wore out in the copying machine, Hepworth was forced to re-make the film twice.[67] It appeared in several programmes during the next twelve months. 'The Dog Detective', a film made by another British studio, Norwood, was clearly influenced by the success of 'Rescued by Rover'. At 730 feet, it was 300 feet longer than its rival and was shown as part of Pringle's North American Animated Pictures at the Temperance Hall.[68] Ralph Pringle was a former Huddersfield variety artist who had switched to cinematograph exhibition in 1900. He eventually settled in Bristol where he established a number of cinema houses while still operating touring companies. After 1914 he suddenly and mysteriously sold all his cinema interests to whoever would buy them and vanished from the industry. He died in poverty in 1922 in Port Talbot.[69]

Ralph Pringle, cinema pioneer. From *The Bioscope* February 13th 1913.

On January 20th 1906 there appeared in the *Leicester Pioneer* an advertisement by one J.W. Rayson of 231, Humberstone Road, Leicester, 'Theatrical agent and entertainment with the Cinematograph'. At the time, he was showing his films with the Imperial Pierrots at the Corn Exchange. His programme included an assortment of old and recent films: 'The Soldier's Return' (1902), 'A False Alarm' (1905) and 'A Henpecked Husband' (1906), and he operated the projector himself at each performance.

The First Talkies

The most significant innovation in the film shows of 1906 was the visit to Leicester of the St Louis Pictures. 'The Gaumont Chronophone - PICTURES THAT TALK AND SING' shrieked the advertisement for the Temperance Hall debut. The device had been first demonstrated at the London Hippodrome in November 1904. It was simply a gramophone mechanically synchronised to a projector. Ten or twelve inch records accompanied the films which were either 165 or 220 feet long.[70] 'By means of this clever invention, the pictures sing and talk and live, so that we get the drolleries both

TEMPERANCE HALL
LEICESTER
FOR TWO WEEKS ONLY,
COMMENCING MONDAY, MAY 21st
STUPENDOUS ATTRACTION
First Visit of the St. Louis
ANIMATED PICTURES.
Introducing the Sensation of the day
TALKING PICTURES.
PICTURES THAT TALK!
PICTURES THAT SING!
PICTURES THAT LIVE!
The Human Voice Reproduced as in Life
See and hear the Famous American Comedian
R. G. KNOWLES
See and hear the Great Australian Baritone
HAMILTON HILL
See and Hear the Prince of Comedy
JOE MACK
See and Hear the Great Pantomime Favourite
ERNIE MAYNE &c., &c.,
Magnificent Series Taken with the
PRINCE OF WALES IN INDIA
GRANDPA AND THE BUTTERFLY
THE SAILOR'S WEDDING
TWO LITTLE WAIFS
LIFE AND TIMES OF NELSON
The Hero of Trafalgar
Over 40 Miles of Pictures Shown Nightly
Each Evening at 8.
POPULAR PRICES 1s. 6d., AND 3d.
A few Reserved seats at 1s. 6d Children Half-price
to all parts except 3d. seats
Doors open 7.30 Early Doors 7 p.m.
Matinee Saturday at 3.

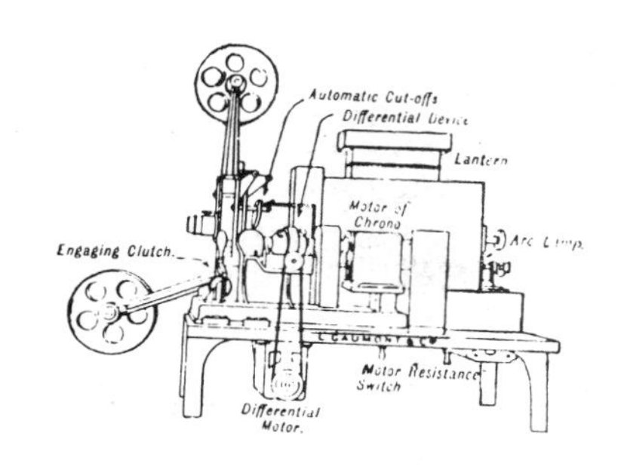

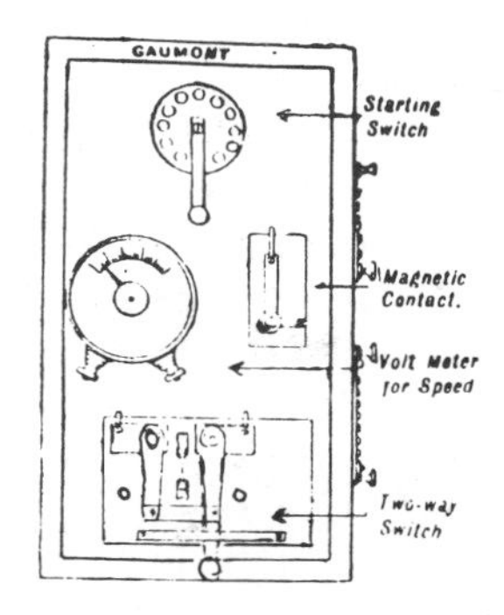

The Synchronising Mechanism.

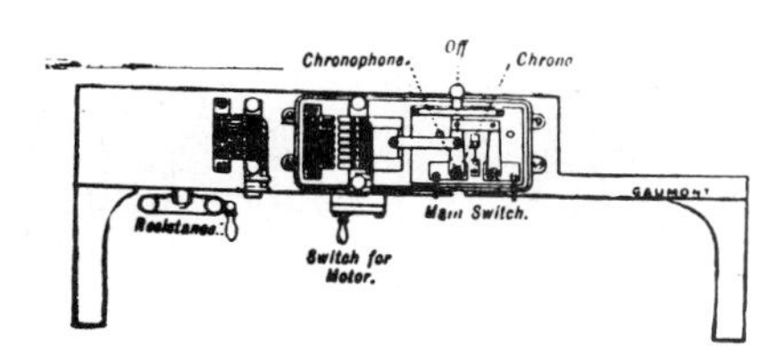

The apparatus for the Gaumont Chronophone, 1906.

in voice and gesture of such well known comedians as R.G. Knowles and Joe Mack reproduced to the very life. Not only are we treated to the humour of such prominent comedians already mentioned, but the voices of eminent vocalists, as for instance the Australian baritone, Hamilton Hill, are heard to perfection. The St Louis Animated Pictures Company claim to have been the first to realise the possibilities of the Chronophone, and by so doing have brought something before the public which cannot fail to add to the enjoyment of this type of entertainment.'[71]

The items described by the reviewer were from a batch of films made by Gaumont in early 1906. Hamilton Hill sang 'The Fireman's Song ', and Joe Mack sang 'Strolling Home with Angelina'.[72]

The novelty took a long time to wear off and the synchronisation in some cases was not as imperfect as is often suggested. Waller Jeffs included talking and singing pictures in his programme in April 1907, and 'Miss Vesta Tilley's

MAN IS BUT MORTAL
and is born to trouble as the sparks fly upwards.
The VOICE of the CHRONOPHONE
will continue for ever to sound through the ages.

Advertisement for Gaumont's Chronomegaphone from their 1906 catalogue.

production 'Please conductor, don't put me off the train' was received with merited applause'.[73]

Amplification of the sound was a major problem. Mechanical amplification by means of vibration-operated compressed air chambers was used by the Gaumont company.[74] With duplex horns placed behind the screen, enough volume was generated for use in medium-sized auditoria.[75] It is not clear from newspaper descriptions what method of amplification was used, but since audibility is not mentioned as an irritating factor, it could be assumed that it was adequate for the purpose.

TONIGHT AT 8
TEMPERANCE HALL, LEICESTER

MR. WALLER JEFF'S SELECT PICTURES
Come and hear for yourselves the Marvel of the Age.
THE CINEPHONE
PICTURES that will TALK, SING, and ACT
Mr. Jeffs' Popular Tour Series,
MOTORING OVER THE ALPS
THE GREAT FLOODS AT MOSCOW
XMAS UNDER THE SEA
BIRTH OF A BUTTERFLY
THE HOSTAGE
THE LITTLE MOTHER

Facsimile of *Leicester Mercury* advertisement January 4th 1909.

Gaumont's own improvement on the Chronophone, 'The Chronomegaphone or Mechanical Concert Party' was shown at the Temperance Hall in May and at the Palace Theatre in August. 'Recent years have seen improvements in the old animated photographs,' wrote the *Post* reporter, 'until now, by means of the Chronomegaphone, they are not only made to move, but also to sing and talk at the same time. Only recently this invention was displayed before the Queen and the Royal Family and Leicester is one of the first provincial towns to be favoured with a visit.'[76]

The Palace programme in August contained three singing pictures by Harry Lauder: 'I Love a Lassy', 'We Parted on the Shore' and 'She is My Daisy'. The items were billed as 'The Illusion of Life', and 'Next to Seeing Him in the Flesh'.[77] Later the same year, the Palace included the Chronomegaphone again for a second series of Harry Lauder Songs, 'Stop your Tickling Jock' and 'I'm the Saftest of the Family'.[78]

Another travelling show brought sound films to the Temperance Hall in October. 'Fabro's Electric Singing Pictures (50,000 Animated Pictures)' used the Chronomegaphone films 'Tala-Indian Love Song (with Stanley and Bain) and 'Won't You Throw Me A Kiss' (with Alf Collins and Miss Horton) and some opera selections. In the same group of films released in September 1907 by Gaumont, there were 22 extracts from 'Faust' and several arias from 'Carmen'.[79]

'This wonderful invention is worked by electric motors, the whole thing being controlled by a central switch-board.'[80] The projector and the amplified gramophone were both operated by electric motors, as opposed to the normal hand-cranking, and clockwork mechanisms. They were electrically-coupled with a manual overide to restore synchronisation, if it strayed for any reason.[81]

Another early sound apparatus, 'The Cinephone', developed by the Warwick Trading Company, was used by Waller Jeffs in January 1909 at the Temperance Hall.[82]

Some showmen who had not obtained one of the 'Singing Picture' devices included in their performances and their publicity 'Illustrated Songs'. During the singing of a popular song, lantern slides would be projected onto the screen. The dissolving scenes could give a pleasing sense of animation, and warrant special comment from the reviewer. 'Miss K. McCabe sang "The Holy City", a beautiful harmony of Music and Photography'.[83]

In its first ten years of existence, the cinematograph had progressed from a scientific curiosity to a commonplace entertainment. The original 80 foot film strips, lasting just over one minute and showing a single incident of actuality, had been replaced by carefully crafted documentaries and scripted dramas sometimes based on well-known literary originals. The demand for films by travelling showmen, keen to advertise the topicality of their programmes, had brought a large number of film-producing companies into being throughout the western world. The cinematograph film was genuinely an international entertainment medium, and audiences, largely starved of visual stimuli in newspapers and magazines, relished the feast of exotic locations and unusual happenings that poured forth from the screen.

The decorative interior of The Palace

Chapter Two

Finding a Home

It was inevitable that, as the popularity of cinematograph entertainment grew and as the steady supply of cinematograph films increased, some showmen would seek to open permanent establishments showing films. But a regular change of programme could prove expensive if the films needed to be purchased rather than leased. By 1906, in America, film hiring had almost completely replaced outright sale. In Britain, at this time, there were only four hiring companies. The common practice was that travelling showmen would purchase a selection of films from the numerous trading companies and tour round with them until they had completed their usual circuit. By this time, the films were well-worn. Some part of their value could still be recouped by their sale to companies who would extract the silver content from the stock. Correspondence in the *Bioscope Weekly* also suggested that some showmen were putting short lengths of old film in envelopes and selling them at one penny a time as 'samples of the films we show'!

The retail price of new film at this time was a uniform 6d (2.5p) per foot regardless of the nature of the subject. Few exhibitors could afford this cost every week, though some had a ready market with other exhibitors for their used films at a reduced rate. An average programme might cost as much as £100. A renter could only expect to get £6 per week for its hire. Theoretically, then, it would take a four month period of rental before a profit point was reached. But, as the film aged, the renter was forced to accept a lower hiring fee thus pushing his profit point further away.

The First Cinema

It was a film renter, Colonel A.C. Bromhead, who opened what is widely accepted as the first cinema in Britain on May 23rd, 1906 in Bishopsgate, London. The two comedy films included in the opening show were made by

. . PROGRAMME . .

SAN FRANCISCO DISASTER.

Showing the Sections of the City Devastated.

PANORAMA OF 4th AND MARKET STREETS.

PANORAMA, DOWN MARKET ST.,

PANORAMA NEAR PALACE HOTEL.

PANORAMA OF UNION SQUARE.

PANORAMA OF CLIFF HOUSE.

All of the Sections shown have been destroyed either by the Earthquake or by the Fire.
Actual Scenes of the ruin and devastation in this beautiful City, as it appears to-day, have been taken for us by our American Agents, and are now on the way to England.

LOST! A LEG OF MUTTON.

THE OLYMPIC GAMES AT ATHENS.

We were appointed Official Cinematographers to H.M. The King of Greece, and held the sole and exclusive Cinematograph Rights for

THE GREATEST SPORTING EVENT IN THE WORLD'S HISTORY.

ARRIVAL OF H.M. KING EDWARD.
ENTRY OF ROYALTIES INTO ARENA.
ROYALTIES TAKING THEIR SEATS.
GRAND MARCH PAST OF COMPETITORS.
THE DANISH TEAMS, including Ladies.
THE SWEDISH AND GERMAN TEAMS.
HEAVY WEIGHT LIFTING.
ROPE CLIMBING EXTRAORDINARY.
And other Events.

IV.

A NAVAL ENGAGEMENT.

This Programme is subject to change without notice.

SPECIAL CHILDREN'S MATINEES. Every Saturday ... at 3 o'clock

The Bishopsgate Bioscope programme for May 23rd 1906.
Courtesy Bishopsgate Institute.

Gaumont, the company for which Colonel Bromhead worked. The rest of the programme consisted of views of the San Francisco earthquake, and scenes taken at the Olympic Games in Athens. Quickly the proprietors, 'The Daily Bioscope Syndicate', opened other cinemas and by circulating their films gained increased cost benefit.

In December 1907, Mr Charles West and his brother opened Leicester's first permanent exhibition of films, and began a new era of entertainment in the city. The site of the cinema was at the top of Cank Street. In 1958, Mr West described it as 'opposite the Edgar Backus bookshop' (in 1993 a picture-framer's shop). Before and after its use for showing films, the Kelly's *Trade Directory* seems to indicate the building's use as a tallow warehouse. Since there were no safety regulations for cinema exhibitions at this time, the doors at either side of the central pay box were both the entrances and the exits. Inside the building, the patrons watched the films from wooden benches. The noise of the projector was drowned in turn with a gramophone operated by the girl in the pay-box, and also a form of mechanical organ. The films themselves averaged 200 or 300 feet in length and were projected continuously with pauses for reel changes. Admission price was 2d.

Drawing made in 1956 by Charles West of the appearance of the frontage of the Cank Street cinema in 1907. *Author's collection.*

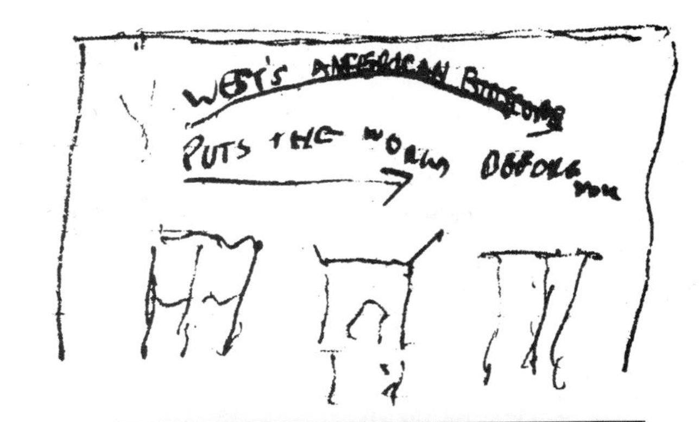

One slogan outside the cinema declared 'West's American Bioscope Puts the World Before You', whilst another optimistically stated 'West's Come to Stay'. To a certain extent this was true, for the site functioned as a cinema for about eighteen months.

Popular comment had predicted only a short life for the venture and often, as he stood outside the building, Mr West heard prospective customers declaring that the cinema was only a craze, like roller skating. At about this time, roller skating was on the wane, but a revival a few years later would provide an number of buildings that were easily converted into cinemas.[1]

La Milo as Lady Godiva, from a postcard. *Author's collection*

An interesting departure from the usual occurred at the Palace in February, 1908, when La Milo, an exponent of artistic statuary, included in her act some moving pictures of herself on the 'Miloscope'. This 300 foot film had been made by the Urban Trading Company in 1906, and showed the poseuse, at home, in her dressing room, and on stage.[2] The Australian-born beauty, whose real name was Pansy Montague, had previously caused something of a sensation by taking the part of Lady Godiva in the Coventry Pageant of 1907. Both the Gaumont and the Urban Companies had produced films of this. The *Kinematograph Weekly* of August 15th 1907 said of the Urban version: 'This should prove of interest to the many members of the public who have followed the discussion, as to the performance, which has raged in the newspapers. It gives a good view of the central figure of the procession, and shows that her dress is beyond reproach'. There is no clue as to which version was included as part of her act.

The Bioscope at the Empire

Live theatre suffered its first blow in Leicester in June 1908, when the New Bioscope Trading Company took a 21 year lease on the Empire, Wharf Street.[3] As a music hall, the Empire had had a precarious existence. It had been closed in 1902 because of bankruptcy only a year after a previous re-opening, and the Chief Constable had opposed an application for a renewal of its licence in 1904.

The *Daily Post* reported that the first manager of the new venture was Mr C.A. Hurley. The Bioscope pictures were the main attraction, but they were supplemented by a variety show. There was only one house nightly, and the claim was that 10,000 feet of film was projected at each performance. Shown without a break, this would account for almost two hours of the evening's programme. More than likely, this figure was most suitable for the advertisement. Some showmen had advertised their shows stating 'Millions of Pictures', and 'Miles and Miles of Entertainment' in much the same way that present day showmen measure their films in millions of dollars.

It would appear that 23 separate films of all types were shown on the opening night, and, amazingly, Méliès' 1902 film 'From Earth to Moon' topped the bill. Trade papers show that this film had had numerous re-issues. Mr T. Ashmell, L.L.C.M. provided the piano accompaniment.[4] A year later *The Bioscope* reported that the business acumen and the courtesy of the manager had made a thorough success of the venture. During the year, the managing director of the company, Mr F.R. Griffiths, had appointed Mr Charles Craig as manager of the enterprise.[5]

A report in the *Bioscope* of May 20th 1909 gives a good indication of a typical programme at the Empire. Of the 14 listed items, it has been possible to

Méliès' film 'From Earth to Moon'.
Courtesy National Film Archive.

identify 12 from 1908 catalogues and listings, and thus give some indication of the length of the film section of the entertainment:

The Pretty Dairymaid (Pathé)	Drama	675 ft.
The Mohawk's Ring, (Pathé)	Western Drama	495 ft.
Electric Hotel (Pathé)	Comedy trick film	495 ft.
Puzzling Enigma (Pathé)		428 ft.
In the time of the Normans (Lux)	Costume Drama	704 ft.
Game of Cards (Lux)		400 ft.
A Zulu's Heart (American Biograph)	Drama	750 ft.
A Guard's Alarum (Urban-Eclipse)	Trick film	430 ft.
Saved by Love (Edison)	Drama	900 ft.
Rent Collector (Williamson)	Comedy	360 ft.
Guardian of the Bank (Cricks and Martin)		570 ft.
House Cleaning Days (Vitagraph)	Comedy	292 ft.
	(total)	6350 feet

'I am an Electrician and a Candid Critic - I get 3/- a week for this. Come and enjoy my show!!!'
A cartoon from *The Bioscope* in 1907.

'Robert's Night Theatre', and 'The Grand Canyon of Arizona' were the two other films. It can be assumed that they would have been at least 300 feet each in length, and thus the whole programme would have run for about 120 minutes. A newsreel and one or two variety acts would have completed the bill.

The Palace and the Pavilion (formerly the Tivoli) continued to show their films as supporting items or as 'chasers' at the end of the programme. Reports in the trade weekly, *The Bioscope*, indicated that the operator in the latter theatre was Mr Walter H. Pallister.[6] The usual travelling shows put in their appearances at the Temperance Hall for one or two week runs, and they continued to attract good custom. 'The popularity of these is due to new ideas and appliances, by which means they been brought to a standard bordering on perfection'[7] suggested the *Daily Post* reporter. The YMCA Hall provided another regular venue for showmen.

Occasionally, the content of the programme was criticised by the *Daily Post* reviewer. 'There are some amusing Bioscope views, but on the other hand there is one set of pictures depicting the funeral of the late Sir Henry Campbell-Bannerman, during which the orchestra played the Dead March, which might well have been left out'.[8] Though the criticism was by no means harsh, it would find favour with the large mass of people who still did not attend the 'pictures' because of their low-class nuance.

During 1909, the popularity of roller skating rinks was revived. In September, the Western Boulevard Rink was taking shape. It had 18,000 sq.ft. of maple flooring,[9] 3,000 sq.ft. more than the Belgrave Skating Rink opened later the same year. It was in the Boulevard Rink that Charles West used to show his films during the interval between sessions. A screen would be pulled down from the roof, and the lights would be dimmed to enable the pictures to be projected. At Christmastime, the management held a party for children under 14, and invited Mr West to give a cinematograph display.[10]

Right: The Pavilion Palace of Varieties. *Courtesy Leicester Mercury.*
Below: An advertising card for the Boulevard Rink in 1909. *Courtesy Philip D. Hall.*

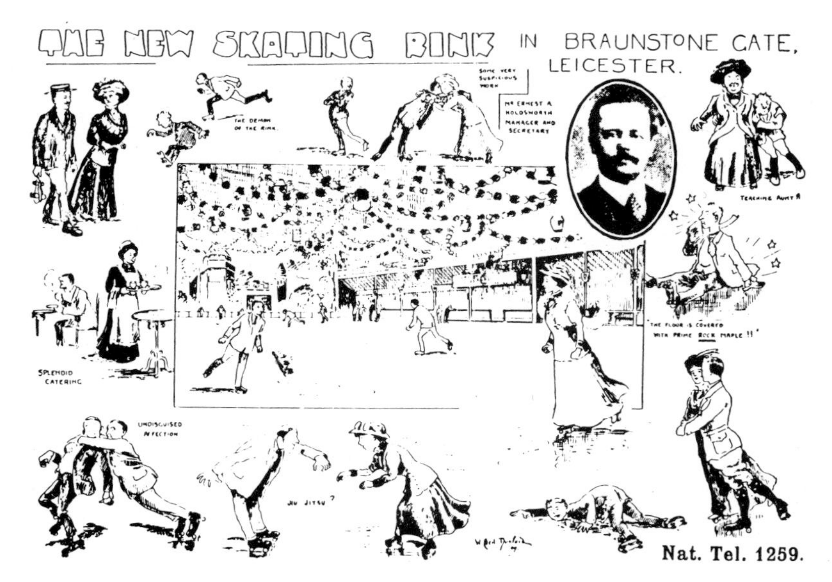

Pat Collins' Wonderland travelling bioscope show. *Author's collection.*

The Cinematograph Act of 1909

The 1909 Pat Collin's Pleasure Fair included a Wonderland, billed as 'the Grandest Travelling Cinematograph Show', but such shows were not far from extinction. Film exhibitions from January 1910 came under the regulations of the Cinematographs Act (1909). The requirements for fire-proof projection rooms and separate re-wind facilities proved to be too cumbersome for most of the portable booths.

Herbert Gladstone's Cinematograph Bill was designed for the safety of the patrons. The highly inflammable cellulose nitrate film had ignited in a number of incidents up and down the country, though there had been no major disasters like those reported from the Continent. Regulation of the Act was to be the remit of the local Watch Committee through the services of the Chief Fire Officer. Licences would be issued to approved premises. They could be revoked by the same Committee either at the time of the renewal or for proven breaches of regulations. The fees for the licence were fixed at £1 per year or, for shorter periods, at 5 shillings (25p) per month.

The first licences were granted to the Pavilion, Belgrave Gate; the Palace; and the Empire, Wharf Street, at a meeting of the Watch Committee on 15th

This cartoon from *The Bioscope* in 1908 suggests the effects of the forthcoming 1909 Cinematograph Act.

March 1910. An application for a licence for premises near the Old Free Library at 50, Belvoir Street was turned down.[11]

Rivalry amongst exhibitors was keen. The London firm of T.J. West, which had a circuit of cinemas throughout the provinces, issued a statement in the *Bioscope* of December 30th 1909 that the picture shows being run in Leicester under the name 'West's Pictures' were not their promotions. There is little doubt

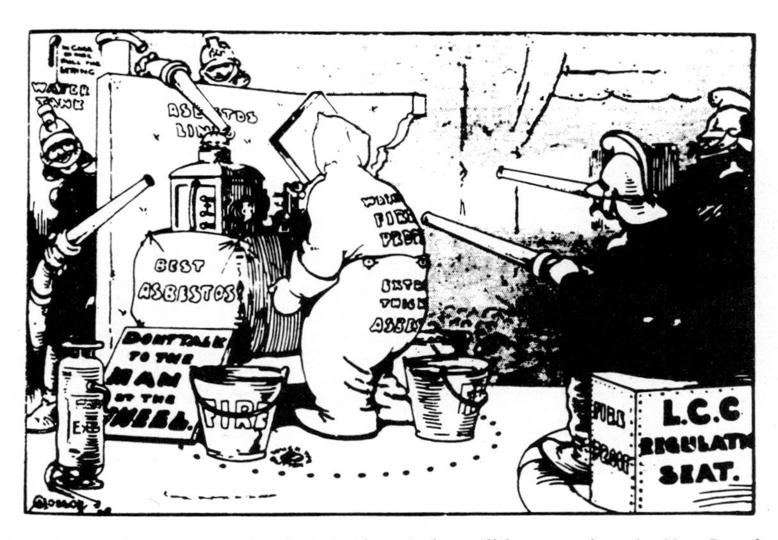

'The safety of the operator. Our Artist's idea of what will happen when the New Regulations come into force on August 1st.' From *The Bioscope* 1908. The London County Council had their regulations in place on August 1st 1908.

The interior and exterior of the Boulevard Skating Rink circa 1909.
Courtesy C.E. John Aston.

that this was referring to the shows advertised at the Boulevard Skating Rink. A regulation projection box was constructed at the rink in 1910, and Charles West began daily showings of films at 8, 9 and 10 o'clock in the evening. 'For fifteen minutes, they form a pleasant diversion from the whirl of the skating', declared the *Kinematograph Weekly* reporter.[12] The Watch Committee confirmed the granting of a licence on May 3rd 1910.

The Empress, Mere Road

The year 1910 had opened with Leicester the owner of no cinema in the true sense of the word. By its close, there were six established Cinematograph Houses. The Empress Picture Palace, Mere Road appears to have begun operating before its licence was confirmed by the Watch Committee. Though the official opening was made by Councillor H.C. Snow on April 19th, the Watch Committee did not approve its licence until the meeting of May 3rd.[13] The keys of the old chapel building had been previously held by Charles West, but faced with the prospect of having to provide himself with hundreds of yards of electric cable from the nearest supply point at Humberstone Road, he found himself without the inclination or the capital. He sold the lease, and established himself at the Boulevard Skating Rink.[14] The design was by Keites and Fosbrooke of Leicester, and approval for the alterations was given on March 18th, 1910.[15] The proprietors, the London Cinematograph Company, paid £395 for the conversion.[16]

The *Leicester Pioneer* introduced the cinema in these words: 'The popularity of the bioscope entertainment in other parts of the country has reached Leicester. The Empress, the first of several projected houses of its kind is situated on the corner of Mount Road, and Mere Road. The hall is well furnished and illuminated and an attractive exterior cannot fail to excite curiosity. There are two houses nightly and a Saturday matinee. The programme is changed twice-a-week. The programme is of a high degree and contains amongst its films the following: 'The Sheep with Six Legs', an instructive film; 'Hidden in a Mattress' - a comedy, 'Flying Dogs' - realism, and 'Roosevelt's Big Game Hunt in Africa' - actuality.'[17]

The 'Sheep with Six Legs' is listed as an 835 foot drama from the French Eclair Company in the *Bioscope* of March 31st. A further indication of the prominence of French productions is Pathé's 379 foot comedy 'Hidden in A Mattress'. 'Roosevelt's Big Game Hunt in Africa' was made by the British explorer/ photographer, Cherry Kearton. President Theodore Roosevelt, initially not wanting any cinematograph pictures taken, turned down an approach to film the expedition by the American company Selig. Somewhat annoyed by the refusal, Selig, already famous for their 'jungle' and animal films, then faked the President's exploits using their own sets and private zoo. Cherry Kearton had already been engaged by the British 'White Hunter', and his 930 foot film was advantageously released by the Warwick Trading Company to critical acclaim. It was the forerunner of many later 'explorer' films that often toured with a narrator.

Mr G. Horton is listed as the manager by the *Kinematograph Weekly* of April 22nd, 1910. 'The premises,' the report went on, 'have been renovated and nicely fitted up, the reserved seats being of leather. A prominent frontage, well-lighted, has been erected. The chief operator, Mr S.B. Peckover, has supervised the fitting up of the Kamms Universal projector in the fire-proof chamber, which also has an exhaust to carry off the fumes. He speaks highly of the machine, never having a mishap in any shape or form'. The reporter had no doubts that the venture would 'catch on', but he thought a winter-time opening might have attracted larger crowds to fill the 420 seats. By May 12th it was only running one house per night.

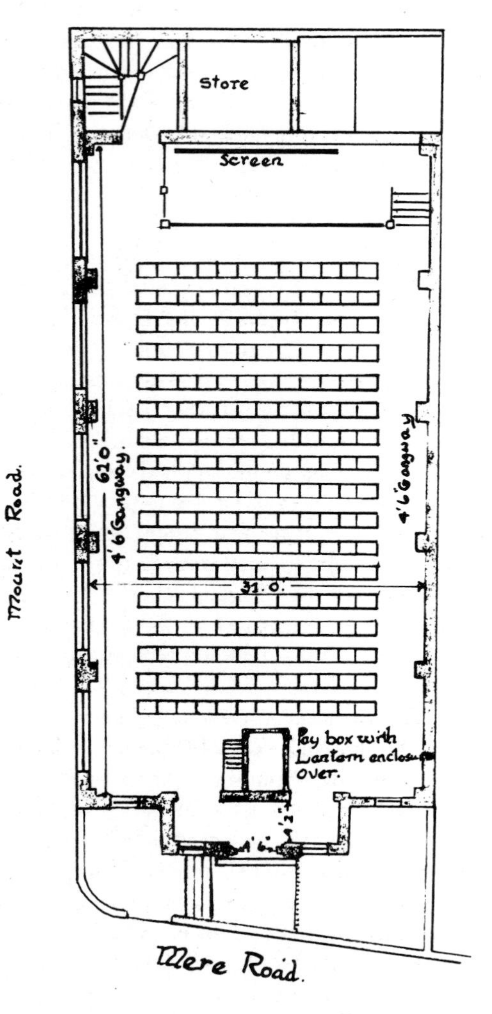

Interior ground plan of the Picturedrome, Mere Road. Submitted March 10th 1911. *Courtesy Leicestershire Record Office.*

In the fortnight before the Empress, Mere Road opened, Waller Jeffs was attracting large crowds to the Temperance Hall with a programme of films and variety. Miss Elsie Foster (comedienne), Miss Clarice May (sketches at the piano), Miss Marie Pascoe (original character songs) and Mr Frederick Mantell and Miss Edith Maynard (sketches and duologues) entertained in between the presentation of the films. The Hall had its cinematograph licence confirmed in the May meeting of the Watch Committee.[18]

The Empress, Belvoir Street.

After another inspection of the Belvoir Street premises, the Watch Committee granted a licence to the London Cinematograph Company to open their second Empress Picture theatre. The Chief Fire Officer, Mr H. Neal, now described the premises in these words: 'The seating in the building accommodates 207 persons, and there is a free access for 3 exits to which panic bolts are attached. The Cinematograph enclosure is a permanent structure outside the building at the opposite end to the exit. The lantern and all necessary apparatus is constructed according to the act.'[19] As with the Mere Road hall, the architects for the alterations were Messrs Keites and Fosbrooke of Market Street. The auditorium was 60 feet long and only 20 feet wide, tapering down to 16 feet. The curtain for the screen was raised like a window blind.[20] The cinema occupied the ground floor of office buildings which were decorated with plaster and concrete stuccos. These were illuminated after dark.[21] The extensive alterations cost £695.[22]

Sir Samuel Faire J.P. performed the opening ceremony on June 16th. He declared that 'living pictures were one of the most effective means of producing amusement and education in people generally. Such entertainment was well worthy of support. There were many attractions for the young which were not always good, but kinematograph entertainments must commend themselves to every right thinking person.' [23] Prices of admission were from 4d (2p) to 1 shilling (5p). The hall was open for the continuous exhibition of films between 3 p.m. and 10.30 p.m., and between 3 p.m. and 5 p.m. a cup of tea and a biscuit was provided for each patron by the manager, Mark Cowen.

Such was the novelty of the Belvoir Street cinema's innovation that the *Leicester Pioneer* published a detailed account of its operation.[24]

> 'The continuous type of entertainment is new in Leicester, though in other towns it is an already established and popular institution, and it may be well, therefore, to explain the system. Generally speaking, and this is the case with the Empress, the house is worked in connection with others in

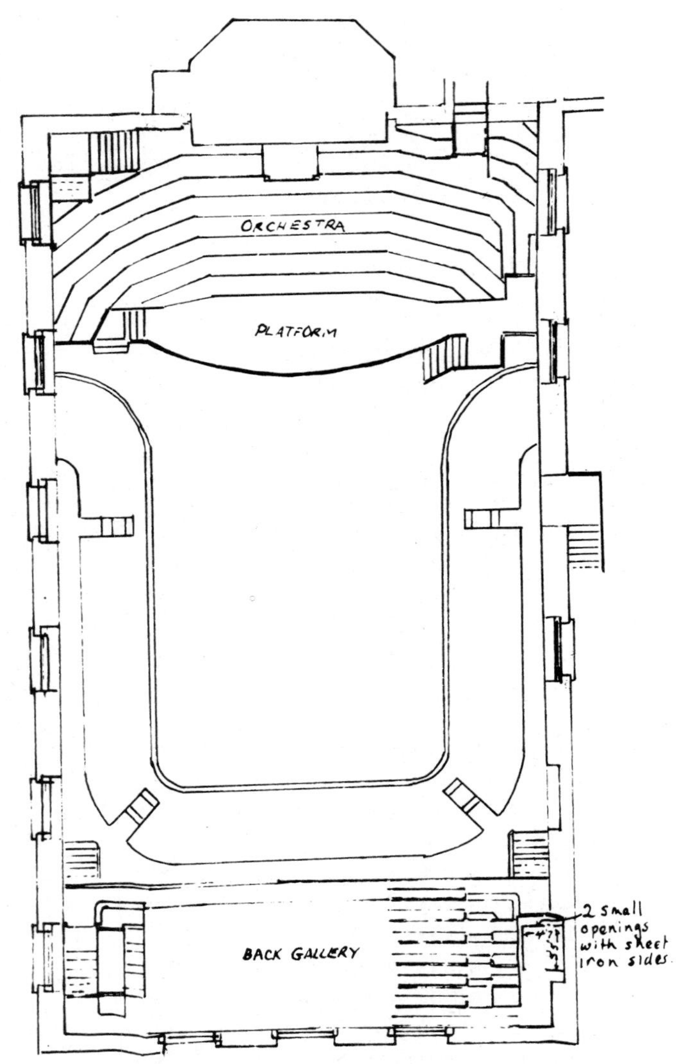

This plan for the siting of a fireproof 'lantern room' at the Temperance Hall, Granby Street, was approved on March 3rd 1910. The positioning of this would have resulted in distorted images on a screen placed in the centre of the stage.
Courtesy Leicestershire Record Office.

various parts of the country, and it is thus possible to show a series of expensively obtained films while fixing the price at a very low figure.
The Empress has a long auditorium most comfortably seated on a rising floor, so that the best seats are at the back near the door. Owing to the fact that the performance continues with only occasional breaks of a minute to change the spools, it is necessary for those entering to be guided to their seats by attendants, whose eyes have become accustomed to the dim light. At the end of the auditorium is a screen upon which, to the accompaniment of a piano, are projected a succession of 10 or 12 films, the series recommencing as soon as the last one has been put through. This occupies approximately 1 hour, but it is obvious that those who wish to see the whole of the exhibition can commence viewing at any point in the entertainment. The pictures are of varied character; some reproducing legends, novel, plays, etc. in dumbshow, others showing industrial processes, beauty spots, resorts, and others represent comedy pure and simple. Some of the pictures are handsomely tinted.'

The London Cinematograph Co. was one of the few companies both producing and exhibiting films. According to Mr Horace Gilbert, and this is confirmed by the approved plans of the building, the pictures were back-projected on to a screen of a special translucent type.[25] There was a change of programme on Mondays and Thursdays.

The opening offerings were 'Cleopatra', 'In the Gulf of Salerno', 'Forbidden Fruit', 'A Tantalising Young Lady',' The Ticket of Leave Man', 'Baffles, Bandit', 'The Biter Bit' and 'Tommmy and the Powder'. In July, the cinema changed to three separate performances on Saturdays 'for the convenience of patrons'.

The two Empresses were, unfortunately, soon in trouble. The trade papers reported good business until the summer, but there were indications from the variety of promotional activities that the clientele was not always large or loyal. For example, singing competitions were tried in July at Mere Road. After August, there are no more reports in the *Kinematograph Weekly*. Empress Picture Palaces, a subsidiary of the London Cinematograph Co., faced their creditors in October 1910.[26] The three share holders were given as F.C. Bostall, W. Freeman and P.W. Willard. The court heard that both cinemas were at that moment closed because Leicester Corporation had cut off their electricity supply. Another cinema that the company owned in Broadmeads, Bristol was also temporarily closed. The running expenses of the two Leicester cinemas were £64 per week, which included £17 for wages and £17.10s for the hire of films. Appointing a liquidator, the court also heard that negotiations were in hand for the sale of the cinemas.

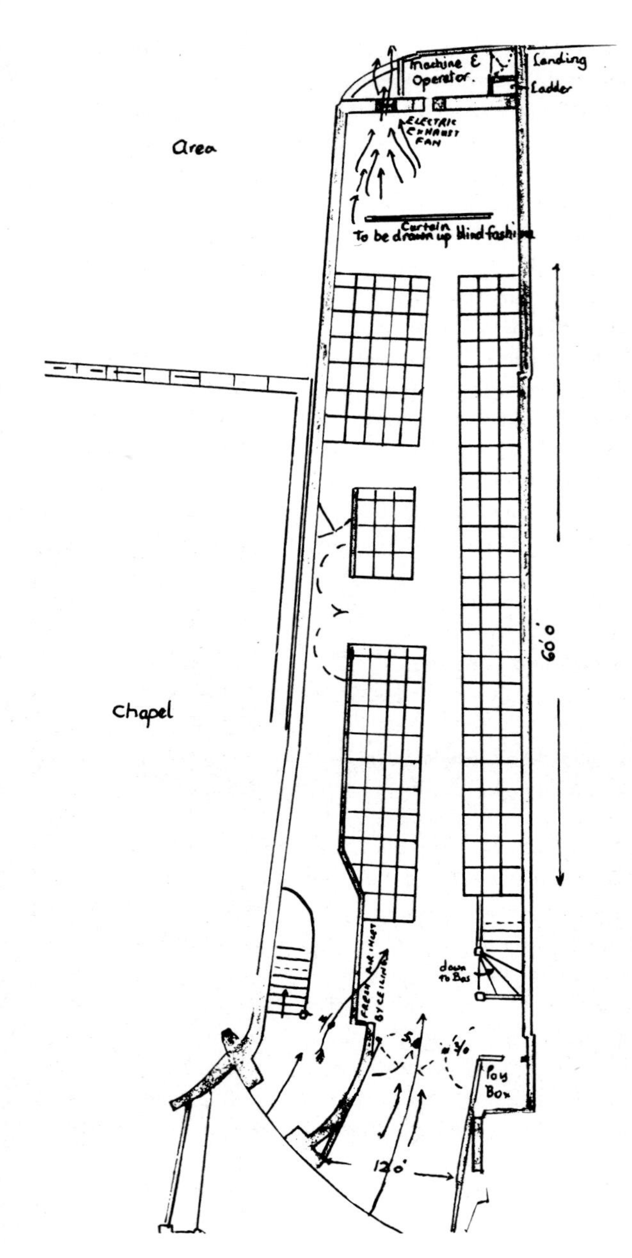

Plan showing the position of the Operator's Room and the rear projection screen at the Empress Picture House, Belvoir Street. Plan submitted by Keites and Fosbrooke on March 18th 1910.
Courtesy Leicestershire Record Office.

References to the re-opening of the Mere Road building are many and confusing. In January 1911, the *Kinematograph Weekly* reported that Messrs Cowen and Brown had opened a re-modelled and re-furnished Empress with a select bijou orchestra, and the latest releases projected by a Kamm's Maltese Cross Chrono, 'with good business resulting'. In February, the *Kinematograph Weekly* further announced that a Mr John Butters had re-opened the Empress, Mere Road as the Picturedrome, that it had been re-modelled and re-decorated, and that it was doing good business. It now only had a continous performance from 7 p.m.

until 10.30 p.m. The music was provided by pianist Jack Eustace and the projection by Mr E. West. There was a further disclosure, at the end of March, that Mr E.C. Clayton of Sheffield had re-opened the old Empress under the name of the Picturedrome to be run in conjunction with his other provincial halls. Mr B. Taylor was announced as the capable manager now experiencing 'good houses'.[27] Hereafter, the cinema was usually referred to as Clayton's Picturedrome.

In May 1911 it was announced that the ownership of the Belvoir Street Cinema had changed to Argyll Picture Palaces Ltd of London, and that Mr H.E. Webbey had become the manager.[28]

During these summer months, things moved very swiftly. There seems to have been a race between the various owners to be the first to get their cinema into operation. Whilst some halls were being built initially for use as cinemas, there were other applications to the Watch Committee for the conversion of existing buildings. One such, by Alfred Macaulay, was for the upper room of the Secular

The Empress, Belvoir Street in 1991. The stucco work was probably part of the building before its conversion to a cinema in 1910. *Photograph by author.*

Mr Bert Dent in 1909.
Kinematograph Weekly

Hall in Humberstone Gate. The Chief Fire Officer reported that there was room for 800 or 900 people to be seated, and that there were two exits only one of which communicated with the outside of the building. He recommended that another exit be built before a licence should be granted. The Watch Committee, however, decided not to entertain the granting of a licence under any circumstances.[29]

The Grand Electric Palace, Silver Street

The Midland Electric Theatres Ltd, a company formed by Waller Jeffs and Partners, were in the course of constructing a cinema in Silver Street next to the Antelope Hotel to accommodate 550 persons.[30] In the meantime, the prospective manager, Mr Bert Dent was showing a programme of Kinemacolor films at the Temperance Hall. He had had management experience at Grimsby and Derby, and had been most recently at the Palace in Attercliffe, Leeds.[31]

Kinemacolor was a natural colour process devised by Englishman George Albert Smith and American Charles Urban. It used a blue-green and a red rotating filter to produce black and white panchromatic positives which in turn were projected through a blue-green and red rotating filter. The taking and projecting speed was twice that of the standard camera (about 32 frames per second) and, with the light also having to pass through gelatine filters, exposure became a problem even in good lighting conditions.[32]

An article in the *Bioscope* of March 4th 1909 only indicated mild approval for the process. The reviewer certainly did not regard the colour effects as reproducing 'the veritable hues and tints of nature' as the adverts claimed. 'The least expert in the audience could tell that a leaden blue was not the veritable

The Kinemacolor projector with red and green filters on the front disc.
Courtesy Science Museum. Crown copyright.

hue and tint of a young lady's arm'. Green and red flashes of light sometimes obscured everything else on the screen, and it was 'the general consensus' that the films produced more eye-strain than conventional ones.

The *Daily Post* reviewer, however, was impressed. 'Kinemacolour *[sic]* pictures at the Temperance Hall continue to draw large audiences. This is not surprising having regard to the novelty of this invention. Here we see for the first time a large and varied collection of beautiful pictures produced in colours. Soldiers drilling in bright uniforms, and Seascapes, and a wide variety of other pictures - interest, news and comedy.'[33] The *Kinematograph Weekly* listed the programme as 'A Shipwrecked Mariner', ' An Indian Bride', 'Betty in Hot Water', 'The Derby of 1910' and Kinemacolor studies. The pictures of the funeral of the late King were shown in black and white. Kinemacolor pictures of the funeral had been taken but they were not shown in Leicester until November when they were held over at the Grand for a second week. Monochrome pictures taken by the Warwick Film Company had been shown at the Mere Road Empress on May 24th.

The programme at the Temperance Hall ran from 3 p.m. to 11 p.m. and local news and trade papers reported excellent business each week. Mr Dent hired a piano to be used at the performance from William Russell's, the piano shop almost next door. He also asked for someone to play it until they could engage a permanent pianist. It was thus that Mr Horace Gilbert first began his connections with the cinema. Mr Gilbert, then an apprentice piano tuner, recalls that he did not fit his music to the pictures but that he played anything that came into his head. When the cinema actually opened, he returned to his apprenticeship.[34]

The Electric Palace, Silver Street.
Elevation of the proposed frontage submitted April 1st 1910.
Courtesy Leicestershire Records Office.

The Watch Committee granted a licence to the Silver Street Theatre on July 19th 1910. The submitted plans show that, above the exterior paybox entrance, there was a semicircular facade with stucco embellishments and the inscription 'Palace of Life'. This was altered to 'The Palace of Beauty' in the finished building. In the foyer, there was a tea-room and buffet. A smaller tea-room was next to the balcony.[35]

GRAND ELECTRIC PALACE,
SILVER STREET, LEICESTER.

OPEN THURSDAY,
JULY 28th, at 6.30 p.m.,

With the Finest Selection of ANIMATED PICTURES ever produced in Leicester, including the

WONDERFUL KINEMACOLOR

ANIMATED PICTURES,
In all the hues and tints of nature.

The Theatre will be OPEN DAILY from 3 p.m. to 10.30 p.m.

CONTINUOUS EXHIBITIONS. NO WAITING

Tea is supplied Free of charge to patrons occupying 1s. and 6d. seats between 4 and 5.30 o'clock.

Come in when you like.
Stay as long as you like.

ADMISSION:- .... 1s., 6d., and 3d.

GRAND ELECTRIC PALACE, SILVER STREET, LEICESTER.

OPEN JULY 28TH, AT 6.30 P.M.

Opening announcement for the Grand Electric Palace in the *Leicester Daily Mercury.*

The Grand Electric Palace, Silver Street in January 1911 as shown in *Kinematograph Weekly.*

The July 28th opening of the cinema had been signalled in a series of advertisements in the *Daily Mercury* in the latter half of July. Continuous performance was promised from 3 p.m. until 10.30 p.m. Between 4 and 5 o'clock, patrons of the 1s (5p) and 6d ($2^1/_2$p) seats were offered tea at no extra charge. The 3d patrons did not qualify.[36]

The *Daily Mercury* reported the actual opening, at length.

> The Grand Electric Palace in Silver Street erected by the Midland Electric Theatres (Ltd) within the past few months was opened this afternoon, the directors of the company holding an invitation exhibition. The Theatre is the only one, at present, run by the company in Leicester, but similar theatres have been opened at Derby and at Nottingham whilst it is contemplated opening others in the counties of Leicester, Nottinghamshire, Derbyshire and Staffordshire shortly. The company runs

Interior plan of the second floor of the Grand Electric Palace showing the position of the Gallery and Tea Room. *Courtesy Leicestershire Records Office.*

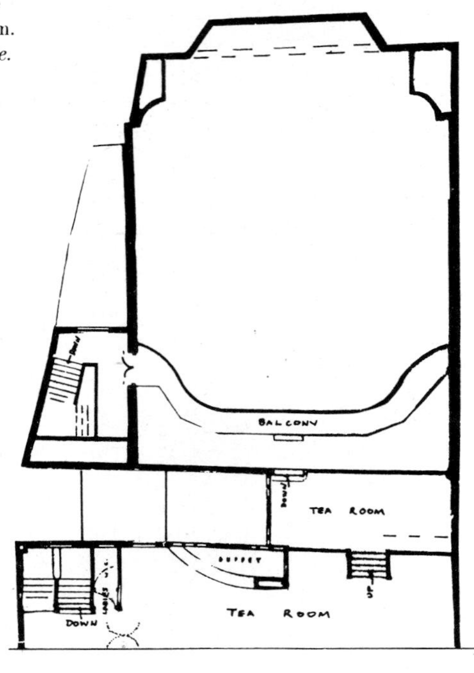

in conjunction with a large London syndicate which supplies films in great numbers from all over the world. These are produced simultaneously, with the result that weekly there is a constant change of programme.

The erection is indeed 'The Palace of Beauty' that it is claimed to be. It is built in white stone and plaster decorated by ornamental designs and illuminated at night by hundreds of semi-hidden electric globes amongst the decorative work. The front is exceedingly striking; the female figure at the centre and top of the building with an upraised lamp, being very effective.'[37]

The *Kinematograph Weekly* described the cinema as spacious with an auditorium 120 by 32 feet and stated that the architect was Mr Arthur Eaton and the builder Mr J. Dickinson.[38]

The inside decorations were in a single colour scheme of Rose du Barry and white. Upholstered tip-up seats were fixed in all parts of the house. The newspaper report estimated the seating as 600, slightly above the approved seating plan. The 'splendidly decorated tea-rooms' which could serve any number of visitors were behind the small balcony. Another feature, not clearly defined on the submitted plans, was a 'family' box with an 'excellent view' capable of seating a private party of twenty people. The interior decorations were by Messrs Chambers and Sons of Leicester.

The opening programme included Kinemacolor films described by the reporter, in a neat summing up of the other available processes, as having 'no tinting, hand-work, stencil-work or similar devices, the work comprising solely the natural pictures upon the original film.' The three short films shown, 'A visit to Brighton', 'Villefranche' and 'A Water Carnival' had been included in the first public presentation of Kinemacolor on February 26th, 1909 at the Palace Theatre, Shaftesbury Avenue.[39] In order to protect the patent the Natural Colour Kinematograph Company only authorized one showman or cinema in each area to have exclusive rights on the special projector and films.[40]

All the other films in the programme had been released during July:

'A Cowpuncher's Ward' (Essanay)	Western Drama	957 ft.
'Pictures from Upper Egypt' (Nordisk)	Travel	302 ft.
'Robert Hyde's Double Life' (Lux)	R. Stevenson copy	659 ft.
'Does She Love Me? (Pathé)	Comedy	510 ft.
'The Broken Vow' (Pathé)	Drama	560 ft.
'Never Judge by Appearances' (Lux)	Comedy	506 ft.
'Who Said Sausages? (Lux)	Comedy	455 ft.
	total	**3289 ft.**

MIDLAND ELECTRIC THEATRES (1911), LTD.

SECRETARY J SEDGWICK, A.C.A.,
TELEPHONE 267.
TELEGRAMS "EQUITY, DERBY"

Registered Office:—
3, St. Mary's Gate,
Derby.

To whom it may concern,

Miss May Greaves has just concluded a two ye?r's engagement with us as pianist, and I can thoroughly recommend her as a first class Picture Pianist. Her reason for leaving us was on account of us installing a complete Orchestra.

Signed... Bert Dent...
Supervising Manager.

Courtesy Mrs Godby.

With the Kinemacolor films, this would give a film running time of over an hour. The ten reel changes could account for a further twenty minutes. Two operators, Messrs Smith and Harrison, were in charge of two ordinary projectors and one Kinemacolor projector from the outset, and this would have shortened the interval between each film. The first manager was Mr J. Eke. and the company secretary was Mr J. Sedgwick. Initially the music was provided by an electric piano, but shortly after the opening the wife of the manager, 'a most efficient pianist', took over.[41]

In April 1911, Mr Frank Dobney was appointed as manager. A new series of advertisements announcing that 'For Kinemacolour Pictures, You Must Visit The Silver Street Electric Theatre', also indicated that the 'Grand Electric Palace' had been dropped in favour of a less elegant but more practical title.[42]

The Boulevard Electric and Variety Theatre

On July 19th 1910 the licence was transferred from the Boulevard Skating Rink to an adjacent building, designed by architects Messrs Ellis and Whitmore, to be called the Boulevard Electric and Variety Theatre.[43] With Mr J. Noble as manager, it opened on July 30th 1910. There were two complete performances at 6.30 and 8.30, and there were matinees on Thursday and Saturday at 2.30. On the Saturday at 10.30 a.m. there was an additional children's matinee. There were 500 seats and its prices of admission were: box seats 1s 6d (7½p),

THE BOULEVARD ELECTRIC THEATRE
Managing Director:- J. NOBLE
COSIEST PLACE OF ENTERTAINMENT IN LEICESTER
Scenery and Artistic Decorations by Mr. E. Leigh (late of Royal Opera House.)
GRAND OPENING, SATURDAY, JULY 30th,
With High-class Coloured and Black and White Pictures, also Grand Variety Entertainment. Entire change of pictures twice weekly, Monday and Thursday.
Special Performances on Bank Holiday Monday, and Tuesday at 10.30, 2.30, 6.30, and 8.30. Remainder of week 2.30, 6.30, and 8.30. First Performance Special Matinee at 2.30 on Saturday, July 30th. All Matinees Pictures only. Prices of Admission: Reserved Seats 1s., Stalls 6d., Pit Stalls 3d. Twice Nightly at 6.30 and 8.30. There will be a Special Morning Performance every Saturday after July 30th at 10.30 for School Children. Admission 2d., 3d., 6d.

Opening announcement for the Boulevard Electric Theatre in *Leicester Daily Mercury*.

reserved seats 1s (5p), pit stalls 6d ($2^1/_2$p), and pit 3d (1p).[44]

The *Daily Mercury* reported on a special 'full dress rehearsal for the opening' on Friday evening July 29th.[45] Once again, the accommodation was over-estimated at 700 seats, but it was reported that 'the comfort of the patrons is well studied,' and that 'the artistic richness and brightness of the decorations are pleasing features'. The advertisements for the opening had indicated that the scenery and decorations were by Mr E. Leigh, late of the Royal Opera House. The projector, of course, was operated by Charles West.

'The animated pictures shown last night,' the writer, somewhat vaguely, but glowingly reported, 'afforded a satisfactory indication of the intention of the manage-

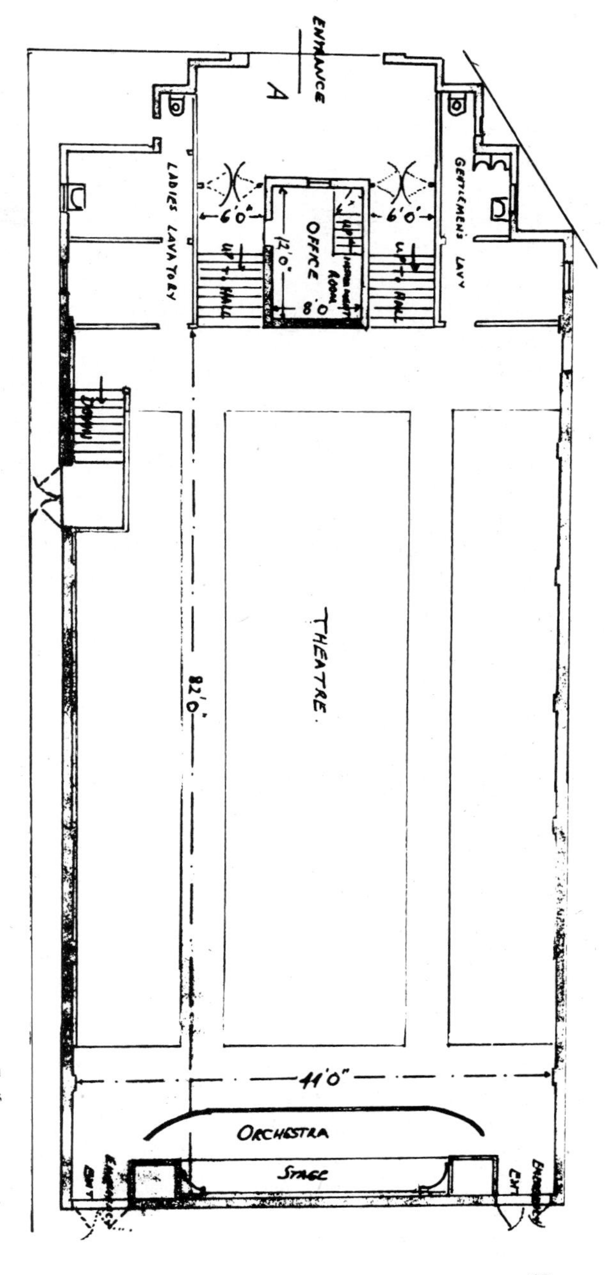

The Boulevard Cinema, Western Boulevard. Ground floor of plans designed by Messrs Ellis and Whitmore and submitted March 1st 1910. The cinema was built alongside the roller skating rink. *Courtesy Leicestershire Records Office*

The building which housed the Boulevard Cinema from 1910-18.
Photographed in 1991 by author.

ment to provide this class of entertainment on the most acceptable lines.' The *Kinematograph Weekly* supplied the titles of the whole programme:

'The Minstrel' (Pathé)	Colour hist. drama	840ft.
'The Pardon' (Urban Film Co.)	Drama	675ft.
'The Precocious Cyclist' (Le Lion Films)	Comedy	380ft.
'The Butler's Revenge' (Cosmopolitan)	Comedy	375ft.
'Over Silent Paths' (American Biograph)	Drama	950ft.
'Accidents Will Happen' (Edison)	Comedy	289ft.
'The Cowboy's Sweetheart' (Essanay)	Comedy drama	978ft.
'The Hindoo's Treachery' (Cricks & Martin)	Drama	780ft.
'It Pays To Advertise'	?	400ft.
	total	**5667ft.**

This would account for about 90 minutes of screen-time, and the whole programme was scheduled to fit into a two hour period with separate performances.

In August, the *Leicester Pioneer* described the new cinema as a 'dazzling and up-to-date show piece'.[46] To begin with, live variety acts, such as that presented on the first night by the Hamoril Concert Party (originally the Leicester Pierrots), were included in the programme. Later in the year, these were dropped, and continuous performances were begun.

The High Street Electric Theatre

On 26th August 1910, the High Street Electric Theatre opened its doors for the first time.[47] The *Bioscope* improbably reported that it was to be called 'The Cinema Electric Theatre.'[48] In July, a letter objecting to the Corporation giving permission for their land to be used for 'frivolous purposes' had been published in the *Daily Mercury*, but there was no other reported opposition.[49] The building was designed by the Birmingham architects, Ward and Bell, under the direction of the London and Provincial Electric Theatres Ltd.[50]

The local and trade press made only passing comments upon its opening, but since most of the exterior of the cinema still stands, the shortage of contemporary description and comment is not so damaging. Above the entrance, the stucco design proclaims the building's purpose. It differs in a number of ways from the architects original drawing. A feature of the interior was the 'oriental' surround to the screen translated faithfully from the plans. This kind of

The Electric Theatre, High Street. Elevation of entrance as designed by Ward and Bell, Birmingham, and submitted April 1st 1910.
Courtesy Leicestershire Records Office

The High Street Cinema in 1991 and close up of the decorative pediment.
Author's photographs.

Above: Interior elevation showing screen area from plans submitted April 1st 1910. *Courtesy Leicestershire Records Office.* *Below:* The Allefex machine as illustrated in *Kinematograph Weekly.*

elaboration became standard in the later Picture Palaces: a mixture of the exotic with the theatrical. There was no gallery and the stalls seating capacity was 700. Two Tyler-Ernemann 'Imperator' projectors enabled continuous performances to be delay- and trouble-free.[51] The first manager was Mr Reynolds Benjamin. A 'Bijou' orchestra consisting of a piano, violin and cello provided the music, and a device called an 'Allefex' provided noises and effects.[52] This latter item, marketed by A. and H. Andrews at £29/15/-, claimed to provide all the necessary noises for a variety of films. Its repertoire included running water, breaking crockery, whistles, pistols and puffing engines, but it was hardly more versatile than the average effects man with his shells, and sandpaper.[53]

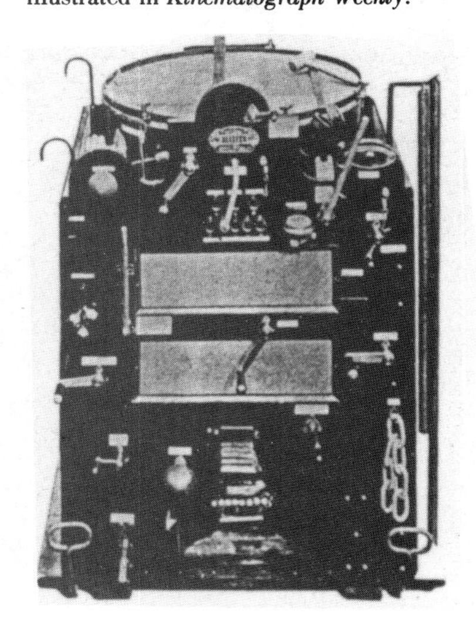

In the same week, the Belvoir Street Pictures advertised 'A picture that sings with the human voice; no gramophone used.' The reporter on the *Pioneer* revealed that 'an unseen singer behind the screen illustrated many scenes vocally.' Another report indicated that the theatre had secured the services of an accomplished pianist, 'whose musical accompaniments are an attraction in themselves.'[54]

The Picture House, Granby Street

The notices accorded to these early cinemas were nothing compared with the publicity given to the opening of the Provincial Cinematograph Company's Picture House in Granby Street.[55] In May 1910, the company was advertising the sale of shares for the purpose of raising capital to build first-class cinematograph theatres in Belfast, Birmingham, Bradford, Bristol, Dublin, Edinburgh, Glasgow, Leeds, Leicester, Liverpool, Manchester, Newcastle, Nottingham, Portsmouth and Sheffield.

The site negotiated for the Leicester Picture House was on the edge of Town Hall Square. This land, belonging to the Council, had for eleven years remained an undeveloped open space behind the Granby Street premises of the Coffee Company. In 1899, the Estates Committee had decided that it was not wanted for public purposes and that it should be let. Its use for the School Board had been considered but not acted upon. It was not big enough for the police department and, in June, the Estates Committee of Leicester Town Council proposed to lease the plot to the Provincial Cinematograph Company for fifty years at a rental of £150 per annum, on condition that at least £3,000 was spent on the building,

The space in which the Picture House was to be built. From a hand-tinted postcard.

and that satisfactory arrangements were made with the owners of the adjoining buildings for proper exits.[56]

In July, when the proposal was referred back to the Council, there was not only a significant amendment, but also a loudly voiced opposition to it. The *Kinematograph Weekly*, in an editorial, accused the Council of trying to milk as much as they could from the agreement with the Provincial Cinematograph Company. Originally, the editor suggested, they had been glad to find a leasee for the plot, but now that they saw the possibility of great profit in the venture, they had raised the rental to £350 per annum and reduced the lease to 21 years. Criticisms of the design which was said to be 'unworthy of the site on which it was intended to place it', were certainly unjustified, in the opinion of the editor. 'It may be news to the municipal dignitaries of Leicester that Provicial Cinematograph Theatres Ltd have a reputation of erecting some of the finest picture theatres in the country'. He went on: 'One of the largest furnishing firms in London - Hampton and Sons - will provide seating and furnishing, and the interior enrichments will be carried out under the supervision of well-known expert in the style of Bartolzzi.'[57]

The Town Council debate produced some acrimony, some humour, and eventually a very large majority in favour of the amendment. Alderman Sawday, in proposing that the lease be granted, attempted to head off 'the moralists' by saying that he failed to see anything degrading or demoralising in the entertainment provided by the picture theatres. He refuted accusations that he was financially interested in the project. He did, however, hold shares in an 'opposition company' giving entertainment at the Temperance Hall.

Councillor Riley opened the case for the opposition, alleging that there was strong feeling in the town against the proposal. By adopting the scheme, he continued, the Town Council would be encouraging a form of entertainment that was inartistic, uneducative, and had a tendency towards the sensational. Such horrors as the Johnson v. Jefferson fight would be exhibited. He also thought that the architect's design for the building was unworthy for the site. Alderman S. Hilton thought that the desire to go to a picture show would soon die away, and the Council would be left 'with nothing to disdain upon'. 'There were already six or seven such shows in town,' he said. Alderman Biggs denied that there was anything demoralising, degrading or debasing in a picture exhibition, and he added that it was in the power of the Watch Committee to exercise supervision of the items exhibited. Councillor Hincks, who was chairman of the Watch Committee, countered the suggestion that it was the element of semi-darkness in picture show entertainment that was upsetting to 'the moralists', by pointing out that Band of Hope lantern slide shows would need to be prohibited if this was

PICTURE HOUSE, LEICESTER.

Top: This drawing, by the architects Naylor and Sale, appeared with the newspaper report of the opening of the Picture House. The entrance to the Café can be seen on the left, and the long panelled corridor, leading to the cinema auditorium, is on the right.

Bottom: An early programme cover for the Picture House. *Author's collection*

seen as a valid objection.

Even after the vote, some concern still remained about the design, since the back of the cinema would face onto the Town Hall Square. Eventually this was approved, the building was built, and a licence was granted on December 20th 1910.

The cinema opened on Thursday December 22nd and on the next day the following report appeared.[58] It is quoted almost in its entirety because it was the first mention of any cinema at all in the *Leicester Daily Post*, considered to be the 'elite' newspaper. An almost identical report was published in the *Daily Mercury* that evening. The *Leicester Pioneer*, the working man's paper, which gave notice of the other cinemas, hardly thought fit to mention the Picture House.

> The latest of Leicester's cinematograph theatres was opened yesterday. It is in as good a position as could be found in the town. Granby Street being quite the central avenue for residents and visitors, it is likely to become one of the best known features of the borough. The theatre itself is admirably built and excellently furnished. It accommodates 600 persons; 500 on the floor of the

theatre and 100 in the balcony, and everything is done to ensure both the comfort of the visitors and the excellence and clearness of the pictures shown. Special attention is given to the ventilation and, amongst other details of the theatre, the operating room is fireproof.

Lady Noreen Bass [59] said it gave her great pleasure to be at the opening of the theatre. She was introduced by Mr J.J. Newbould. She was struck, she continued, by the beauty of the building and was sure from what she had heard from the managers that the pictures would be worthy of the house, and would be amusing, interesting and intellectual. Events that were going on in the world were of the highest educational value. She hoped that the Picture House would become a source of interest for the people of Leicester.

The pictures consisted of the following: 'Glimpses of Wild Bird Life' in lovely colours; 'The Royal Mint' and ' A Day with a Foxhound', two brand new instructional films; 'Winona', a western love story; and 'A Living Blackboard', a trick film. Also a newsreel film was shown of the funeral at 9 o'clock that very day of the three policemen shot at Houndsditch. The utmost despatch must have been used in developing the photographs and making the cinematograph film. The enterprise displayed in this respect speaks well for the future success of the picture house.

The Building

When the Estates Committee of the Corporation asked for sanction to lease a portion of the Town Hall Square to the Provincial Cinematograph Theatres Ltd, doubt was expressed as to the wisdom of such a course. It was felt by some that the building would not be an improvement to the town, and by others that the entertainment was not necessary, artistically or educationally. But the Committee had their way, and today, Leicester is in possession of one of the best and cosiest picture theatres in the country. The front entrance is in Granby Street through part of the premises of the Coffee House Company. It has been carefully designed to harmonise with the general style of the buildings by which it is surrounded. One enters through a portico with granite pillars over a marble pavement into an Old English lounge with an ingle nook and comfortable fireplace. The walls are encased in oak panelling and the furniture is in strict keeping with the surroundings. The vestibule beyond, the artistic treatment of which is in keeping with the other parts of the theatre, has been designed to shut out both light and draught from the main hall.

One of the more striking features about the hall is the balcony at the back, access to which is gained from the lounge. The floor rises in tiers and as the seats are 3 ft. apart from centre to centre, they afford the maximum of comfort. The seating downstairs is arranged in three groups by two lateral aisles and ample spacing gives exceptional comfort. The proscenium arch is surmounted by plaster work with caryatids [60] supporting the roof trusses, and dividing the wall space into bays, which gives a particularly handsome appearance to the interior.

The Theatre was built by Messrs Herbert and Son, to the plans of Naylor and Sale, Derby, who have designed all the picture houses for the company. The furnishing throughout has been executed by Messrs. Inglesant. The general colour scheme is scarlet relieved by reseda green. All the seats have been designed with a view to comfort; those on the balcony are probably the most luxurious ever used in any theatre. To avoid the discomfort usually associated with cinematograph theatres, special attention has been paid to the ventilation, provision having been made whereby the air is completely renewed 8 times an hour without draught.

When it is added that a cloakroom and a parcel office have been provided, and that light refreshments may be obtained, it will be seen that the comfort and convenience of vistors have been thoroughly studied.

The programme of films will be changed each Monday and Thursday, with the exception of special items which it may be considered advisable to introduce and withdraw in accordance with popular demand.[61]

The Tyler/Ernemann Imperator Projector (hand-cranked version) as installed in the Floral Hall, High Street, and Picture House Cinema.
Kinematograph Weekly

Cost of admission was: stalls 6d, balcony 1s and children half-price. Opening time was from 2 p.m until 10.30 p.m. with continuous performances.[62] The chief

Mabel Greaves, one of the pianists at the Picture House in 1911.
Courtesy Mrs Godby.

projectionist was none other than Charles West, leaving his Motiograph projector at the Boulevard and taking over the two Tyler Ernemanns here.[63] The musical accompaniment was provided by seventeen year-old Miss Mable (May) Greaves, beginning her long association with cinemas and musical accompaniment in the town.

The Floral Hall Picture Theatre

At the same time, a new picture house was being finished on part of Palace of Varieties site in the old Floral Hall, which had been disused for several years. Frank Matcham and Co., the theatrical architects, designed the alterations, and the building work was carried out by G. Duxbury and Co. of Leicester. It opened on Boxing Day 1910.[64]

The *Daily Post,* , in a brief description, said: 'The long corridor entrance hall is gaily planted on each side with trees, whilst the hall itself is comfortable. At the back is a lounge with easy chairs and tables.' The *Kinematograph Weekly* implied that it was correct to retain the original name of the hall because so much of the new decoration had been carried out in the floral style. The lounge was in the form of a pergola with wicker chairs and palms, and there were lattice work flowers in the corridor designs. The furnishings were by Inglesants and there was seating for 600, all in tip-ups.[65]

The projectors were ordered and fitted in record time. On Thursday evening December 22nd, Will Day of the Tyler Apparatus Company took an

order to fit out the hall. On Friday, two Tyler-Ernemann Imperator machines and accessories were despatched from London. 'The hall was wired, the machinery installed and the whole thing passed by the County Council *[sic]* in record time, and a show was given to the public just after mid-day on Monday, December 26th, - less than four days from order to performance!' The current for the projector arcs was obtained from a generator on the premises.[66]

The first programme contained a colour film 'David and

Left: The Floral Hall in the 1950s. *Courtesy Carl Jennings Collection.*

Below: Belgrave Gate *circa* 1913 with the Floral Hall Picture Theatre. *Author's collection.*

The rear entrance of the Floral Hall in the 1950s. *Courtesy Carl Jennings Collection.*

Goliath' and several interest films. Opening times were from 3 p.m. to 10.30 p.m. and admission charges were: lounge 1s., stalls 6d, and pit 3d. Afternoon tea was served, in the lounge, free of charge between 4 p.m. and 5.30 p.m. Films were changed twice per week and the programme ran continuously. The manager, Mr George Reynolds, was also manager of the Palace Theatre, so that the day-to-day management of the cinema was in the hands of Mr Pearce, who had previously been chief operator at the Holloway Empire, London. Mr Arthur Rawson was appointed as pianist.

A Projectionist's Day

An impression of the daily routine of a cinematograph operator can be gained from an apochryphal article printed in the *Bioscope* of July 28th 1909. Of first concern was the care and maintenance of the electric motor supplying the direct current for the carbon arc illumination. Next, the projector or projectors needed a thorough cleaning. At midday, the 'boy' arrived with the new batch of films. These were checked for torn sprocket holes and for any heavy joins that might jump the sprocket wheels. Black spacing was placed between two short films on the same reel, so that the programme didn't 'jump straight from a deep dramatic into a silly Continental comic without a break.'

After half-an-hour break for dinner, the operator got back for a 2 p.m. start. In the sequence reported, he had one stoppage because of a blown fuse, but nothing more till until 3.45 p.m. He then heard that the Council Inspector was on the premises. He hoped that the manager would keep him downstairs for a few minutes, so that he could check the box. He trusted the 'handle' to the boy

'Operators we have met'. *Left:* The novice. *Centre:* The dude. *Right:* The general utility man. From *The Bioscope* September and October 1909.

whilst he put the smother blanket properly in place from its more permanent job of keeping out the draught from the ventilation hole. He brought in the water and sand buckets from the roof outside. 'There isn't much room when they are in the projection box'. When he had put the cover back on the spool box, he was ready for his inspection.

At 5 p.m. whilst he was out having a cup of tea, the carbon got a 'crater'. He was supposed to have his break in the box, but 'nine hours in that oven is no joke'. He returned to discover that the 'boy' had put on the wrong film. Before the day was out, he had a film break, and a fault with the reel catching on the spool cover. He mused on the fact that audiences sat patiently through a quarter of an hour between acts at a live theatre, and yet they stamped their feet with impatience for a stoppage of less than three minutes in the cinema. The stoppages caused the programme to over-run, so, risking the manager's anger, he missed out the last film.

With the close of 1910, the first great phase of Leicester's cinemas ended. During the next few years more were to be built, at an average of two per year, but there was never to be the same kind of race encountered in the first years. The cinematograph hall was now legitimate by dint of an Act of Parliament, but this was protective not promotional; regulatory rather than reinforcing. Cinemas needed to be controlled by legislation, the argument went, because the highly inflammable film stock made them potentially hazardous. The hidden agenda was that the regulations would also restrict the presentation of undesirable material. The trade had welcomed the intrusion, seeing it as a 'powerful factor in securing a high class of entertainment'.[67]

A 1910 offer to prospective cinema proprietors in *The Bioscope.*

Chapter Three

Finding an Audience 1911-14

It is difficult to estimate the actual size of the audiences that made up the general clientele of the cinema. Trade statistics for the period are almost non-existent and at best are conjectural. The steady growth in cinema building would suggest that there was a surplus to draw on, and that cinema-going was becoming a pastime of more and more sections of society.

Its cheapness originally gave it major support from the working-class and, to some large extent, the subject matter of the majority of the films patronised the taste of popular culture. New cinema buildings began to cater for segregated audiences. The long wooden benches provided in early converted public halls gave way to individual seating, sometimes with tip-up seats, and, often, with clearly deliniated price areas. The building of balconies and galleries also gave some sections of the public the opportunity not to 'rub shoulders with the masses'. As an industry the cinema was looking for a little more prestige and generally called its audiences 'patrons'.

The gradual emergence of the 'feature' film gave more purpose to a cinema visit, especially when 'classic' stories were portrayed. Short films became diversions rather than the main fare. But the proliferation of cinemas had produced a shortage of suitable films and re-issues and duplications were commonplace. It was not unusual to see the same film appearing under different titles at different cinemas. For example, in January 1911 the Picture House had 'Dido and Aeneas' and the Floral Hall 'Ancient Carthage'. This was almost certainly Ambrosio's 'Dido Forsaken by Aeneas', a 1055 foot costume drama released that week.[1]

During 1911 there was a return to an earlier use of the cinematograph. On two occasions[2] the Pavilion used it as a means of showing outside and linking action in a play. In 'The Adder's Tooth', the main action took place in an editor's office, and the linking scenes between the office and the bankrupt editor's home were shown by means of the Bioscope. In 'An Indian Romance', the *Bioscope* 'records early incidents in the story'.

Surprisingly, too, Waller Jeffs' New Century Pictures occupied the Temperance Hall in January, 1911. Good business was reported despite the obvious competition from six other film programmes and the return of La Milo to the Palace. It proved to be Jeff's last visit to the city. Shortly afterwards, the Temperance Hall had its licence revoked because, on his annual inspection, the Fire Officer deemed the exits to be inadequate and badly sign-posted.[3]

The Coronation of King George V

The Coronation of George V in June caused some hectic competition amongst the exhibitors. Once again, the Palace advertised in advance with more fortunate results than in 1902. The Picture House arranged with Mr Charles Hubert, the aviator, to fly from London with films of the Coronation to enable them to be shown on the same day. The plane was to have flown to Rugby and the films were to have been picked up by car and brought to Leicester. However, the bad weather prevented this and the films taken shortly before 11 a.m. were immediately developed, put on a special train and shown that evening at the Picture House.[4] The Silver Street Cinema (The Grand Electric Palace) obtained films from several production companies, so that as many scenes of the Coronation as possible could be seen by their patrons. It was, of course, the only place able to show the scenes in Kinemacolor. A number of films in this process ventured into the realm of historical and contemporary drama. In January 1911 'By

'The Coronation of King George V'.
A three-frame strip of Kinemacolor film showing the alternate red and green sensitive exposures.
Courtesy Science Museum. Crown copyright.

A famous newsreel poster of April 1912 *(Kinematograph Weekly).*

Order of Napoleon' was advertised at the cinema as a special attraction. Since it was only 500 feet long, and passed through the projector at twice the speed of conventional film, it could only have lasted just over four minutes. It may certainly have been enhanced by the playing of the newly installed 'select orchestra'.[5]

Pictures of sensational news stories were still very popular with audiences. Local and national news bulletins were always contained in the programmes under titles such as 'The Leicester Pictorial News', 'The Topical Budget', 'The Topical Times', and Pathé's 'Animated Gazette'. The Palace and the Pavilion showed the news plus a short subject film in their live variety programmes.

Prosecutions under the Cinematograph Act

In January 1911 the Watch Committee had passed a resolution that persons found smoking in the 'operating chambers of cinemas' would be prosecuted. The first such prosecution was in February 1911 against Joe Noble, proprietor and manager of the Boulevard Cinema. In his defence, Mr Noble said that it ought to be the under-manager before the court, since he was the one on duty, when the offence took place. He indicated that he had already served notice on the under-manager and the operator. The magistrates agreed that Mr Noble had done all that he could to prevent breaches of the regulation and restricted his fine to 40s 6d. (£2.03) [6]. Though no one other than Mr Noble is named in the report, management movements reported by the *Kinematograph Weekly,* give the information that Mr N. Horton was replaced by Mr W. Lapworth at the turn of the year. The Boulevard Cinema was again in trouble in December 1913 when the Chief Fire Officer reported them for obstructing a gangway.[7]

The Coliseum, Melton Road

Towards the end of 1911 the skating rink craze once again hit the city and the Boulevard began to entertain large crowds. The Belgrave Skating Rink was in difficulties, however, because the Licensing Committee would not grant it a music licence. To get over this, the Belgrave Skating and Social Club and Institute was formed.[8] Membership was hard to come by and advertisements, placed in the newspaper to recruit more members, refer to it as 'the persecuted rink'. Plans for the conversion of a portion of the hall into a cinema were already before the Watch Committee in September 1911. In February the following year plans were approved for a full conversion into the Belgrave Cinematograph Theatre and, on March 19th, a licence was granted for film exhibitions to begin.[9]

As 'The Coliseum Cinema' it was the largest in the city with a seating capacity variously estimated at between 1,900 and 2,000.[10] The site between Herbert Avenue and Windsor Road still had plenty of room for further

The Coliseum in September 1913. The advertised film is 'The Zulu King', a 14 minute Lubin comedy released in Britain on September 4th 1913.
Courtesy C.E. John Aston Collection.

development and in December 1912 a Grand Café was opened. Shortly after that a billiard hall with 25 tables was fitted out by Messrs Riley and Co.[11]

The Annual General Meeting of Provincial Cinematograph Theatres Ltd. in March 1912 summed up the reasons for the increase in the number of cinemas. 'A year ago, most people classed cinematograph theatres with skating rinks, and looked upon them as passing crazes. Now, the general opinion seems to have changed round to the view that cinematograph theatres of the right kind have come to stay permanently.' The P.C.T. had reason to rejoice. The *Bioscope* of March 14th had reported its declared profit for the year at £35,000.

As more new cinemas were built, the established ones endeavoured to keep their previous clientele, and to preserve some notion of 'house' loyalty. Cycles could be stored free of charge at the Empire, Wharf Street.[12] Soon after its opening 'The Imperial' gave free admission to old age pensioners who showed their cards.[13] The Coliseum had already done this for its Monday matinees from December 1912 and the manager, Charles Burgess, estimated that there had been 10,000 admittances under the scheme.[14]

The mode of operation is as follows:—The Disc Record is placed upon the Gramophone and the Needle is dropped into the starting cut provided on the edge. At the Kinematograph the Operator now adjusts the film in his machine with the picture marked "start" opposite the mask. He then moves the switch handle G (Fig 1) from right to left, which movement connects the Synchroniser and simultaneously gives the starting signal to his assistant at the Gramophone.

The Simplex Synchroniser for the Animatophone.

The Sound of Music

In January the High Street Cinema introduced the Animatophone, another attempt to present viable sound-synchronised films. Synchronisation was achieved by means of a battery-activated 'governor', chain-driven from the projector. With the 'Start' frame in the projector gate in the projection room, and the gramophone needle in the 'start' groove by the screen, the mechanism could be set away with a switch. The operator then turned the projector handle so that he kept the needle pointing to the central calibration (see illustration). The Animatophone was only employed for a small number of musical items, but as usual poor amplification proved its downfall, and the company was wound up in late 1911.[15]

The Picture House, noted for the educational value of its programmes, changed its pianist for a quartet, who according to the paper were 'all capable musicians, and to a large extent are responsible for much delightful entertainment.'[16]

The Floral Hall continued to use a pianist and the paper comments on his efforts too. 'The music is a credit to the pianist and is changed every evening'.[17] This may have been more by accident than design, since it was rare to find scored incidental music, except for the illustrated songs.

The Picture House Quartet became so popular with the patrons that a special musical interval was provided. Apart from this, the players always made the music 'fit in' with the subject matter of the film. 'The way in which it has been chosen to illustrate the theme of emotion, pathos, and tragedy has always been notable. Last night, the orchestra under the direction of Mr W.H. Carter played selections from Falla, Elgar, Lehar, Lestange, Adams, Tschaikowsky, and others whose melodies transport'.[18] This critic was so obsessed with the musical content of the programme that the next week, he failed to comment upon any films and merely listed the items played, complete with the names of the composers.[19] Film criticism had not yet arrived. All films seemed to be good, and some were better than others.

If the *Daily Post* reporter had music on the brain, his plight was not as sorry as that of the young suicide who was reported to have had 'picture shows on the brain'.[20] The unfortunate incident occurred in London, but its sentiments must have been nationwide. The Chairman of the Theatres Committee of the L.C.C. said that if any reasonable definition of harmful or criminal life in pictures shown in picture palaces licensed by the council were given, he would bring it before his executive. 'Of course,' he continued, 'if they were going to exclude pictures having reference to criminal law, then they would have to exclude 'Babes in the Wood' or 'The Forty Thieves'. It would be just as reasonable to have censorship over religious houses, on account of the large number of people who have committed suicide from religious mania'. The film industry was only a few months away from submitting its films voluntarily to a Censorship Board.

Film sources in Britain

A comment by the American Vice-consul at a Sheffield lecture gives a good idea of the types of films being shown in the cinemas at this time. 60% of the films shown in Britain were American, 15% Italian, 10% French, 7% British and the rest from other sources such as Scandinavia and Belgium. 'The American films', he said,' mostly dealt with the so-called Western Drama with stirring action in the open. The French films tended more towards the comic with close-work, where the facial expression and detail count. The French also excelled in historical costume plays in colour. Their photographic excellence is undoubted. The British film producers have gradually improved their photography and their subject matter is of the higher level that cinema shows are approaching. In a broad way, the English makers are tending towards the military drama, and street scenes, and are generally along a high plane, in that they educate and enlighten.'

The Vice-consul offered the opinion that the popular films of five years ago were home dramas; that the western drama had occupied that position two years ago, but that now there is more and more demand for real people and real things. 'Managers confidently state that the day is coming when the tragedies of history as subject matter will supercede entirely the mythical battles of cowboys and "badmen".'[21] This, of course, well fitted the philosophy of the *Daily Post* without it being reflected in the actual programmes of the local cinemas.

The Imperial, Green Lane Road

Proposals for new cinemas were mostly concerned with fresh locations and large seating capacities. But the Imperial Playhouse, Green Lane Road, was built not far away from the original Empress Picture House, Mere Road, now under

The Imperial, Green Lane Road in 1991. *Author's photograph.*

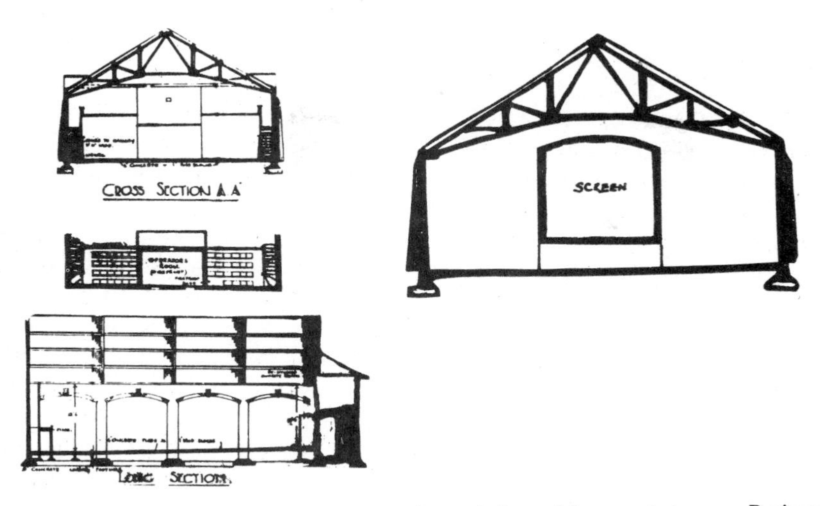

The Imperial, Green Lane Road. Interior elevation and plans of the operator's room. Designed by T. Henry Bowell and submitted September 20th 1912.
Courtesy Leicestershire Records Office.

new ownership and re-named the Picturedrome. Neither was of any great size; the Picturedrome holding 420 and the Imperial 460. The Imperial was built in two months for Messrs Mynard and Co. (a partnership headed by Mr Alfred Mynard, Mr Roland M. Wright and Mr Albert W. Robins) to a design by T. Henry Bowell of the Market Place, Leicester. It had a small gallery with 46 seats and a 15 feet-wide screen. It opened on Thursday December 5th 1912.[22]

Metropolitan Pictures at the Temperance Hall

December was, in fact, a busy month for the exhibitors. The Temperance Hall, which had been closed for cinematograph performances since June 1911 because the Fire Officer considered the exits from the gallery were inadequate, was re-licensed on December 17th 1912. The actual construction of the exits and the fixing of illuminated 'Exit' signs had taken place in November 1911 and the hall had been used for concerts and public gatherings. Under the management of Metropolitan Electric Pictures, film performances were renewed there in January 1913 on all vacant dates in the hall's diary.[23]

The Belvoir Street Picture Playhouse

The Belvoir Street cinema (The Empress) which had been closed for over a year, and whose licence had been allowed to lapse, was also granted a new licence under new management on December 17th 1912. Continuous performances were given from 2 p.m. till 10.30 p.m. The new proprietor was Mr A. Alexander, and the new manager was Mr Harry Cassidy.[24] Previously, the parent company was the London Cinematograph Company, who had followed Empress Picture Houses into liquidation in 1911.[25]

The *Pioneer* commented on the re-opening: 'The pretty little picture house in Belvoir Street has re-opened as The Belvoir Picture Playhouse. Really excellent pictures are submitted, and considering that the pictures have to be operated from behind the screen, they are delightfully clear.'[26] There was only one price of admission, 3d. This was cheaper than when it originally opened.

The Lyric in 1993. *Courtesy Brian Johnson.*

The Lyric Cinema, Knighton.

The next stage of cinema expansion was to bring screen entertainment to the very doorsteps of growing surburban housing estates. In January 1913 plans to convert Knighton Public Hall, built in 1892, into a cinema were approved by the Watch Committee. The architects were Wakerley and Wells who provided a seating capacity of 354 in the stalls and 90 in the small gallery.[27] It had been licensed for 14 days in September 1910, on condition that the apparatus was fixed in compliance with the Act, but no further application had materialized, and the minutes do not reveal who the applicant was.[28]

The new enterprise was the concern of Lyric (Leicester) Ltd, a company registered on February 11th 1913 with a share capital of £3,500. The directors of this were Messrs B. Jackson, T..Thompson, S.T. Crowe and W.H. Shaw and the general manager was Mr John A. Taylor. Their registered office in Manchester immediately identified the leasees as belonging to the H.D. Moorhouse Group.[29]

With the clear intention of allaying the fears of the mainly lower-middle-class neighbourhood, the company staged the official opening on February 13th as a private matinee for local residents. The formal opening

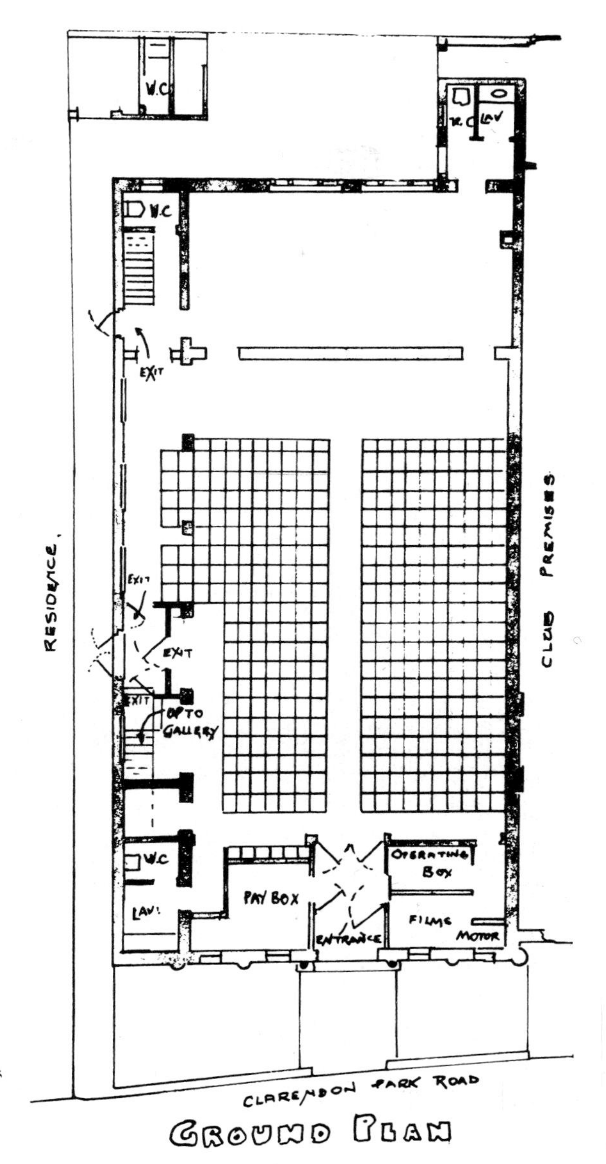

The Lyric, Clarendon Park Road. Interior ground plan as designed by Wakeley and Wells and submitted January 28th 1913.
Courtesy Leicestershire Records Office.

The Lyric (Leicester) Limited.

Managing Director:
Mr. H. D. MOORHOUSE.

Registered Office:
93, MARKET STREET,
MANCHESTER.

Telephones:
2046 City, Manchester.
2272 Leicester Central.

Kindly address all Communications to the Registered Office of the Company, and not to Individuals.

Knighton Cinema,
Clarendon Park Road,
Leicester, Feb 6th 1915

During Miss Greaves term under my management (four months) as Pianist, I have found her perfectly willing & her ability as a musician, is of a very high order.

F. Horsfall.
Manager.

of the programme was by Mr C. Holland (of H.D. Moorhouse Cinemas) and during an interval he remarked on the quality of the pictures shown and on the benefits that theatre would bring to the locality. Mr W. Ferrar, the manager, said that he was determined to maintain the popularity of the house by providing every possible comfort and convenience.

'The theatre is furnished throughout in a luxurious fashion. It is scientifically heated and ventilated, and the atmosphere is regularly treated with an active disinfectant. The seats are of the tip-up variety richly upholstered. A large seating gallery has been erected on one side of the hall with semi-private boxes. The programme will be changed on Mondays and Thursdays and there will be continuous performances from 6.00 p.m. until 10.30 p.m., with the exception of Mondays, Thursdays and Saturdays, when there will be matinees at 2.30. Prices of admission are sixpence and one shilling, and half-price for children under 14 at matinees. The attendance since the opening has been highly satisfactory and the fine programme and capital orchestral music has been much appreciated.' [30] In July the *Bioscope* reported that it had changed its name to the Knighton Cinema.[31]

The Olympia, Narborough Road

Plans for a new cinema on the Narborough Road had been approved on 28th September 1912. Building started almost immediately. 'Olympia (Leicester) Ltd' had been registered as a company on September 26th 1912 offering £3,500 in £1 shares. Directors were shown as B. Jackson of the White Hart Hotel, Leicester, and Messrs S.A. Rhodes, T. Thompson and S.T. Crowe. The registered office was again in Manchester.[32]

The design was by Albert E. King of Loughborough.[33] The Olympia was opened on Thursday March 6th by Mr B. Jackson, who is listed as one of the directors of the Lyric. This was not the only link, for they adopted the same private invitation ploy to sweeten the local residents of 'the high-class residential neighbourhood', and the proprietors, Olympia (Leicester) Ltd also had as their general manager and secretary, Mr John A. Taylor. The resident manager was Mr Frank Gray.

The 'handsome red-brick building was crowded almost to its capacity of 1,250. Tastefully arranged ferns and palms serve to set off to advantage the

The Olympia, Narborough Road. The front elevation from plans submitted on October 18th 1912. Designed by Albert E. King. The 1912 motif was simplified in the eventual building. *Courtesy Leicestershire Records Office.*

The Olympia, Narborough Road *circa* 1914. *Author's collection.*

beautifully decorated interior which is well provided with exits, and fitted with the latest in velvet plush tip-up seating accommodation. A fine rake to the floor ensures an undisturbed view of the screen from all parts of the house. The singing licence, the application for which was adjourned by the Leicester Licensing Committee 3 weeks ago has now been granted. The performances will be continuous every evening from 6p.m. to 10.30 p.m. and matinees will be given three times a week. Prices of admission are 3d., 6d., and 9d.' [34]

In October 1913 the company of Leicester Enterprises was set up with a capital of £11,000 in £1 shares in an agreement between J.F. Johnston and A.S. Evanson for the lease of the Olympia Picture House. The directors are shown as H.D. Moorhouse, B. Jackson and J.F. Johnston.[35] There was no change in the day to day management of the cinema.

The Belgrave Cinema

Plans for a new cinema to be built on a site between 101 and 109 Belgrave Road were submitted to the Watch Committee on June 9th 1913 The design by Seale and Riley of Horsefair Street was for a single storey auditorium 66 feet wide and 96 feet long. An announcement in the *Bioscope* of July 3rd 1913, that building had commenced, suggested that the opening was originally scheduled

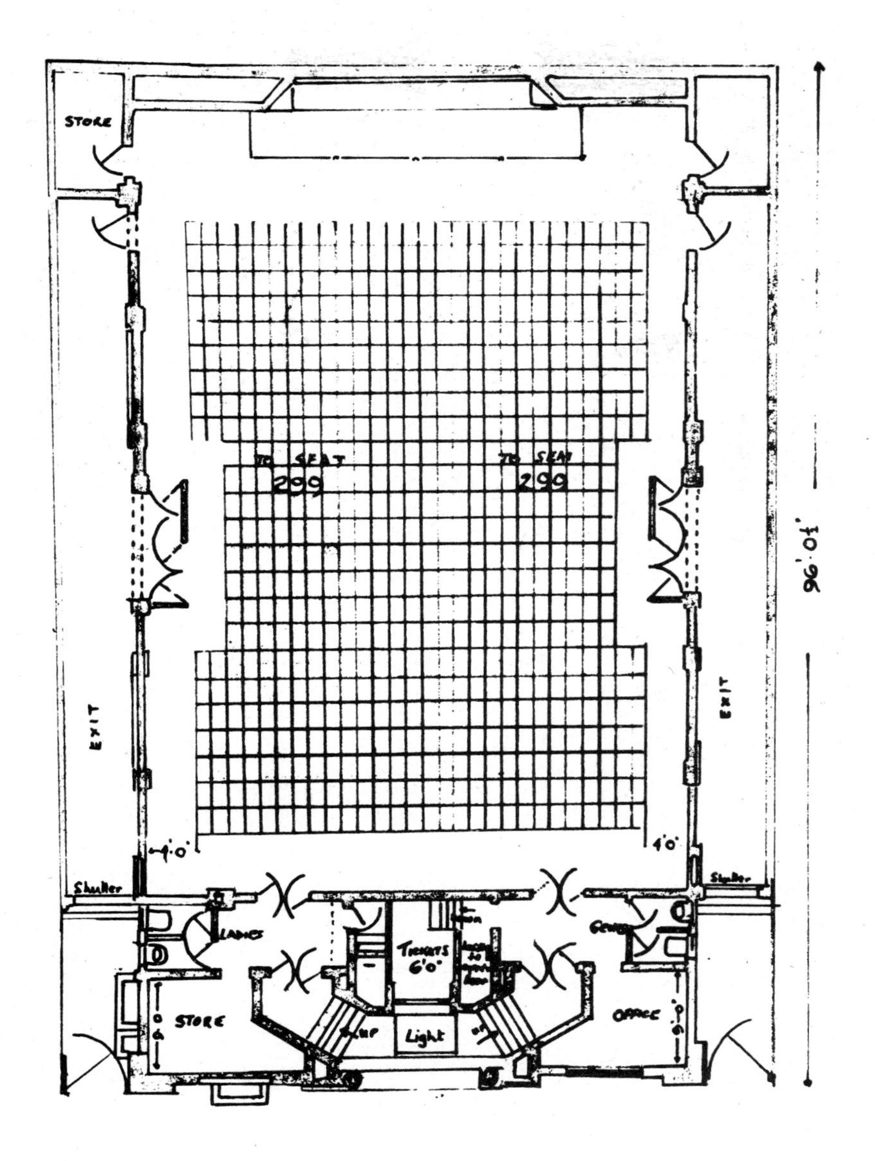

The Belgrave Cinema, Belgrave Road. Ground plan submitted May 6th 1913.
Courtesy Leicestershire Records Office.

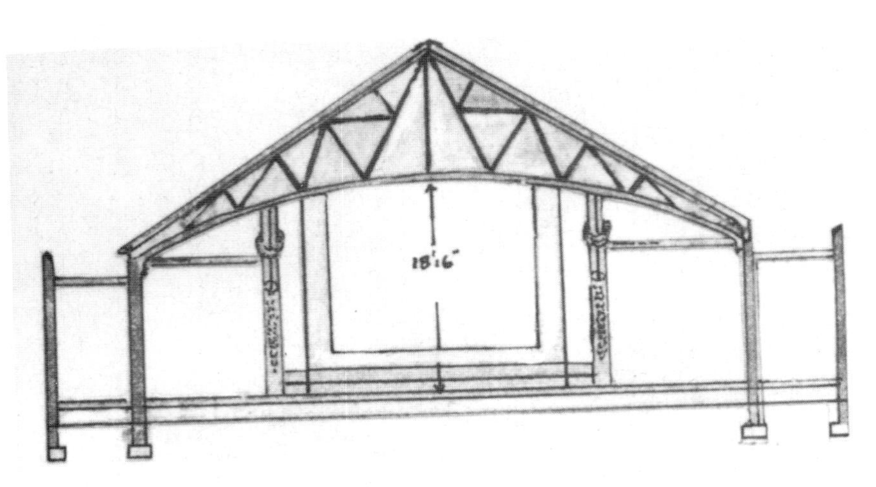

Above: The Belgrave Cinema. Cross section showing screen area. From original designs by Seale and Riley. *Courtesy Leicestershire Records Office.*
Below: The Belgrave Cinema on its closure in 1960. *Courtesy Leicestershire Museums.*

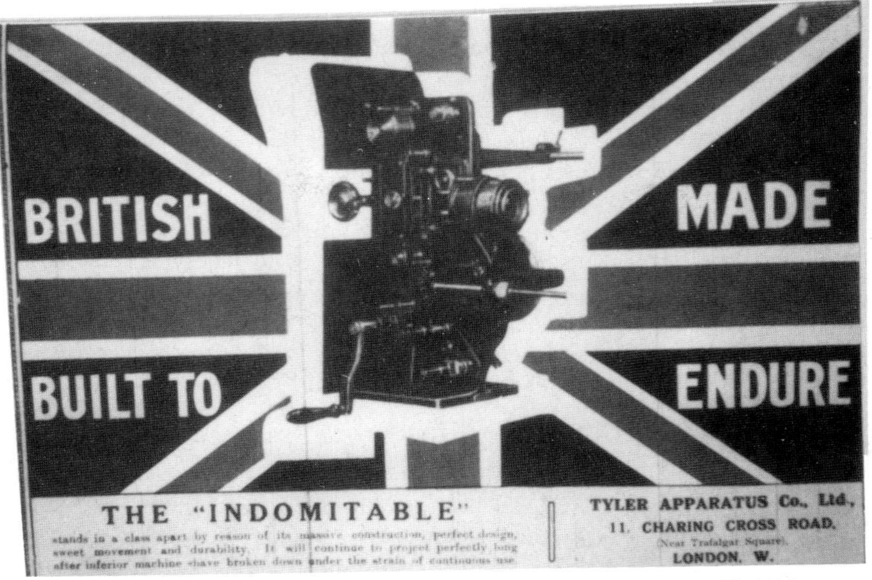

The Indomitable as advertised in *Kinematograph Weekly* of February 13th 1913.

for an August date. The actual opening date was October 6th 1913. The *Bioscope* of October 16th highlighted a number of its innovative features:

'An important addition to Leicester's already lengthy list of picture houses was made with the inaugural opening of the Belgrave Cinema. The last word in picture houses it undoubtedly is, and situated in a teeming industrial centre, there is every reason for predicting a brilliant future for the latest comer.

'Directly opposite is the huge British United Hosiery Works with its 6,000 workers, while the well known home of Wolsey is within a stone's throw. The house which has a seating capacity of between 800 and 900 is splendidly fitted with comfortable wide plush tip-up seats supplied by Messrs Beck and Windibank of Birmingham, from every one of which a fine view of the screen is to be had. The projector is an 'Indomitable'. (This was a version of the Imperator also by Tyler)

'One novel feature is the panel roof lighting, in which powerful electric lights placed in the roof and fitted with reflectors throw a peculiarly pleasing and mellow light into the building below through coloured glass panels inserted into the ceiling. Another is the building on either side of long covered passages running the entire length of the building giving ingress and egress to the body of the hall. These passages are well-lighted and each will hold 300 of the waiting public, thus obviating the forming of queues in the street outside.

'The proprietor and manager is Mr W H.B. Emson and his assistant manager is Mr Nelson B. Brown, late of the Imperial, Green Lane Road. Singing and musical licences (except for brass instruments) have been granted.'

There were packed house during its opening weeks. A tram car route which passed by the front of the cinema had the potential of extending the Belgrave's clientele. Mrs Edith Black, who was later listed as manageress of the cinema, claimed in the *Bioscope* of October 13th 1927 that she acted as manageress from the opening.

Picture House Second Anniversary

The Picture House celebrated its second anniversary with a special programme and a souvenir booklet. 'The public taste', said the reviewer, 'has considerably advanced during the past couple of years with regard to moving pictures, as well as other things, and the management of the Picture House has not only kept pace with the improvement, but led the way with such films as

'The Seige of Troy', 'Henry VIII' (with Violet Vanburgh and Sir Henry Beerbohm Tree), 'With Scott to the Pole' (shown in three separate series), 'The Love Story of Queen Elizabeth' (Sarah Bernhardt) and many others.'[36] It is possible that the special programme was designed to be a retrospective, since it included 'Foolshead Buys a Christmas Tree' which dated back to 1910, and 'Foxhunting' to 1911.

In July 1913, almost the last act of the manager, Mr L.F. Barnett, before he moved to another position in the Provincial Cinematograph Company, was to engage a second orchestra, so that it could have continuous music from 2 p.m. until 10.30 p.m. Both orchestras were under the direction of W.H. Carter. An interim manager from Edinburgh, Mr G. Parrington, took charge of the cinema until Mr R. Lowndes Salmon was appointed in September.[37]

Film Fans

Some cinemagoers had become very regular patrons, and the first British fan magazine, *The Pictures*, had been issued in October 1911 to cater for their enthusiasm. During 1913 Vitagraph comedy films featuring Flora Finch and John Bunny were specially mentioned in the *Daily Post* reviews. When 'the popular Vitagraph actress, Florence Turner' visited Leicester in July 1913 she was

Left: 'Queen Elizabeth' with Sarah Bernhardt. *Courtesy National Film Archive.*

Right: The first British cigarette card set devoted to the cinema (1913). *Author's collection.*

honoured with a civic banquet. The first British Cinematograph Actors cigarette card set was issued by the Major Drapkin Company in 1913 and Picture Play Chocolates and Moffat's Dainties both included give-away portraits.

The cinema was beginning to find a 'better' clientele and its worth was highlighted in a paragraph from a series of articles on 'Present day Leicester':

'Reference must be made, of course, to the picture theatres which have now become such a feature of modern life. In this town and its suburbs, there are at least ten. Those in the centre of the city with their continuous performances are much frequented by visitors to the town, shoppers with a few hours to spare, and even many business men, who patronise them for a quiet smoke after lunch, to say nothing of the regular patrons, and children who go 'by appoint-

Top: A cinema promotion of 1913.
Author's collection.

Right: Moffat's advertisement of 1913.
Author's collection

ment' week in week out. The pictures are of such varied subjects that they are not all likely to please the same individual, and it would be better if the London plan of classification was adopted, and the pictures run in series, indicating the times to the patrons.'[38]

The penultimate statement may be a reference to the beginnings of 'A' and 'U' classification by the newly functioning British Board of Film Censors set up by the industry itself. As if to support the very last item, the Picture House installed an electric clock-face indicator, in the entrance and the lounge, that pointed to the number of the film being shown.[39]

The feature film was still something of an innovation. A standard programme at this time would be made up as follows:

'Taking Care of Baby' (Tannhouser)	Comedy drama	525ft
'Life in the Mexican Army' (Urbanora)	Interest	300ft
'The Illumination - a Story of Roman Times'	length unknown	
'Cupid's Window' (Gaumont)	Comedy drama	835ft
'The Office Boy's Birthday' (Edison)	Comedy	600ft
'In Picturesque Morocco' (Gaumont)	Travel	430ft
'Annie Crawls Upstairs' (Edison)	Drama	1000ft

The whole programme probably ran for about 90 minutes.[40]

Feature Films

When 'Les Misérables' was shown at the Picture House from January 20th until January 31st 1913 it was announced with increased advertising and reviewed with overwhelming epithets. Extracts from the reviews were used as advertising for the second week. *Leicester Mail*: 'Magnificent acting'; *Leicester Advertiser*: 'Beautifully arranged'; *Leicester Pioneer*: 'We can only speak with greatest praise'; *Daily Mercury*: 'Everyone was kept enthralled'; *Daily Post*: 'Powerful acting'.

The film was $2^1/_2$ hours long and yet during the day from 2 p.m. until 7.45 p.m., the usual continuous performance took place. All seats could be reserved for the 8 p.m. performance and there was no continuous performance ticket issued after 6.30 p.m. Prices were increased to 2/6d (13p) for the balcony and 1/- (5p) for the ground floor with limited standing at 6d (3p) and 1/-.[41] It was re-run in March as an afternoon matinee with all seats reserved at 1/- and 2/- (10p).[42]

More feature films followed during the year: the Italian 'Theodora', and the British productions of 'Ivanhoe' (8,000 feet), 'The House of Temperley' (4,500 feet) and 'David Garrick' (3,000 feet). Audiences were becoming more willing to sit through a developing story.

Showmanship and publicity were on the increase. When the 4,500 foot British and Colonial film 'The Battle of Waterloo' was shown at the Silver Street Cinema in October 1913 the manager, Mr Horace Springett, arranged for 'soldiers' dressed in period uniforms to accompany sandwichboard men through the town. The enterprise certainly paid off, and 'all Leicester flocked to the cinema'. [43]

Cinemas and Holy Days

Normally, the cinemas were closed on Sundays, Christmas Day and Good Friday, but there were occasional applications by various cinema managers for permission to show films of a religious nature on these days. The first request was from the manager of the Coliseum for permission to open on Good Friday 1912 to show 'Sacred Pictures'.[44] For a Christmas opening, the Coliseum was joined in its application by the Imperial, the Picturedrome, and the Silver Street cinemas.[45] None of these applications was granted. Some exhibitors became aware that the licensing laws only applied for the showing of flammable film stock. West Riding County Council stopped one man from exhibiting films in his public house. The publican continued to give shows by using 'non-flam' stock. However, the shows did not have the desired effect as his clients drank less when they were watching the films.[46]

When the manager of the Coliseum attempted to circumvent the Act by applying to use non-flam film on Sundays April 20th and 27th, his request was first of all referred to the Mayor. It was finally turned down in May on the grounds that local bye-laws forbade the opening of cinemas on Sunday regardless of the film stock. An editorial in the *Daily Post* commented that it was better to have two projectionists at work rather than ten drunk men, and that the cinema had done much to stop Sunday drinking in other places.[47]

Leicester sees a serial

A monthly serial in the American magazine *Ladies' World* called 'What Happened To Mary' had resulted in the making of a film series with the same name and the same ingredients. The star was, appropriately, Mary Fuller. The film appeared at the Floral Hall as a bi-weekly on Sept 16th 1913,[48] an obvious inducement to patrons. By the time the ninth episode had been shown, the *Daily Post* reviewer commented 'It makes us long for more, like the serial tale that

Marc MacDermott and Mary Fuller in Edison's film 'What happened to Mary'. *Author's collection.*

ends at an exciting point.' For the benefit of the people who could not see all the episodes, the *Post* obligingly gave a weekly resumé.[49] By Christmas, and the twelfth instalment, the series was over.

Plans for more Cinemas

The 1915 *Kinematograph Yearbook* (giving statistics for the year 1914) lists Leicester as having 14 cinemas for a population of 227,222. In round figures, this is a disadvantageous ratio of 1 cinema per 16,000 persons. Coventry had a ratio of 1 per 13,000, Nottingham 1 per 12,000, Birmingham 1 per 11,000, Leeds 1 per 8,000 and Manchester 1 per 7,000. To keep pace with cinema developments in other towns, Leicester needed much more entrepreneur interest and investment.

Plans had been submitted for a proposed cinema at the corner of Vaughan Street and Hoby Street in December 1912 but it was not until 1914 that the building was completed.[50] It was referred to as the Alhambra Picture Theatre. The design was by H. Langley of Berridge Street, Leicester.[51]

In July 1913 plans for a new cinema in the Market Place in connection with the Continental Café were approved conditionally on the understanding that no queues would be allowed to form outside the theatre. In June 1914 the plans re-submitted for amendment were turned down and not until July 1914 was there provisional agreement for the building of the theatre.[52] Within one month of this, however, the Great War had begun, and the plans were not resurrected until 1924.

Chapter Four

The War Years 1914-18

The war years were obviously going to be a period of go-slow in cinema expansion as investments became doubtful and as employees and employers became mobilised. But 1914 opened with optimism and enterprise.

Christmas 1913 had seen good business in the town centre cinemas with capacity crowds at most of them. The Silver Street Cinema had opened its

The Tudor cinema (undated photograph). *Courtesy Leicester Mercury.*

enlarged balcony on Boxing Day 1913 and, with other re-arrangements, it was now listed as a 1,000 seater house, against its original 650. In August 1913 the adjoining premises had been acquired to facilitate the expansion. Ices and afternoon tea were still served in the higher priced seats. The two Kineto projectors were efficiently managed by the chief operator, Mr W. Harrison.[1]

The Tudor Cinema

Throughout the winter and spring, the Alhambra Theatre was being constructed in the Tudor Road district. Plans had been approved by the Watch Committee in December 1912.[2] The architect was H. Langley of Berridge Street.[3] Reports of building progress originally suggested an opening before the Easter Holiday although delay in furnish- ing arrangements held up the safety inspection and the opening was postponed until Easter Monday, April 13th. As seems often to have been the case, the issuing of the Cinematograph Licence was not confirmed until the next meeting of the Watch Committee on April 21st.

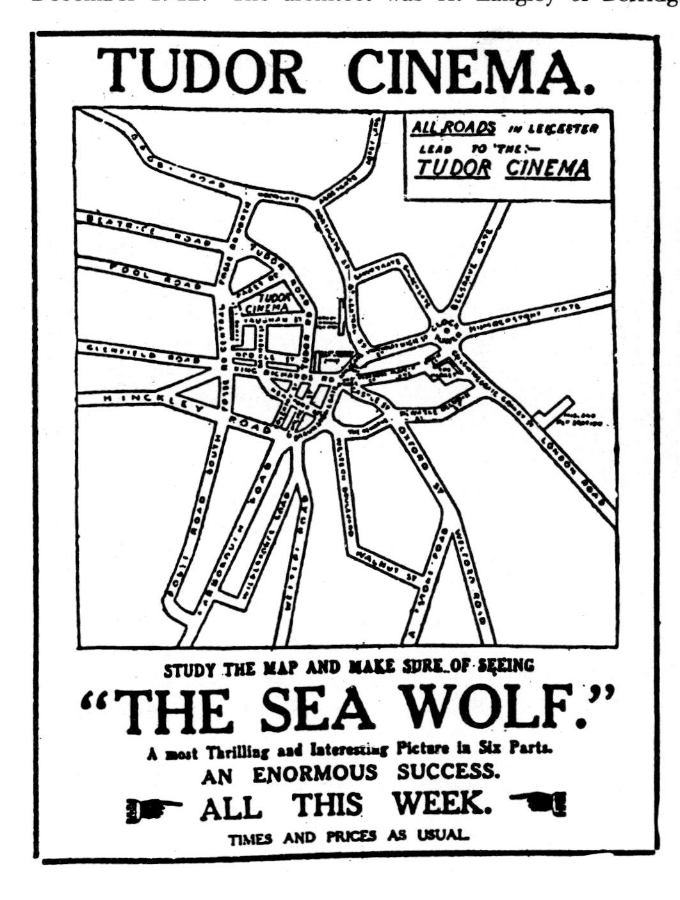

An advertisement from the *Leicester Mercury* of November 26th 1914.

The *Bioscope*, in its progress reports, continued to use the name Alhambra up to its report of April 23rd 1914:

'An important addition to Leicester's already lengthy list of houses, to say nothing of nightly bioscope features at the variety theatres, was made when the Tudor cinema opened with Mr Heather White as manager. The brick building though not outwardly elaborate is very solidly built, while inside, the arrangements are everything to be desired, the 'rake' of the floor ensuring an uninterrupted view from every one of its 1,250 seats. These are upholstered in red plush, the greater part being tip-ups of a generous width. A plentiful supply of exits, up-to-date lighting, etc., figure in an excellent scheme. The screen used is the largest in the town, being 24 ft. by 20 ft. and the projector, a motor-driven Vulcan, with a 144 ft. throw is manipulated by Mr R.F. Thompson with excellent results. At the inaugural performance in the afternoon, a crowded house waxed enthusiastic over a capital programme which included 'To Headquarters' and 'The Stolen Plans'. So far, nightly audiences have been entirely satisfactory.'

There was no gallery in the original design, and the site on the corner of Vaughan Street and Hoby Street had the possible use of three pay boxes. The 'Vulcan' Projector was an all-British product from the London firm of Pearson and Sopwith Ltd.

Prior to the cinema's opening, the original owning company, Alhambra Ltd with Mr Edmund Tyler as chairman, had gone into liquidation and sold its assets to a consortium of businessmen trading as Leicester Pictures Ltd for £2,000. Although there is no

A hand-cranked version of the British Vulcan projector. *The Bisocope.*

evidence of any co-ownership, the Tudor and the Belgrave Cinemas shared programming over the next few years. It is possible that, as independent cinemas, they came to some agreement with the renters in order to show films on a 'second-run' basis rather than be forced into the 'last-run' category.

The Star, Belgrave Gate

Plans for the Star, Belgrave Gate, designed by T. Henry Bowell, had been submitted to the Watch Committee in January 1914. The 100 x 65 foot building occupied a site between Painter Street and Memory Lane. It had accommodation variously estimated between 800 and 960 seats.[4] The proprietors were Messrs A. Mynard, A.W. Robins, and R.M. Wright, who were also the owners of the Imperial, Green Lane Road.

An appreciative audience watched the opening film 'The Accusing Skeleton' on July 30th. This 3,000 foot drama was an early production of the Warner Brothers before they acquired their own studio. The *Bioscope* report on August 6th gave a good impression of the building.

> 'Situated in the centre of a working-class district, the new house has accommodation for 930 persons, and is replete with every convenience in the shape of up-to-date heating, ventilation and lighting. As in the case of the Belgrave, opened a year or so ago, covered and well-lighted corridors run on either side down the entire length of the building. These, in turn, communicate at intervals with the body of the house. Large crowds are thus able to wait their turn in comfort and without disturbing the traffic. A fine rake and an unimpeded view of the screen of generous proportions are further advantages, whilst numerous exits ensure a rapid emptying of the house. A 'Tiger' projector completes the up-to-date outfit and shows a first class picture.'

The manager was Mr George H. Finnis, who after the second week's exclusive showing of 'A Gambler's Wager', shared his programming with Mr W. Jefford-Parsons at the Imperial.

The Shaftesbury.

The Shaftesbury on Overton Road was designed by Seale and Riley of Horsefair Street for Messrs Cayless and Chamberlain and they used designs similar to those in their Belgrave Cinema. First reports of the purchase of the site had appeared in the *Bioscope* in June 1912 with a suggested opening date of

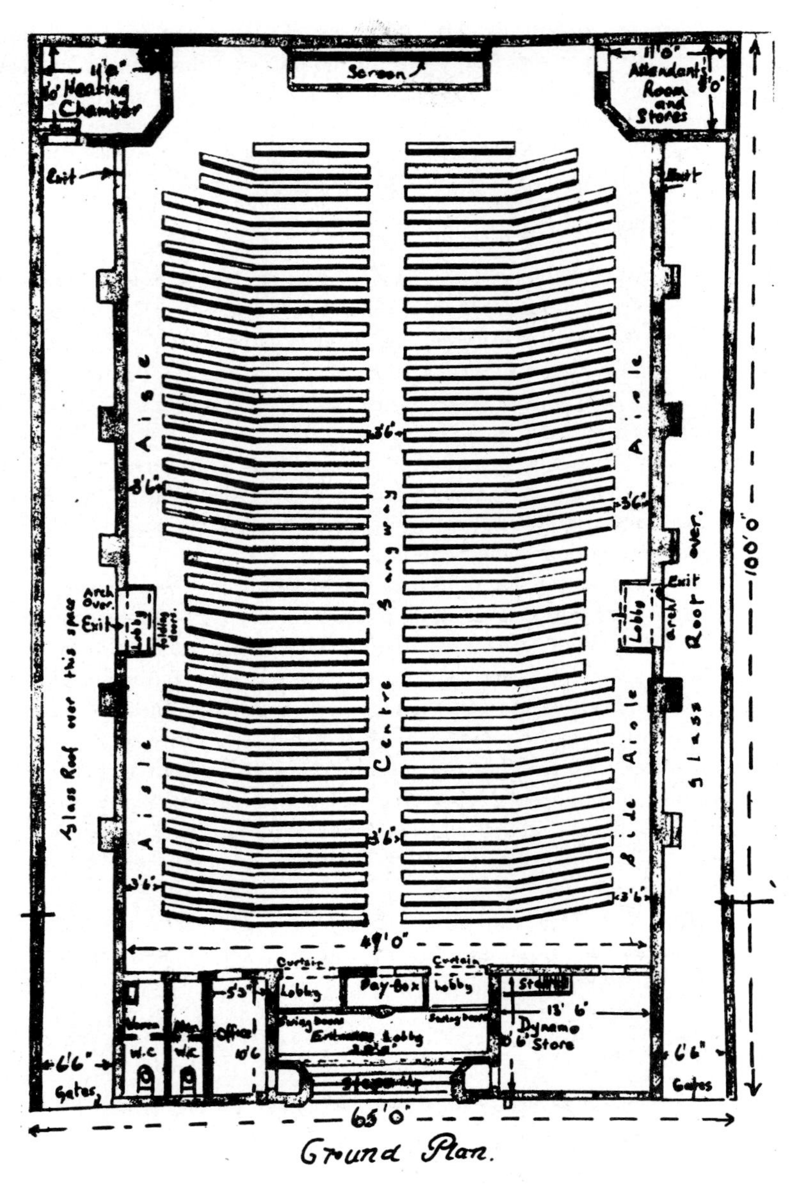

Ground plan of the Star Picture House, Belgrave Gate.
Courtesy Leicestershire Records Office.

Top: The Shaftesbury cinema in 1955.
Courtesy C.E. John Aston Collection.

Bottom: The Shaftesbury in 1991. *Author's photograph.*

An advertisement from *The Bioscope* for a popular brand of seating.

August Bank Holiday that year. But submitted plans were not provisionally accepted by the Watch Committee until April 29th 1914.[5] It was opened on October 8th.

'Following on the lines so much approved by local licensing authorities in recently erected buildings, the new structure, occupying a commanding position on Uppingham Road, includes a well-lighted annex running the entire length of the building, and communicating at intervals with the interior of the hall. Inside, the building is unimpeded by obstruction of any kind, and aided by a fine rake, ensures a capital view of the screen from each of its 830 seats.

'The seating arrangements, wide and comfortable, and of the crimson plush tip-up variety throughout, have been carried out by Messrs Turner of Birmingham. The building contractors were the local firm of Chitham and Co. Yet another feature is the panel roof lighting, the even and subdued scheme having a pleasing effect. Plentiful exits, up-to-date ventilation, radiator heating, etc,, all figure in an excellent ensemble. The proprietors are Messrs A. Cayless and T. Chamberlain, and the manager is Mr Horton. The projector is a Tyler 'Indomitable', and a packed house on the opening night testified its approval by a hearty 'send off'.[6]

Cinema programmes seemed mostly to last about two hours with six or seven subjects included in each. A comparison of the programmes of two of the central cinemas for the first week in January 1914 reveals that some of the films were to be found at both.[7]

Picture House

'King Gontran the first' (Eclair)	Comedy	869 ft.
'A Railroader's Warning' (Kalem)	Drama	1,020 ft.
'The Labour Struggle' (Kalem)	Drama	1,620 ft.
'Not as Rehearsed' (Hepworth)	Comedy	675 ft.
'The Science of Palmistry'	(no details known)	
'Their Mutual Friend' (Vitagraph)	Comedy	1010 ft.
'The Topical Budget'		c.250 ft.

Floral Hall

'King Gontran the first' (Eclair)	Comedy	869 ft.
'A Railroader's Warning' (Kalem)	Drama	1,020 ft.
'The Harvest of Flames' (Rex)	Drama	1,500 ft.
'Calino, Water Diviner' (Gaumont)	Comedy	400 ft.
'Boy wanted' (Edison)	Comedy	600ft.
'A Modern Steel Plant' (Flying 'A')	Interest	316 ft
'In the Midst of the Jungle' (Selig)	Drama	2,495 ft.
'The Topical Budget'		c.250ft.

All the films that can be indentifed were brand new releases, except 'In the Midst of the Jungle' (from October 1913), and demonstrate that the town centre cinemas were on a first-release footing.

Increasing competition was beginning to lead to a larger number of 'exclusives'; that is, film titles that were rented for showing at only one cinema or cinema circuit in each location. The exclusive nature of the programme became a particular watchword for the advertising. As films lengthened into four and five reel features, this tendency became more and more prevalent.

Sometimes, in an attempt to demonstrate an exclusivity that was not present, the titles of the films were changed. In the same week, the Picture House advertised a film 'How to get Rid of a Burglar' and the Floral Hall 'Lottie Coin's Ghost'. The synposis of each describes a character called Lottie Coin who is waylaid by burglars and who puts on a ghostly disguise to confuse them. The patron might not know this before entering the cinema. It was a 1054 foot film in the Ham and Bud Comedy series, and its real title 'Lotta Coin's Ghost' contained a pun that obviously eluded the reviewer. [8]

In July 1914 the Coliseum began a policy of changing the programme every day. This was only broken once during the rest of the year, when Madam Ada

POST CARD.

FOR THREE DAYS ONLY,
Commencing THURSDAY, Jan. 1st, 1914,

MLLE. NAPIERKOWSKA
IN

PSYCHE

A beautiful coloured Kinematograph version of the delightful mythological legend.

at

ELECTRIC THEATRE,
HIGH STREET, LEICESTER.

A postcard advertisement for a Pathécolour costume drama.
Courtesy C.E. John Aston Collection.

White was engaged for three days to synchronise her singing to the film 'The Rosary'.

The central cinemas tried to create a high-class image for themselves in an attempt to woo patrons. The Picture House was always conscious of this, and seemed especially generous in its announcement that it was introducing a special Pathé educational matinee section to be shown once a day. This 45 minute collection of films on natural history and science was timetabled just after the close of the school day. It was, in fact, a ploy that cost them the handsome amount of £1. 1s. 0d per week. Pathé's clever advertising clearly impressed the management of the Picture House: 'Special educational matinees attract the best kinds of patrons and get a reputation for high-class shows'.[9]

One of the most popular films of the year was 'Sixty Years A Queen', a dramatic reconstruction of some of the events of Queen Victoria's reign. Produced by the British firm of Barker's and marketed by the young G.B. Samuelson, it played to record crowds firstly at the Olympia and then at the Coliseum. It was clearly evident that as war approached, film production and presentation were heavily underlined by patriotism. 'The British Army Film', as it was billed, was shown in two parts at the Picture House; part one from Monday to Wednesday, and part two from Thursday to Saturday. Three weeks later, a special Military night was arranged at the Picture House in front of His Grace the Duke of Rutland, the Mayor, the Sheriff of Leicestershire, and the local Army hierarchy. [10]

The back page of a Picture House programme of 1915.
Author's collection.

More Talkies

But novelty was still a good crowd puller, too. 'Have you heard of Edison's new invention?' asked the advertisement, 'MARVELLOUS TALKING PICTURES at the Picture House Next Week'. The Edison Company had been attempting to marry sound to pictures since the earliest Kinetoscopes. Some of the later models had been equipped with a crude form of sound supplied to the viewer by means of stethoscope-like earphones.

In a long review of the Kinetophone entitled 'Grand Attraction - Talking Pictures That Are Nearly Perfect', the *Daily Post* critic for the most part enthused about the invention. 'Right at the beginning one wishes to state that they are not yet perfect. On the other hand they are hardly at all imperfect.' The films were introduced by a man walking onto the screen stage: 'The speaker picks up a plate, and then proceeds to point out that when he throws it to the ground, you will hear it smash. He does so and you hear it all. Then you sit back and think that this is all mechanical, and that there is no man, no plate, and no sound, just applied mechanics.'[11]

The nearness to perfection is explained later in the article; 'Just at first you notice that the spoken word and the sound word do not exactly synchronise. You will be tempted to say that the gramophone and the speaker (the actor) are out of time. In a second or two, the two begin to work together perfectly.' The introductory film was followed by a pierrot

HAVE YOU HEARD OF
EDISON'S
NEW INVENTION?

"The Kinetophone"
MARVELLOUS
Talking Pictures
COMING TO
THE PICTURE HOUSE,
GRANBY STREET,
MONDAY NEXT.

Look Out for Further Announcements.

Edison's Kinetophonee achieved its effect through a long endless belt connecting the gramophone to the projector via a braking synchroniser. Despite this it performed well and audiences endorsed the claims of the advertisement. Advertisement from *Leicester Daily Post* of March 16th 1914.

entertainment, a lady violinist, a prima donna, and a dramatized version of 'Faust'

The reviewer was of the opinion that 'the invention will revolutionise the picture theatre, and any picture theatre not installing one in the next 12 months will have to close its doors. This is an exceedingly short period to predict, but ultimately theatres on these lines must come.' The novelty enjoyed a four-week run at the Picture House, the sound films being interspersed in an ordinary programme. In April, the *Mercury* reviewer announced that Clarendon Pictures have introduced a device whereby 'speaking pictures' can be shown without the ally of the gramophone. He describes the film at the Belvoir Playhouse as being taken from Alfred Berlyn's poem 'Coming Home'.[12] There was no great technological breakthrough, however, since the series of eleven 1,000 foot Clarendon Speaking Picture films which contain this title were shown to the trade in November 1913, and were designed for synchronisation with a gramophone, or with a live on-stage voice.[13]

Live readings accompanying films were not uncommon. One such in May 1914 at the Olympia arranged by 'the genial manager, Mr F.D. Gray' was read by Mr Cyril Grantham as accompaniment to 'a series of pictures depicting a young man's early crime and subsequent efforts to reform.'[14] Though the title of this film is not recorded, it seems likely to have been 'The Convict's Dream' one of the one-reel Kinemapoem series released in February 1914.[15]

The most famous 'elocutionist and originator of speaking pictures' was Eric Williams. In 1910 he had been involved with the stage actor Harry Hinton in a voice-behind-the-screen presentation of D.W. Griffith's American Biograph film 'The Convict's Sacrifice'. Although the venture had been a critical success, it became obvious that films needed to be specially made for the technique to work to its best advantage.

In April 1914 the *Bioscope* reported that he had just completed the thousandth presentation of his own film 'The Surgeon's Child'. The poem by Fred Weatherley had been dramatised in 1912 with Eric Williams as the coachman in the film, and the narrator on the stage.[16] He had appeared in Leicester in 1913, and he was booked for a return engagement at the High Street Cinema in October 1914 with his latest 'Speaking Films', 'The Lifeboat' from the poem by George R. Sims and Tennyson's 'The Charge of the Light Brigade'.[17]

The Importance of Cinema Music

Live musical accompaniment was very essential to each cinema, and the augmenting of an orchestra for special films, or the appointment of a new conductor never passed without some mention. In March 1914 the Silver Street Cinema appointed Mr Cyril Godwin, 'well-known in Midland musical circles' as the conductor of its new orchestra.[18] Miss May Greaves, who had been a pianist there since 1912, was required to find another post. She continued her highly-rated career at the Lyric.

Soloists were regularly engaged to provide vocal accompaniment to appropriate films. Ada White, the local contralto, sang to the film 'The Rosary' at the Olympia and the Coliseum in March and December, and Mr W. Payne was called in to give vocal life to 'The Wastral' at the Coliseum in May.

In February 1914 the licensing authorities granted a music licence to the Mere Road Picturedrome, in the name of the acting manager Frank J. Harris, for the period 2.30 p.m. till 10.30 p.m. Normally, cinemas did not need a music licence as long as the music was only a subsidiary part of the performance. A number of court cases had been reported in the trade press concerning the illegal playing of musical interludes and concerts in cinemas, and it would appear that the proprietors of the Picturedrome were insuring against such an eventuality. Most Leicester cinemas took out a music licence as a matter of course at the time of their opening.[19]

The Cinematograph Exhibitors' Association

The protection and the promotion of the exhibiting part of the industry was the remit of the Cinematograph Exhibitors' Association which had been formed in 1912. During its first two years of existence, it had set up a number of district branches. One of the most successful was that of the Northern Central Branch based in Manchester with its secretary, H.D. Moorhouse. He was managing director of a thriving circuit which already had three cinemas operating in Leicester. In April 1914, at the White Hart Hotel, Mr Moorhouse presided at the inaugural meeting of the Leicester Branch. Those present elected Mr B. Jackson as chairman of the branch, Mr

H.D. Moorhouse. The founder of the H.D.M. Circuit and of the Leicester C.E.A. Branch. 1926 drawing from *The Bioscope.*

'The Adventures of Kathlyn' a Selig serial shown in Leicester during 1914. *Author's collection.*

W. Emson as the treasurer, and Mr Charles Burgess as the secretary.[20]

Good Friday film performances took place on April 10th 1914. The Picture House showed 'The Last Days of Pompeii', and according to the *Daily Post* most cinemas put on special films.[21] Sunday opening was still hotly debated up and down the country. It was now permitted in Belfast, Birmingham, Bradford, Bristol, Cardiff, Dundee, Durham, Edinburgh, Glasgow, Glastonbury, Leeds, Lincoln, Manchester, Newcastle, Norwich, Preston, Reading and Warrington. There were reports of improvements in street conditions and reductions in drinking from some of these places, but Leicester stuck firmly to its six-day policy.[22] Christmas Day opening was also not permitted but extended hours were the general rule on December 24th and December 26th.

In the same week that war broke out, the Floral Hall screened a second serial entitled 'The Adventures of Kathlyn'. This Selig film, although billed as a serial, was a series of independent pictures about the same girl and her adventures in the jungle with an assortment of wild animals and villains. It ran for a period of 13 weeks.[23]

The First Effects of the War

The *Bioscope* carried a number of articles speculating on the immediate effects of the war in the weeks following the declaration. Mr R. Lowndes Salmon, the manager of the Picture House, who had just returned from an extended holiday through Belgium and Luxembourg, was of the opinion that there was little immediate adverse effect resulting. He thought that the supply failure of some

The Floral Hall interior *circa* 1913. Drawn by author from a photograph.

continental films would be offset by the resurrection of 'numberless excellent re-issues'. The most clear effect would be the calling up of the reserves. He had already lost six of his staff and two of his operators to this end.[24]

The *Bioscope* was quick to begin printing a Roll of Honour of those men in the industry who had volunteered for the colours or who were called up as reservists. Mr Lowndes Salmon's eight employees were the first to be listed; Mr Andrews to H.M.S. Dominion, Messrs A. Pratt and Simmons to the Leicestershire Regiment, V. Greaves to the 10th Hussars, Messrs E. Brown, Thomas Moore, and C. Warner to unspecified units, and Mr Harmer to the Leicestershire Special Reserve.[23] Mr W. Wignall and Mr W. Smith, both of the Silver Street Cinema, went to the Royal Marines and the Lancers respectively.[25]

Manpower changes were not all linked with war-time pressures. Mr Fred Trueman Towers Snr took over from Mr G.F. Reynolds as manager of both the Floral Hall and the Palace Theatre of Varieties at the end of April. Mr E.W. Pearce remained as the assistant at the Floral Hall. Captain H. Worsley became manager of the High Street Cinema in place of Mr Kingstone Trollope in August

The Pleasures of Cinema-going

At the end of the year, the *Daily Post* critic reflected on the pleasures of cinema-going. 'In these days, when picture houses abound, one wonders what we did without them. The opportunities to escape from weather like we are now having, and at the same time to be accommodated with comfort and entertainment were far less in the old days than now. It is necessary only to find a good cinematograph house, and there you are.'[27] Greater comfort had been brought to Leicester's oldest cinema house during the latter part of the year. The Picturedrome had closed on September 21st for extensive alterations and it re-opened on November 26th with tip-ups replacing the former bench seats.[28]

Germany and the High Street Cinema

During 1915 the Belvoir Street Playhouse closed down and the High Street Cinema was in danger of closure. On December 8th 1914 a sub-committee of the Leicester Watch Committee were asked to review the renewal of the licence of the High Street Cinema since the Directorate of the

IMPERIAL PLAYHOUSE. HIGH STREET.

MONDAY, SEPT. 20th, FOR THREE DAYS.

THE MASTER DIPLOMAT.

IN THREE PARTS.

Featuring FRANCIS X. BUSHMAN.

EXCLUSIVE FOR LEICESTER.

High Street cinema name change.
Leicester Mail September 20th 1915.

Company owning it and the majority of the share capital was German. A petition had been presented to the Committee by 300 trade and professional people urging refusal of the renewal. The manager, Captain Worsley, was present at the Committee meeting, and he stated quite openly that the capital of London and Provincial Electric Theatres Limited was £56,000 of which £2,196 was held by 66 British shareholders. The rest of the stock was held by bankers or individuals in Mannheim, Germany. Dividends of 15% had twice been paid by the company, and further dividends of 18% and 12% had also been paid in its four years of existence. Any profits to the company would be held by the company's bankers until hostilities ceased and there was no danger of 'trading with the enemy'.

The sub-committee decided by nine votes to five not to take any action until they had received a report from London County Council on the same subject. They, thus, renewed the licence for a period of three months pending further inquiries.[29]

There was no reason to doubt the patriotism of the manager Captain H. Worsley. In February 1914 he arranged for the proceeds of specially purchased tickets from St Paul's vicarage to go to the Belgian Refugee Fund[30] and in October 1914 he had entertained 42 newly-arrived Belgian refugees with a free afternoon film performance. On March 16th 1915 the licence was renewed for the rest of the year.

In April Captain Worsley was posted to the Royal Engineers at Glen Parva barracks and in May he was at the head of a military parade down the High Street in support of a recruiting campaign. Later in the year the licence was transferred from London and Provincial Electric Theatres Ltd to Messrs Chambers and Smerthwaite of London and the cinema was, with ironic genius, renamed 'The Imperial Playhouse' in the week beginning 20th September 1915.[31] The new manager was Mr E. Nicols.

The Cinema as Recruiting Agent

Patriotic films with titles such as 'England Expects', 'On His Majesty's Service' and 'If England Were Invaded' began to flood the screens. Recruiting programmes became regular features of the wartime cinema. Usually an Army Council film was shown in addition to the normal programme. This was followed by patriotic speeches by both military and civilian personnel. Captain R.W. Pritchard of the National Service League had spoken at several such events at the Picture House. In October 1914 his preamble to the showing of the film 'Kitchener's Army' was terminated by an opposing view. During the playing of the National Anthem it was observed that one member of the audience had remained seated. Sensing the feeling of the the rest of the audience, the manager quietly asked him to leave. He refused to budge and as the Anthem finished an angry demonstration followed. It is alleged that the man then attempted to mount a seat with a view to making a speech. This act, apparently, gave the manager grounds for his forcible removal. 'With the willing aid of a few stalwart Territorials who were present, his exit was speedily effected.' 17 men were recruited that evening.[32] In the lounge of the Picture House, a printed Roll of Honour of employees of the 100 Provincial Cinematograph Theatre

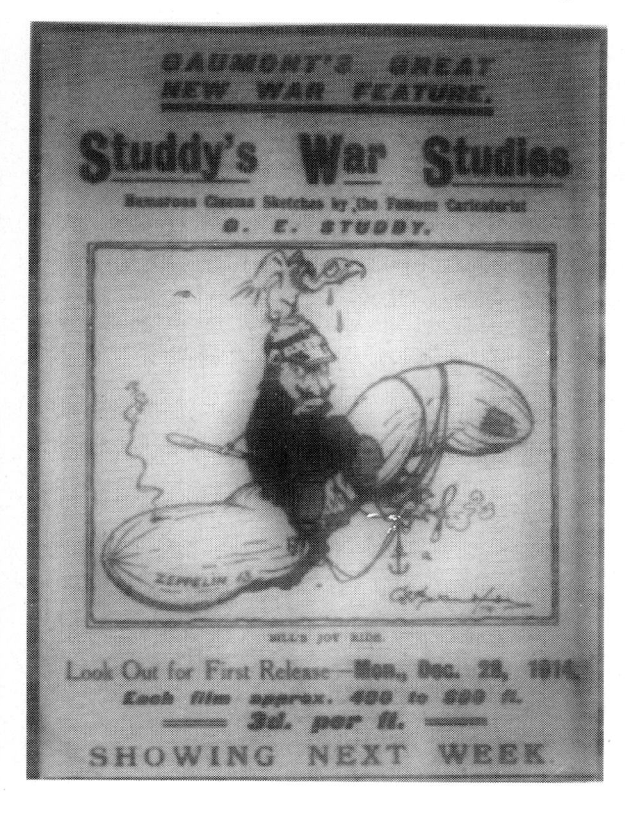

Topical wartime amusement. 'Lightning' sketches by G.E. Studdy. From *The Bioscope.*

staff who were in the colours, was framed and mounted and suitably draped with a Union Jack.

In January 1915 'Defenders of the Empire' at the Picture House was a front for a recruiting speech.[33] In May at the Tudor the recruiting film 'Wake Up!' was shown as part of the programme in a special recruiting week. On successive nights the speakers, after the presentation, were the Mayor of Leicester Alderman J. North, Mrs Pankhurst, Mr Laurence Cowan (author) and Colonel Mosse, the chairman of the Leicester and Leicestershire Recruiting Council. It was reported that the total number of recruits, after the first four nights, was 80.[34]

Though not a recruiting film, the British and Colonial film 'The Life Story of Florence Nightingale' had particular appeal as the local hospitals filled with returning wounded. Mr Springett at the Silver Street Cinema contacted all of them and the reviewer noted many nurses uniforms in the audience on the night he was in attendance.[35]

Throughout the hostilities, war-related charities and appeals featured in collections and competitions at the cinemas. Though patriotism and benevolence were the overt motivations, they ultimately produced increased attendance. One such promotional event was reported by the *Kinematograph Weekly* on January 31st 1918. Oliver Rogers, the newly appointed manager at the Imperial Playhouse High Street, requested his patrons to retain their Entertainment Tax Ticket whilst the correspondingly numbered entrance ticket was retained by the cinema. On the Saturday night, a ticket was drawn by the manager and the ticket owner was presented with a £5 War Bond.

Occasional news of cinema employees in 'the colours' filtered through to the trade press. Mr W. Wignall, a former doorman at Silver Street, who was last heard of in June 1915 on the 'Majestic', sunk by enemy action, turned up the next month uninjured but badly stressed from his startling experiences. Mr Trevor Godwin, who for many years was first violinist with his brother's orchestra at the Silver Street Cinema, was reported to have lost an eye on the Somme in November 1916.

The First Cinema Organ in Leicester

In September 1913 the Floral Hall had added a balcony, 'The Family Circle', to its amenities in an attempt to maintain the standard of its clientele. Now, much to the pleasure of the *Daily Post* critic, they installed an electrically-operated orchestral organ.

The Floral Hall interior in the 1950s. *Courtesy Leicester Mercury.*

'It is generally agreed,' he intoned, 'that an important essential for the success of an up-to-date motion picture house is the provision of an adequate and suitable supply of music. In this direction, the management of the Floral Hall made an important and novel move when the music hitherto supplied by a solitary piano was, for the first time, superseded by the more orchestral-like music produced from a new instrument that has been installed. It may be described as an organ-piano combination in which the characteristics of both instruments may be employed simultaneously or separately. The organ is blown by an electric motor, and in the absence of an organ loft, the pipes have been erected on one side of the stage with imitation pipes on the opposite side to maintain the balance. This instrument is not to be confused with many of the purely mechanical contrivances that are often met with in picture theatres'. It was supplied by Messrs Nicholson and Ward of Walsall. Mr Arthur Rawson was engaged as the principal organist to play from 2.30 p.m. to 5.30 p.m. and from 7.30 p.m. to 10.30 p.m. [36]

Films of the Year

After the war films, the principal films of the year were mostly costume epics. The American contributions were the Famous Players Film 'Tess of the D'Urbervilles' starring the stage actress Minnie Maddern Fiske, and the Mary Pickford four-reeler 'Mistress Nell' with her husband, Owen Moore, playing Charles II.[37] The Picture House showed the four-reel French film 'Marguerite of Navarre' in January. A reviewer described its 'skilled tinting' and 'its colours faithful to nature'.[38] One British contribution to this genre was a three-reel pageant-drama 'Kismet' starring Oscar Asche and Lily Brayton, and given the right oriental atmosphere by appropriate musical selections by the Picture House Orchestra.[39]

Leicester's Premier House of Entertainment

TO-DAY, FRIDAY AND SATURDAY

MR.
NORMAN
WILLIAMS
ENGLAND'S FAMOUS BARITONE

From the Royal Opera House, Covent Garden, Royal Albert Hall, & Queen's Hall, London.

Mr. Norman Williams will sing at 4 and 7.30 p.m. daily—this week and all next week

ALSO
EXCLUSIVE ENGAGEMENT OF
Mons Hugo Lenaerts
Celebrated Violinist—from the Royal Opera House, Antwerp

The Picture House Orchestra, always a feature of this popular Theatre, has been augmented and is now the finest Orchestra in the Midlands.

Exclusive and very powerful Three-part Drama
THE VICTIM
An absorbing human story crowded with exciting incidents

Splendid Comedy
Wiffles–Victim of Jealousy
Full of laughter

MRS. MURPHY'S COOKS
Another delightfully amusing Comedy

ALSO
"LITTLE BOBBY" (Comedy); "SCENES IN TONKIN" (Coloured Film); CURRENT EVENTS Etc., Etc.

The Picture House
Augmented Orchestra
Granby Street, LEICESTER
Continuous Performance, 2 to 10.30 p.m.
TAKE HER TO THE PICTURE HOUSE

Leicester Mercury (1915).

Music was still so important to the *Daily Post* critic that the departure of the quartet's chief violinist, Mr Frank Muston, was reported in his column.[40] Another popular member of the Picture House orchestra was Winifred Cockrill, a former harpist with the Scottish and Beecham Orchestra. Her twice nightly solos were 'almost as big an attraction as the pictures'.[41] Theo. Kieule, 'one of the best violinists in the district' was engaged to enhance the orchestra at the King's Hall.[42] Mr Cyril Godwin, in charge of the Silver Street Orchestra, was often singled out for praise, along with Mr Jules Guitton at the High Street Cinema.

The Floral Hall interior in the 1950s. *Courtesy Leicester Mercury.*

'It is generally agreed,' he intoned, 'that an important essential for the success of an up-to-date motion picture house is the provision of an adequate and suitable supply of music. In this direction, the management of the Floral Hall made an important and novel move when the music hitherto supplied by a solitary piano was, for the first time, superseded by the more orchestral-like music produced from a new instrument that has been installed. It may be described as an organ-piano combination in which the characteristics of both instruments may be employed simultaneously or separately. The organ is blown by an electric motor, and in the absence of an organ loft, the pipes have been erected on one side of the stage with imitation pipes on the opposite side to maintain the balance. This instrument is not to be confused with many of the purely mechanical contrivances that are often met with in picture theatres'. It was supplied by Messrs Nicholson and Ward of Walsall. Mr Arthur Rawson was engaged as the principal organist to play from 2.30 p.m. to 5.30 p.m. and from 7.30 p.m. to 10.30 p.m. [36]

Films of the Year

After the war films, the principal films of the year were mostly costume epics. The American contributions were the Famous Players Film 'Tess of the D'Urbervilles' starring the stage actress Minnie Maddern Fiske, and the Mary Pickford four-reeler 'Mistress Nell' with her husband, Owen Moore, playing Charles II.[37] The Picture House showed the four-reel French film 'Marguerite of Navarre' in January. A reviewer described its 'skilled tinting' and 'its colours faithful to nature'.[38] One British contribution to this genre was a three-reel pageant-drama 'Kismet' starring Oscar Asche and Lily Brayton, and given the right oriental atmosphere by appropriate musical selections by the Picture House Orchestra.[39]

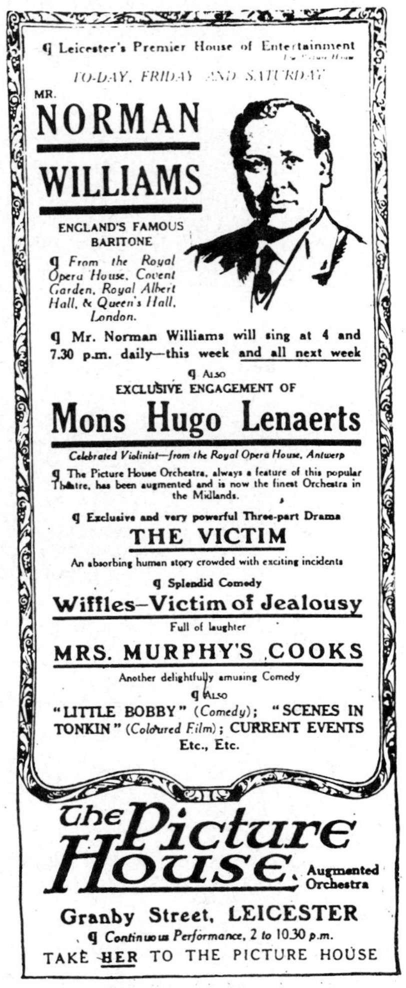

Leicester Mercury (1915).

Music was still so important to the *Daily Post* critic that the departure of the quartet's chief violinist, Mr Frank Muston, was reported in his column.[40] Another popular member of the Picture House orchestra was Winifred Cockrill, a former harpist with the Scottish and Beecham Orchestra. Her twice nightly solos were 'almost as big an attraction as the pictures'.[41] Theo. Kieule, 'one of the best violinists in the district' was engaged to enhance the orchestra at the King's Hall.[42] Mr Cyril Godwin, in charge of the Silver Street Orchestra, was often singled out for praise, along with Mr Jules Guitton at the High Street Cinema.

Film Stars

The names of the film stars were now regularly appearing in the reports and the advertising. Prior to 1912 it had been the policy of the producers not to reveal the names of the players. In some cases this was at the request of the players who did not want their descent into the vulgar circles of the photoplay to be recorded. But it was also clear that the producers did not want to provide the 'stars' with a reason for demanding higher fees. The interest of cinema patrons, and the resultant production of 'fan' magazines, soon forced the distributors to attach names to the familiar faces previously known by such titles as 'The Vitagraph Girl' or 'The Biograph Girl'. More and more 'star' picture postcards were given away by distributors to encourage collections and 'brand' loyalties. By

Publicity cards for two 'Transatlantic' serials of 1915. *Author's collection.*

1915 every film by the 'famous cinema comedian Charles Chaplin'[43] was given prominence and quite rapidly it became standard practice to include the names of players both in the advertisements and the reviews.

In September 1915 the Olympia Cinema had been sold by public auction at the White Hart Hotel. The auction realised £4,025. Although press reports do not reveal the name of the new owner, it is fair to assume that it was H.D. Moorhouse. The leaseholders 'Leicester Enterprises Ltd' were not affected by the change [44].

Immediately afterwards, the Coliseum and the Olympia jointly staged an interesting publicity stunt by having G. Hewitt, the author of the British wartime story 'A Soldier's Girl', introduce the film made from his book. The advertisment for that programme gave the intriguing information that 'Miss Olive Gordon who was saved from ruin, and her sister Miss Phyllis Gordon, who saved her, will appear at each performance.' During the week there would have been quite a lot of 'toing and froing' between the cinemas to meet the staggered timings of the showings. All this for a film with a running time of less than 40 minutes[45].

The King's Hall Cinema, Granby Street

Two new cinemas opened during 1915, both conversions of existing halls. The King's Hall, part of the Grand Hotel in Granby Street, opened on Thursday, July 29th.[46] The associated café was open from 12 noon, but the cinema presentation did not begin till 2.00 p.m. Prices were one shilling or 6d. Admission to the café and Winter Garden was free. The opening programme included an exclusive presentation of the film drama 'One of the Many', the Charlie Chaplin comedy 'A Night Out' and the Topical Gazette. The *Bioscope* reporter in the August 12th edition went into raptures about the cinema's elegance, without, unfortunately, including photographs as well.

'A wide and stately staircase richly carpeted leads to the second floor of the fine block of buildings comprising the Grand Hotel. Marble and mahogany of massive design comprise the walls and supporting pillars. A suitable rake of the floor ensures a fine view of the 14 ft. screen from every seat in the house- the capacity, including the balcony, being upwards of 700.

'The whole is carpeted throughout in luxurious style while subdued lighting effects, tasteful curtains and drapings make a most pleasing impression. The projection machines used, of which there are two, are the last word in Gaumonts. The commodious seats of tip-up design, and with rows generously spaced are upholstered in plush compressed by a new process. The colour scheme is rose-du-barri. There is also a private box in the circle decorated in French gray.

Adjoining the circle, approached by a second handsome short stairway, is a combined lounge and smoke room luxuriously appointed, the spacious magnificence of which is fittingly spanned by handsome twin domed-shaped glass roofs of noble proportions.

'Returning to the lower level, and crossing an imposing landing giving from the body of the theatre, a large, lofty and most pleasing caf is situated. It is a corner room overlooking one of the cities busiest thoroughfares on two sides.

'Music of the very best is to be featured, and it will be rendered by a two-manual organ, a grand piano and a highly skilled orchestra of nine under the direction of Mr Shirley North. The proprietor of the Grand Hotel Company is Mr W.E. Stevens. The opening on July 29th was quite informal.'

The Temperance Hall frontage - not unlike its Cinema-de-Luxe days.
Courtesy Leicester Mercury.

The Cinema-de-Luxe

The Temperance Hall was re-granted a licence on September 1st in the name of the Vanguard Picture Company, after the completion of further alterations to exits as required by the Watch Committee. The re-opening on September 6th prompted the following from the *Daily Mercury* reporter: 'The Opening of the Leicester Temperance Hall as a high class cinema adds an exceedingly comfortable and well-managed place of entertainment to those already existing in easy reach of the centre of town. It is evident from the all round excellence of the programme on the opening day that the management are determined to stand high in popular esteem.' Unusually for a city centre cinema the continuous programme was only presented between 5.30 p.m. and 10.30 p.m., instead of from 2.30 p.m. There was to be a change of programme on Mondays and Thursdays, and admission prices were 3d and 6d.[47] The manager, Mr J.H. Schofield, had come from Brighouse, Yorkshire.

The inaugural programme included 'The Jungle Queen' a drama with wild animals very much in evidence; 'The Guiding Light', a touching story with a lighthouse as its background; and 'One kind of Friend', a tragic drama. The comedies were 'Leading Lizzie Astray', 'Scottie loves Ice cream' (a British half-reel film made by Bamforth's at their Holmfirth studio), and 'Podgy Porkins' Plot' (a ten-minute British film made by the Martins Film Company). When the licence was renewed in January 1916, the cinema had been renamed the Cinema-de-Luxe.[48]

Prosecutions

Since the implementation of the Cinematographs Act, the Leicester Chief Fire Officer and the Watch Committee had been very thorough in demanding strict adherence to its tenets. In December 1913 the licensee of the Boulevard Cinema, Mr Tertius B. Blakesley, was prosecuted for obstructing the gangway of the Theatre,[49] and in September 1915 the licensee of the Star was successfully prosecuted for allowing overcrowding at the cinema.[50] The pressure on managers was enough to prompt many comments in the trade journals. 'At the Great Coliseum, Melton Road things are still humming. In the face of the strictly enforced 'no standing' order, this house is fortunate not only in its unusual seating capacity (2,000), but also in its possession of an adjoining lounge and café and a well-equipped billiard room.' [51]

Encouraging the Patrons

Patronage of the cinema was clearly on the increase, especially at holiday times. Very fine weather in the summer usually decreased the audiences, though reports often praise the ventilating systems in the local theatres for providing comfortable atmospheres even during the hottest spells.

The new manager at the Lyric (Knighton Cinema), Mr F. Horsefall, announced that from September 4th 1915 there would be two houses nightly.[52] Business had been reported as satisfactory, but the cinema had a very small seating capacity and this seemed to be a move to increase patronage with only a minor increase in outlay.

Leicester Mail advertisement of September 20th 1915.

An advertising card given to patrons at the Silver Street Cinema extolled the joys of attendance:

'One or two nights a week YOU reserve for Pictures and for the FIVE following reasons you should get on the car and visit THE SILVER STREET PALACE

1. It is Leicester's Original Picture Theatre.
2. Absolutely the clearest Pictures in town and when you leave, there is not the usual headache caused by eye-strain.
3. At least two special Feature Films exhibited daily.
4. The only Picture Café in town where patrons can enjoy Tea and the Pictures at the same time.
5. Cars stop one minute from the Theatre from every route in town.'

Unfortunately no actual example of this card has survived, and the only evidence of its existence is in a report in the *Kinematograph Weekly* in October 1916.

Several cinemas were in the process of carrying out minor and major enlargement plans. The Picturedrome re-equipped and re-seated in December 1914. The Picture House had submitted plans for very extensive alterations and an accommodation improvement from 900 to 2,000. But, it was clear that the shortage of labour and materials would prevent or restrict their execution. A

WHARF STREET, LEICESTER.

Lessees - - - THE NEW BIOSCOPE TRADING Co., Ltd.

MONDAY, FEB. 7th, 1916 and Every Evening

OUR MOTTO: "DREADNOUGHT"
THE ALL BRITISH FIRM.

MONDAY, TUESDAY and WEDNESDAY,
GREAT VITAGRAPH DRAMA

WOMAN IN THE BOX

Thrilling Dramatic of the Courts.

GREAT LOVE DRAMA

THE CLIFF GIRL

WHOLE WEEK.-New Bio. Varieties.

JACK CREW

ECCENTRIC COMEDIAN.

THURSDAY, FRIDAY and SATURDAY,
DON'T MISS THIS!

LITTLE BLONDE IN BLACK

THE MYSTERY DRAMA.

THE EBONY CASKET

GREAT PHOTO-PLAY.

TIMES & PRICES AS USUAL.

PICTURE MATINEE, SATURDAYS at 2-30

'Dreadnought' was the name of the projector used at the Empire.
Courtesy I. Patterson.

Encouraging the Patrons

Patronage of the cinema was clearly on the increase, especially at holiday times. Very fine weather in the summer usually decreased the audiences, though reports often praise the ventilating systems in the local theatres for providing comfortable atmospheres even during the hottest spells.

The new manager at the Lyric (Knighton Cinema), Mr F. Horsefall, announced that from September 4th 1915 there would be two houses nightly.[52] Business had been reported as satisfactory, but the cinema had a very small seating capacity and this seemed to be a move to increase patronage with only a minor increase in outlay.

Leicester Mail advertisement of September 20th 1915.

An advertising card given to patrons at the Silver Street Cinema extolled the joys of attendance:

'One or two nights a week YOU reserve for Pictures and for the FIVE following reasons you should get on the car and visit THE SILVER STREET PALACE

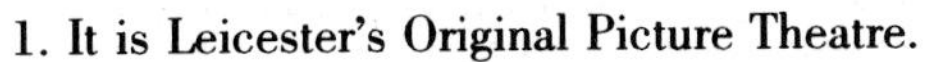

1. It is Leicester's Original Picture Theatre.

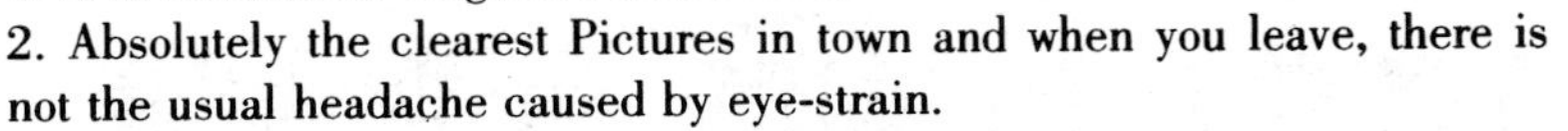

2. Absolutely the clearest Pictures in town and when you leave, there is not the usual headache caused by eye-strain.
3. At least two special Feature Films exhibited daily.
4. The only Picture Café in town where patrons can enjoy Tea and the Pictures at the same time.
5. Cars stop one minute from the Theatre from every route in town.'

Unfortunately no actual example of this card has survived, and the only evidence of its existence is in a report in the *Kinematograph Weekly* in October 1916.

Several cinemas were in the process of carrying out minor and major enlargement plans. The Picturedrome re-equipped and re-seated in December 1914. The Picture House had submitted plans for very extensive alterations and an accommodation improvement from 900 to 2,000. But, it was clear that the shortage of labour and materials would prevent or restrict their execution. A

WHARF STREET, LEICESTER.

Lessees - THE NEW BIOSCOPE TRADING Co., Ltd.

MONDAY, FEB. 7th, 1916 and Every Evening

OUR MOTTO: "DREADNOUGHT"
THE ALL BRITISH FIRM.

MONDAY, TUESDAY and WEDNESDAY,
GREAT VITAGRAPH DRAMA

WOMAN IN THE BOX

Thrilling Dramatic of the Courts.

GREAT LOVE DRAMA

THE CLIFF GIRL

WHOLE WEEK.-New Bio. Varieties.

JACK CREW

ECCENTRIC COMEDIAN.

THURSDAY, FRIDAY and SATURDAY,
DON'T MISS THIS!

LITTLE BLONDE IN BLACK

THE MYSTERY DRAMA.

THE EBONY CASKET

GREAT PHOTO-PLAY.

TIMES & PRICES AS USUAL.

PICTURE MATINEE, SATURDAYS at 2-30

'Dreadnought' was the name of the projector used at the Empire.
Courtesy I. Patterson.

Bioscope report of October 14th 1915 indicated that only the frontage of the cinema might be altered and even that was doubtful until the war's end.

Possibly because of the problem of filling live variety acts, the Pavilion increased the amount of time it devoted to film in its programmes. The Empire was now almost completely a cinema house, and though it closed at the end of 1916, it was reported as playing to crowded houses during 1915. There had been a change of management from Mr Fred Pollard to Mr F.R. Griffiths, who was the managing director of the leasees, the New Bioscope Trading Company.[53]

A successful evasion of the 'no standing' rule was perpetrated at the Silver Street Cinema as reported by Mr Springett.[54] He was astonished to see an 'elderly and rather diminutive woman' kneeling between the rows of seats. She had come in with a friend and could not find a seat next to her. She confidently told the manager that the regulations didn't say anything about kneeling!

A correspondent to one of the local papers even went into verse to mock the 'guardians'.

'They went into a Picture House,
As lively as three elves,
To see if gangways were all clear,
And they stood in them, themselves!'

The *Bioscope* reporter suggested that it made up in merit what it lacked in poetry. [55]

The 'Five Nights' Affair

But the most sensational action of the Watch Committee during the year was to stop the showing of the film 'Five Nights' at the Silver Street Picture House. The five-reel film, based upon the romantic novel by Victoria Cross and made at the Ealing Studios of Barker Motion Photography Ltd., starred Eve Balfour and Thomas MacDonald. It had been given an 'A' certificate by the British Board of Film Censors and it had been shown without problems in Liverpool, Cardiff and Bristol. But, prior to its Leicester showing, the Watch Committees of Preston and Birmingham had caused the film to be withdrawn.[56] This, no doubt, had alerted the Chairman of the Leicester Watch Committee to its notoriety. The cinema's advertisements in the previous week had not been slow in adding fuel to the fire by describing it as 'The sensation of 1915. The most talked about novel ever published'.[57]

It was reported in the *Bioscope* of October 21st, by Mr H.H. Springett, that 'Crowded houses, by no means an unusual state of things at Silver Street, had followed the programme throughout with appreciative interest during Monday and

Above: Kinematograph Weekly advertisement of July 1915.
Right: Leicester Mercury advertisement of October 13th 1915.

Tuesday, and, despite the fact that many clergymen were present, no word of complaint was heard concerning the star film. Indeed, rightly surmising that the widely discussed 'Five Nights' was the chief reason for the presence there of the reverend gentlemen, I took the opportunity of asking their respective opinions of the film as from time to time they came out, and in no case was there any fault found, while at least one of them - who admitted that he was there to lodge a protest if, in his opinion it should be necessary - waxed frankly and warmly eulogistic upon the merits of the film.'

On Tuesday night, the film was witnessed by members of the Leicester Watch Committee, including the Chairman, Councillor W.E. Hincks. They subsequently expressed strong disapproval to Mr Springett, and suggested that the showing of the film was not in the best interests of the public. They decided to take no action that night, but asked Mr Springett to attend a special Watch Committee meeting the next day. At this meeting, he was warned by the Chairman that 'Five Nights' must not again appear. Mr Springett then got in touch with his head office by 'phone and the film was withdrawn. A notice was placed on the door saying, 'We regret that owing to unforseeable circumstances the contract for the showing of 'Five Nights' has been cancelled'. Fellow managers rallied round to enable Mr Springett to remain open that day. Mr Frank

FLORAL HALL PICTURE THEATRE.
MONDAY, TUESDAY, & WEDNESDAY.
A Superb Photo-Play Version of the enormously successful Play now nearing its four hundredth performance at the ROYALTY THEATRE, LONDON.
THE MAN WHO STAYED AT HOME.
See Bills and Programmes for Eulogistic Press Reports.
GRAND ORCHESTRAL ORGAN.

GRAND ELECTRIC PALACE,
SILVER STREET.

TO-DAY & DURING THE WEEK.

POSITIVELY FOR SIX DAYS ONLY.

ENORMOUS ATTRACTION.

FIRST TIME OF EXHIBITION IN LEICESTER.

THE FILM THAT IS SWEEPING THE COUNTRY.

FIVE NIGHTS

By VICTORIA CROSS (In 5 Acts).

An Adaptation of the most talked of Novel ever Published.

THE SENSATION OF 1915.

SPECIAL ORCHESTRAL MUSIC.

CONTINUOUS EXHIBITIONS
EACH DAY 2.30 TO 10.30.

APPROXIMATE TIMES OF COMMENCING:—
2.30, 4.30, 6.30; AND 8.30.

ADMISSION .... 3d., 6d., and 1/-.
NO HALF-PRICE ALL WEEK.

THE PICTURE HOUSE.
GRANBY STREET, LEICESTER.

JOHN STRANGE WINTER'S THRILLING STORY.
"GRIP."
IN THREE PARTS.
Also—"HUNTING A HUSBAND" (Vitagraph Co.).
"A PEACH AND A PAIR" (Nestor).
"MAUD AND THE MISER" (Comedy).
"IN THE LAND OF BULLRUSHES" (Coloured), etc.

TUDOR CINEMA

MONDAY, TUESDAY, and WEDNESDAY.
"THE WISHING RING."

Harris of the Picturedrome, Mere Road, a cinema that did not open until the evening, offered the Silver Street its whole programme for the afternoon show. Even so, that afternoon, Mr Springett reported that he was £20 down on his usual takings.

In his Tuesday entertainments column, the the *Leicester Mail* reviewer had declared, 'My opinion of naughtiness, - better say alleged naughtiness, in the fashion of nervous sub-editors, - of Victoria Cross's famous book is not worth having. There will no doubt be a stampede to see the film, which the management have secured with commendable enterprise. The film was rebuked by the Preston Town Council, and the Censor rebuked the Preston Town Council for casting aspersions on his efficiency.' The *Evening Mail* film critic also found little to object to. 'Five Nights' is a work that lends itself to dramatisation, and the skill which has been put into the task of filming the story makes the production a brilliant success. Miss Eve Balfour is splendid as Viola and Mr. T.H. Macdonald in the role of Trevor Lonsdale, the artist round whose emotions and experiences the story is woven, presents an intensely human interpretation of the part. As Susee, the wayward wife of a Chinaman, Miss Sybil De-Bray is strikingly good. Indeed, it may be said that both play and players are excellent, and the result is a more than usually attractive series of pictures. One feature of the film which strikes the observer is that while many of situations are daring, the combination of skill on the part of the players and the artistic staging prevents any obtrusion of the unpleasant. The scenes in the artist' studio which roused some opposition in other towns, do not strike the writer as being objectionable. Judged from the stand point of art, they are well conceived, cleverly carried out and in good taste.[58]

When interviewed by the *Leicester Mail*, Councillor Hincks said that the film was unpleasant and unsavoury. 'Whilst we have no desire to restrict reasonable discretion and liberty,' he went on, 'there can be no question whatever that the wholesome minded men of the world would not tolerate an exhibition of the calibre of "Five Nights". The use of the word "Art" like "Charity" covers a multitude of sins, and to talk of this film being artistic and delicate is "piffle".' Leicester and Preston were not alone in opposing the exhibition of the film, and it was banned in Weston-super-Mare, Bath, Walsall, Brighton and. finally, London.[59]

Censorship was the subject of a directive from Whitehall, to which the Town Clerk, Mr H.A. Pritchard, replied:[60]

'I am requested to point out that in Leicester, there has been a decrease in the number of youthful delinquents since the War, and it is the opinion of the Chief Constable that the Cinematograph Exhibitions in Leicester have not been the cause of more than one or two prosecutions since they have been licensed.'

The Chief Constable and the Watch Committee were in favour of a Central Censorship Board for films to be issued with certificates for general distribution, but they did not want the power of final approval taken from them. 'This control', the Town Clerk went on, 'is as necessary for films which are in parts suggestive, as for those which might induce mischief, if not crime, in the minds of the younger part of the audience.

'One film ("Five Nights") has been summarily stopped here, and in others parts have been eliminated. All of these have been suggestive and bordering on the indecent.

'It has been the custom here for members of the Watch Committee themselves to regularly visit the various cinema exhibitions in order that they might see the character of the films exhibited.'

The only other film that is mentioned in the minutes before this date is 'Midnight at Maxim's' which the Committee viewed at the King's Hall on January 6th 1916. They took exception to several sequences, the content of which is not described in the minutes!

Of course, there was official censorship of the war-time newsreels, a fact not disguised by the *Daily Post* reviewer: 'Although the military authorities, we imagine, exercise the power of the censor over the pictures, we get a good impression of the type of Indian soldiers who will fight on all fronts.'[61]

The Cinema Commission was sitting during 1917 and a number of interesting facts were presented to it by Mr J. Brooke Wilkinson, the Secretary of the British

Board of Film Censors. He stated that in 1916 7,061,681 feet of film was viewed. 4,430 subjects were passed for Universal exhibition, 904 for Adult exhibition, 25 films were rejected, and 502 were taken exception to.[62] A short film called 'Pruning the Movies', showing 'in humourous terms how some people might censor the pictures', was exhibited in Leicester in 1915.[63]

The Evington Cinema

In March 1916 a petition was organised by some local residents to prevent the building of a cinema on East Park Road. On April 4th the Watch Committee approved the plans prepared by architect Ernest H. Smith of Dover Street, after defeating an amendment that the public of the neighbourhood should be consulted. In May, land was purchased by William A. Jennings, a Leicester boot manufacturer, on behalf of the Evington Cinema Limited, and building began.[64]

A licence for the Evington Cinema was granted to Mr W.A. Barker on October 17th 1916. The cinema had had its grand opening the day before, with a free matinee (excepting War Tax). A ladies' orchestra provided the musical entertainment, and Messrs Wilford, Stork, Pace and Pierpoint were also included in the programme. The *Leicester Mercury* reported that, at the invitation of the management, a large company assembled for a view of the house. 'The building, which is of an artistic appearance, has been designed with the idea of catering for the greatest possible comfort of its patrons. The exterior is in the Renaissance style, and the interior is Jacobean with comfortable seating accommodation, both on the ground floor which slopes to the front so that everyone is allowed a clear view of the screen, and in the balcony.' The spacious entrance

GRAND OPENING
OF THE
EVINGTON CINEMA
EAST PARK ROAD (Opposite St. Peter's Road),
MONDAY, October 16th, 1916.
MATINEE 3 P.M.
FREE ADMISSION (excepting War Tax),
Shewing the World's Best and Latest Photo Plays.
First Attraction Including
Mde. JANE HADING
In a great Cinematograph Production and Thrilling War Story,
entitled
"THE SPIRIT OF FRANCE."
ORCHESTRAL MUSIC. CAFE AND LOUNGE.
EVENING from 6.30.
PRICES 2d., 4d., 6d., Balcony 9d. (Tax Extra).

Leicester Mercury advertisement

A poster for the film which opened the Evington. *Kinematograph Weekly* August 17th 1916.

lounge also contained a small café. The reporter saw a successful future for the venture, given that it was catering for an area of the city not yet served by a cinema. The admission prices (excluding War Tax) were 2d, 4d or 6d in the stalls, and 9d in the balcony, and the programme commenced each evening at 6.30 p.m. The opening film was the patriotic wartime drama 'The Spirit of France' starring, Mme Jane Hading and Raphael Duflos.[65] It was a French film made by Film d'Art from the novel 'La Flambée'.

The *Kinematograph Weekly* reporter, again without any illustrations, attempted to convey the grandeur of the building.[66] 'Of all the cinemas I have visited during the past few years, I cannot remember that any of them have left behind a more comfortable impression than that of the latest newcomer, the Evington. Outside and in, the place is a triumph of thoroughness, and a work of which the architect Mr Ernest Smith may feel justifiably proud.'

The description, whilst highlighting some of the same items that appeared in the local newspaper reports also gave some unique details. The entrance to the cheaper seats was 'via a wide well-lighted corridor on the left, running the entire length of the building, from which doorways at intervals communicate with the interior. The rake to the floor is the steepest I have seen, so that the screen 18 feet x 17 feet above a handsome platform (a new feature this, doubtless with an eye to the increasing popularity of lecture films and the like) is well within the

The Evington cinema frontage in 1991.
Author's photograph.

view of everybody. Below the stage is the Orchestra stall, the orchestra with a single exception being composed of ladies. The accommodation is approximately 900. There is a fine semi-circular balcony holding 200 seats communicating with the daintiest little tea-room lounge imaginable. This in turn leads one through glass doors to an open air balcony of sunny aspect. The tea-lounge opens at 3 o'clock and the cinema at 6 o'clock. There will be three matinees weekly. Gaumont machines are being used with the usual excellent results.'

Amongst the subscribers to the Evington Cinema Ltd partnership were Messrs W.R. Hallam, W.A. Flemming, Harry Bowerman and J.A. Hartopp and A.F. Chapman. The secretary was H. Macaulay Brown. The most significant subscriber was, however, Mr George H. Scarborough, who was in the shoe trade with D. Henderson and Sons Ltd. of St Saviours Road. His faith in the suburban cinema persisted even when business was poor, and by the mid-twenties he was the major share holder in Evington Cinema Ltd. Over the next 14 years he built or acquired six more cinemas in the city and three in the county. He was National President of the Cinematograph Exhibitors' Association in 1946, and he was honoured by that Association in 1951 for 25 years' service on the general council. He died in 1972.[67]

In March 1918, the licence of the Evington Cinema was transferred to the same Charles E. West, who had opened the Cank Street Cinema in 1907. After employment at the Picture House for a year from 1910, he had gone back into Variety for five years, returning to Leicester in 1916. He introduced a permament orchestra to the Evington, and at times took a turn on the clarinet, himself.[68] He joined the company as a director and as booking manager.[69]

Above: Charles West in 1948 *Leicester Mercury* photograph.

Below: Kinematograph Weekly advertisement January 3rd 1918.

Proposals, Closures and Transfers

On May 3rd 1916 plans for a new cinema in Nedham Street were approved and in June plans for cinemas in Aylestone Road and Melbourne Road were passed. None of these materialised during the war years. The Lyric, Knighton, then under the management of Mr A.A. Forknall, did not renew its licence in January 1917. The lease for the Boulevard Electric Theatre expired during the year and its projectors and

BOULEVARD ELECTRIC THEATRE,
WESTERN BOULEVARD, LEICESTER.

RANDLE & ASPELL

Have received instructions from the Directors of the above Company, owing to the lease expiring.
TO SELL BY AUCTION.
On THURSDAY next, JANUARY 10, 1918, at 11 o'clock prompt,
THE VALUABLE

OPERATING MACHINES

537 TIP-UP CHAIRS in Red Plush and on Iron Standards, ELECTRIC FANS, SWITCHBOARDS, ELECTRIC FITTINGS, PIANOFORTE, and numerous other items, as particularised in catalogues to be obtained from Auctioneers.

On View Morning of Sale

or by appointment with the Auctioneers. Offices, 32, Halford Street, Leicester.
Telephone 837. Telegrams: "RANDLE, Auctioneer, Leicester."

furnishings were auctioned on January 10th 1918. A *Kinematograph Weekly* report the following week suggested that the buildings would be demolished and replaced by a textile mill.[70] The skating rink had apparently been closed for some years. An advertisement in the *Leicester Mercury* in October 1914 had offered the Boulevard Rink for sale, and asked for tenders for demolition and clearance of the site. Fortunately, the buildings still remain with their interiors and exteriors little changed.

Ownership of the lease on the King's Hall changed in December 1918. The new owner, Mr H.B. Stone of Nottingham, replaced the whole management structure. Mr J.H. Walter, who had been manager since November 12th 1917, was succeeded by Mr A. Whitworth Cheetham from Birmingham. Mr J. Fielding Crompton, the leader of the orchestra, was replaced by Mr Frank W. Muston.[71]

The newsreels were dominated by war footage, 'as interesting as the censor will allow'.[72] 'John Bull's Animated Sketch Book' and the Kineto animated maps of the war front presented both humourous and morale boosting propaganda at the expense of the Germans, and the Turks. But, in September 1916, the feature length documentary 'The Battle of the Somme' provided ample evidence of the real cost of the war, even though, as we now know, and contemporaries must have suspected, it had been somewhat massaged by the War Office. A quotation from Lloyd George accompanied the newspaper advertisement: 'If an exhibition of this picture all over the world does not end war, God help civilization.' The reviewer reported that 'music mostly of a lightsome character helps to soften some of the incidents depicted.'[73] Other official war documentaries followed.

Sundays and Holy Days

The policy of not allowing cinemas to open on Sundays was adhered to except in certain circumstances when the proceeds were donated to War Charities. On Sunday February 18th 1917 the Picture House and the Evington were given permission to open in aid of the Kitchener Memorial Fund. Even though the performance was for such a worthy cause, and the time of opening was from 7.45 p.m. to 9.45 p.m., there were some protests from places of worship.[74]

The programme at the Evington was veiled in the form of 'A Picture Entertainment and Sacred Concert' with the main screening being the two-reel Tannhauser film, 'The White Lady', starring James Cruze. Another film, 'The Indian', was also shown after several sacred songs by Miss Louise Hill and Mr Fitz Hallam. Miss Lettie Nourish sang 'Land of Hope and Glory' before the National Anthem closed the proceedings. One of the accompanists, Mr

PROGRAMME

GRAND PHOTO PLAY (*Tannhauser*). TWO PARTS.
"THE WHITE LADY."
Featuring James Cruze, of "The Million Dollar Mystery" fame.

SONG .. .. "Abide with me" .. .. .. *Liddle*
MISS LOUIE HILL.

SONG .. .. "The Last Call" .. .. *Sanderson*
MR. FITZ HALLAM,
London and Provincial Concerts.

K.B. FILM .. "The Indian" .. ..

SONG .. .. .. Selected .. ..
MISS LOUIE HILL.

SONG .. .. .. "Babylon" .. *Stephen Adam*
MISS LETTIE NOURISH.

SONG .. "Soldier, what of the Night?" *J. Airlie Dix*
MR. FITZ HALLAM.

SONG .. .. "Land of Hope and Glory" .. .. *Elgar*
MISS LETTIE NOURISH.

Chorus. Land of Hope and Glory, mother of the Free,
How shall we extol thee, who are born of thee?
Wider still and wider shall thy bounds be set;
God, who made thee mighty, make thee mightier yet.

(*The audience are requested to join in the above Chorus.*)

GOD SAVE THE KING.

ACCOMPANISTS .. MISS MAUDE HARVEY AND MR. T. ASHMELL.

Our thanks are due to
The Management for the use of the Theatre.
The Staff.
The Artistes, all of whom have given their services free.
The Printers.
The Leicester Billposting Co. for posting bills.

The programme for the Sacred Concert and picture entertainment on Sunday February 18th 1917 in aid of the Kitchener Fund.
Courtesy Leicestershire Records Office.

T. Ashmell, had at one time been resident pianist at the Empire, Wharf Street.

Good Friday opening was permitted in 1916 after 3 p.m. 'subject to the approval of the programme'. Approval was not given in 1917, but in 1918 opening could take place after 3 p.m. 'subject to approval' and as long as the employees got double pay and an alternative holiday.[75] Christmas Day opening followed similar lines. It was not granted for 1916; but, for 1917 and 1918, opening was possible after 3 p.m. with double pay for the employees, and approval of the programmme by the Chairman of the committee. In

1918 approval was also given for extended opening times on Boxing Day and the following two days from 11 a.m. to 10.15 p.m.[76]

The Influenza Epidemic

The influenza epidemic of November 1918 nearly caused the closure of all public places including cinemas. Earlier in the year the City Council had passed a bye-law which required the exclusion from cinemas of all children of school age and below if the local health officer had signed a closure order on local schools because of infectious diseases.[77] The current crisis occasioned a meeting called by the Watch Committee at which the managers of places of entertainment voiced their opinions.[78] Mr Trueman Towers (manager of the Floral Hall and the Palace) suggested that places of amusement should remain open to provide people with a relief from their anxieties. Mr F. Gray (manager of the Olympia) estimated that there had been a fall in receipts of between 30 and 50 per cent. Alderman T. Windley, chairman of the Sanitary Committee, said that there must be sufficient time for ventilation between performances. It was observed that the system in operation at the Picture House, Granby Street completely changed the air in the theatre ten times per hour. A decision was deferred until there could be a full meeting of exhibitors and owners. At this later meeting, it was decided

Granby Street *circa* 1914. The entrance to the Picture House is on the right.
Postcard in author's collection.

that, starting on November 4th, performances would be restricted to 7 to 10 p.m. in the suburbs with matinees an Mondays and Thursdays, and from 2 p.m. to 5 p.m. and 7 p.m. to 10 p.m. in the centre of town.

The next week brought even worse attendance figures, but a decision was taken to return to normal hours of opening on what turned out to be Armistice Day, November 11th. Influenza deaths in Leicester had been alarming, and a well-known figure in cinema circles, Miss May Towers, succumbed to the epidemic in November. She had been the pay-box cashier at the Picture House for several years.[79]

The Watch Committee Ban Another Film

The Watch Committee met at the King's Hall on February 11th 1918 to view a film called 'Jimmy Dale, Alias the Grey Seal' and, without any minuted reasons, decided against its presentation in Leicester. This 15-part serial was shown without problem in other towns, but an advert in the *Kinematograph Weekly* of February 21st, clearly defending the reputation of the film, indicated that the story of the film was being serialised in two of Cassell's journals. 'Doesn't this prove that it is wholesome and good?' it concluded.

During the War years, the cinema had proved itself to be an excellent provider of entertainment and a ready vehicle for morale boosting. In the process, with an increased input from the U.S.A., the nature of the programme had changed. A single main film and a series of shorts, had become so normal by February 1916, that the *Daily Post* critic was able to talk of the 'feature' film.[80] Advertisements and reviews printed in the newspapers indicated the common programme format of a four- or five-reel feature with a further hour's worth of shorts and a newsreel. The one-reel animated cartoon had arrived as well.

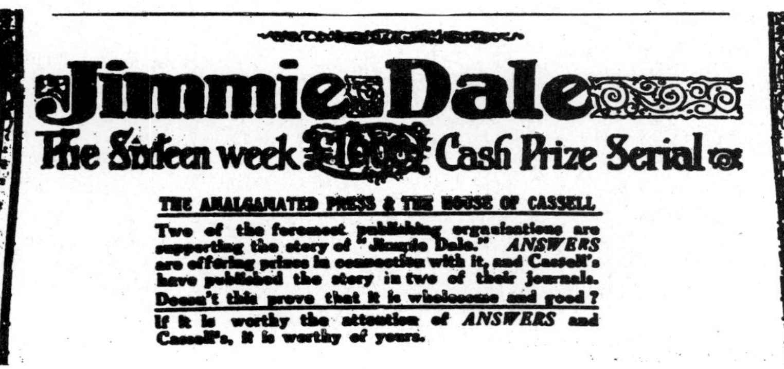

Cinema exhibition was becoming more assured, some might say 'brash'. It attempted to tackle any subject under the sun from the inconsequential cavortings of the Keystone Bathing Beauties in 'Hula Hula Land'[81] to the social problems of an industrial society in Lois Weber's 'The Price of a Good Time.'[82] It had developed a new art form in which drama, photography and music combined to present a new view of the world and it had brought the skills and mimes of practised comedians to a wider public than could be contained in, or encouraged into, the halls of variety.

And yet, there were those looking to other technological changes that the first twenty years of cinematography had only hinted at. The *Daily Post* printed extracts from a speech made by John Tippett, the managing director of the Transatlantic Film Co. in January 1917.[83] His evidence was that attempts to perfect a talking picture machine had, so far, not met with any success. He suggested that the main reason was that the sound did not appear to match the position of the speaker on the screen. 'A great advance will have been made when with screens 20 or 30 feet wide, the voice can be thrown from one character on the extreme right to another character on the extreme left.'

The writer of the 'Here and There' column of the same issue was of the opinion that the reason for failure was the inability of the picture and phonograph to synchronise properly! Surprisingly, neither of them mentioned amplification as a problem.

The popularity of the cinema had increased during the war years, and cinematograph shows reminiscent of the fairground booths had been transported to the troops in France. Few young cinema patrons could remember a time without the 'Flicks', and the peace would bring with it fresh opportunities to make their acquaintance.

Two serial stars on cigarette cards.
Left: Pearl White in 1916.
Right: Kathlyn Williams in 1920.
Author's collection.

Chapter Five

The Post-War Era 1919-23

In June 1919, during a visit from King George and Queen Mary, Leicester was created a 'City'. The preparations, the decorations and the pageantry had caught the public imagination and Mr J.H. Walter, the new manager of the Picture House, arranged an exclusive showing for an extended newsreel of the occasion made by London Films. The 1,500 feet of film played to crowded houses for three weeks.[1]

The Sovereign Cinema

With the cessation of hostilities, the demobilised cinema managers began to take up their old jobs, and some of the previously-planned cinemas were now built. On December 22nd 1919 'The Sovereign Cinema' with 797 seats was opened.[2] Approval for the building had been given on April 1st. Leicester's Watch Committee had granted a licence for the building as early as October 1st. The distinctive half-timber design by Seale and Riley of Horsefair Street was very apt for the Woodgate site. Its large roof-mounted ventilators were another notable feature. Prices of admission were 4d, 6d, 9d and 1/- in the stalls, and 1/3d in the balcony. The Sovereign Picture House Company Ltd was under the directorship of Messrs S. Feinhols, W. Moss, J.E. Whittle and W.J. Reeve;

SOVEREIGN PICTURE HOUSE, Woodgate.

ALL NEXT WEEK.

Tarzan of the Apes.

Gripping and Full of Thrills.
Supported by Full Star Programme.
Prices: 4d., 6d., 9d., 1s., Balcony 1/3

The New Super Cinema.

Leicester Mercury advertisement.

company secretary was Mr A.F. Chapman.

The title of the film for the opening programme is not recorded, but 'Tarzan of the Apes' starring Elmo Lincoln was the presentation for its second week. This had already been shown the week before at the Floral Hall.

The Sovereign.
Above: Exterior. *Drawing by author after photograph.*
Below: Section through auditorium.
Courtesy Leicestershire Records Office.

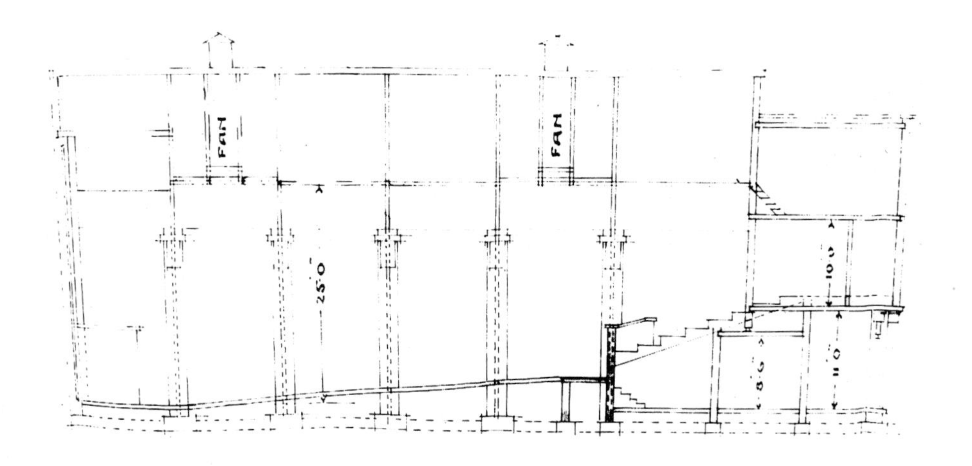

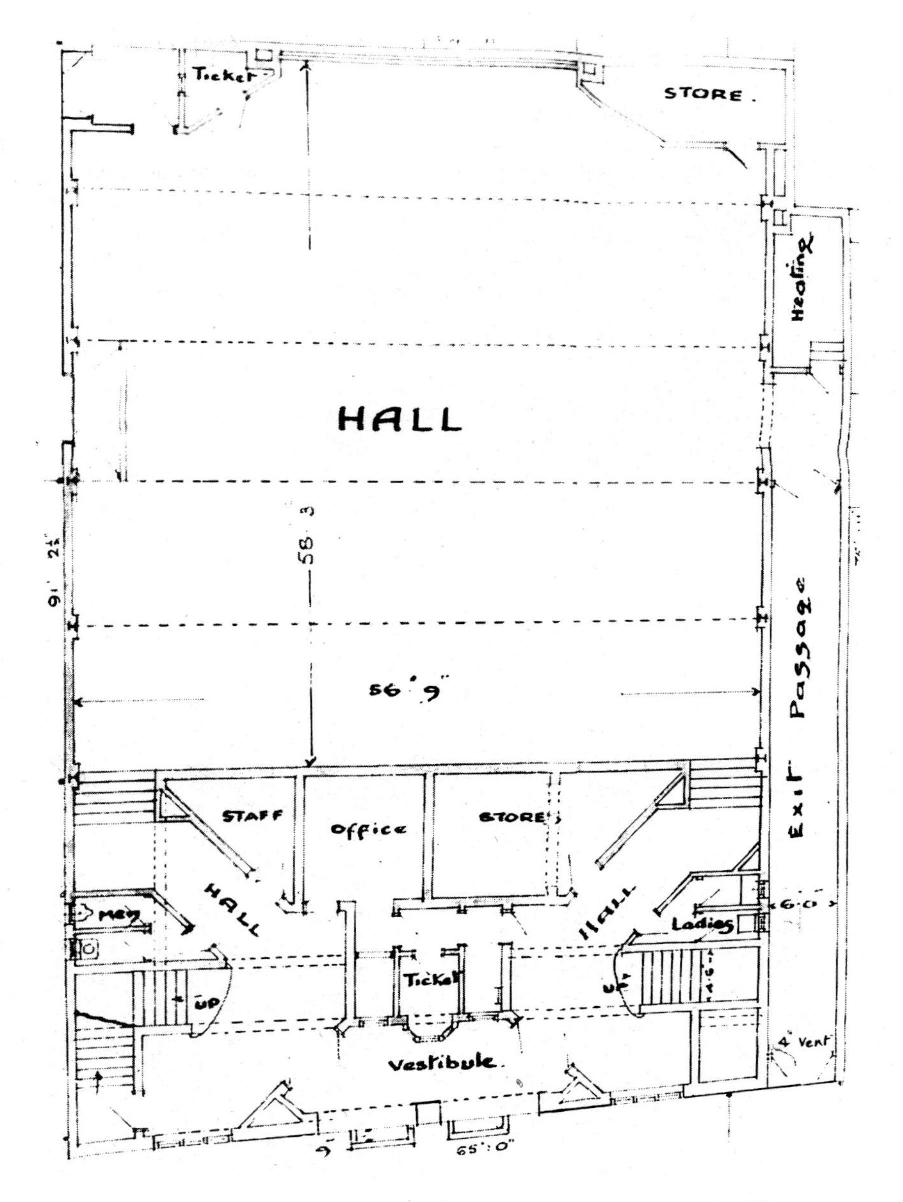

Ground plan of the Sovereign. *Courtesy Leicestershire Records Office.*

The Melbourne Cinema.

The Watch Committee granted a licence for the 944 seat 'Melbourne Cinema' on May 4th 1920[3] and it was officially opened on Tuesday May 18th. Plans for the cinema had originally been submitted in July 1916 and demolition on the site had been reported in the *Bioscope* in November of that year. A Government Department order relating to wartime shortages of materials caused the work to be halted. As with his Evington Cinema design, Ernest H. Smith, of 26, Dover Street, Leicester managed to combine style and practicability. The site in this case was less open and the building fitted perfectly into the surroundings.

The *Kinematograph Weekly* of May 27th was quite lavish in its reporting of the opening by Alderman W.J. Lovell J.P., the Deputy Mayor, who also happened to be the chairman of the Watch Committee.

'The building, a handsome and impressive structure is situated at a part of the city known as 'Five Ways'. As there is a tramway stop immediately opposite,

The Melbourne *circa* 1970. *Courtesy Leicester Mercury.*

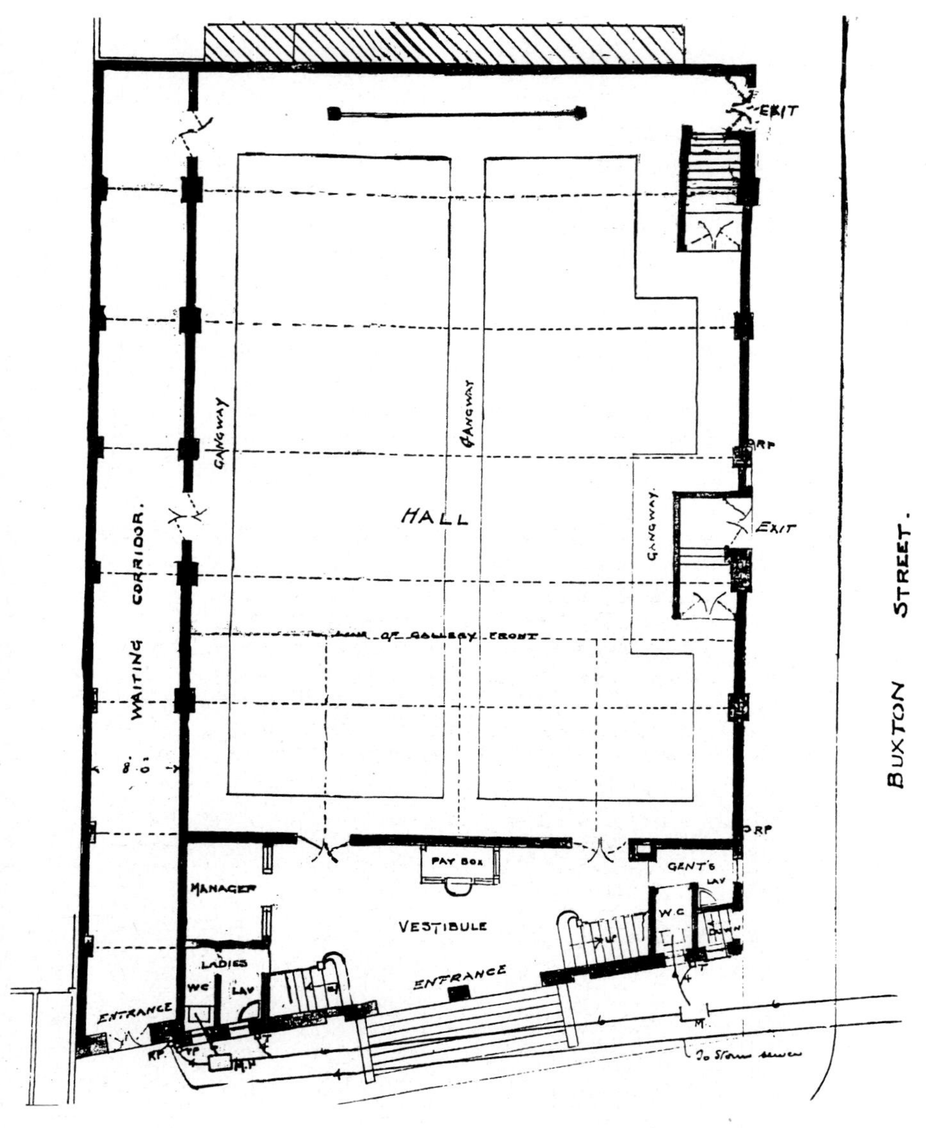

Ground plan of the Melbourne. *Courtesy Leicestershire Records Office.*

the value of the position can be appreciated. It is built of blue brindle brick and Derbyshire stone, and the entrance hall is approached by a wide staircase. In the hall are situated the box office, and the manager's office. Two staircases also of stone lead to the balcony, café and balcony lounge. The seating accommodation for upwards of 1,000 is entirely tip-up, those on the ground floor being of leather [the original plans only showed seating for 750 [4]]. The lighting is a feature - a soft subdued rose effect being got by the artistic shades used. The ventilation and heating, the latter being by radiators, is said to be the best in the city, while the good offices of the Chief Fire Officer (Mr Neal) were secured in regard to the installation of fire extiguishing apparatus, with the result that the directors have instituted more than required by the local bye-laws. In addition to the front exits, two exits on the ground floor are provided, one on each side of the proscenium.'

In declaring the hall open, Alderman Lovell said, to enthusiastic applause, that the building was not only a credit to the architects, the directors and the neighbourhood, but also to the city. 'There were many', he continued, 'who deprecated the opening of so many Kinemas, but it must be remembered that they only met a demand by the public for the provision of clean, wholesome and educational entertainment.' He congratulated the directors for 'securing as manager the services of Mr H.H. Springett, who had managed another house in the city for many years (the Silver Street Cinema), and who had a good name with the Watch Committee.' Fred Trueman Towers, son of the Manager at the Floral Hall and Palace had replaced him in January 1920. The formalities at the new cinema closed with little Dorothy Pallett, the daughter of one of the directors, presenting Mrs Lovell with a bouquet, and with Mr F.W. Southorn, another director, asking for a vote of thanks for the Deputy Mayor.

Programming in 1920

A Silver Street Cinema handbill for May 3rd 1920 gives some idea of the shape of a town centre cinema programme. The mid-week programme change was complete except for the Chaplin film. This re-issue of the 1915 Essanay film 'A Woman' has been retitled 'Charlie, the Perfect Lady'. It was common practice to re-title re-issued comedies. At this time also, some early Fatty Arbuckle one reelers were entirely renamed and re-presented locally. The serial in the first half of the week had been trade-shown over a year previously, but the serial for the second half of the week was being shown exactly on its release date.

In 1956 Mr Trueman Towers recalled that in his first days as manager at Silver Street circle patrons were served with a cup of tea and a piece of cake whilst the films were being shown. Even when the café was opened, the screen

SILVER STREET

PICTURES.

Manager . . . . F. TRUEMAN TOWERS

CONTINUOUS EXHIBITIONS DAILY FROM 2 P.M.

MONDAY, MAY 3rd, & during the Week.

MONDAY, TUESDAY AND WEDNESDAY,

Fruits of Desire

Five Part Drama.

CHARLIE CHAPLIN in
Charlie, the Perfect Lady

LEAH BAIRD in
WHEN WOMAN WARS

Serial.

HIS SPEEDY FINISH

Comedy.

CYNTHIANA

Two Part Drama.

GAUMONT GRAPHIC

THURSDAY, FRIDAY AND SATURDAY

The Game of Liberty

Five Part Drama.

CHARLIE CHAPLIN in
Charlie, the Perfect Lady

The Mystery of Thirteen

Serial.

Featuring **FRANCIS FORD and ROSEMARY THEBY.**

WHEELS AND WOES

Comedy.

ORCHIDS

Two Part Drama.

GAUMONT GRAPHIC

Afternoon Teas. **THE PICTURE CAFE.** Afternoon Teas.

ORCHESTRAL MUSIC DAILY

Conductress . . . . Miss MARIE VAUGHAN, A.R.C.M.

For a Taxi at any time, ring up West End Garage, 103 Kirby Road. Phone No. 964.

Popular Price (including Tax) - 5d., 9d. & 1/-
Balcony, Cafe and Lounge - - - 1/3

Phone 1774.

Management reserve right of Admission. No Money Returned.

A handbill for May 3rd 1920. *Courtesy Leicestershire Records Office.*

could still be seen from at least four tables. The café remained open until 9 p.m.. A four-piece orchestra was under the direction of Miss Marie Vaughan.[5]

Management Changes

Captain Worsley, former manager of the High Street Cinema, was appointed manager of the King's Hall in December 1920 when he was released from his Army Service. He replaced Mr Arthur G. Emms who had held the appointment since July 1919 when the lease of the cinema had been sold 'for a very big figure' to Tom Wright of Nottingham, owner of Victory Cinemas. Mr Emms was now moving to take up the managership of a new cinema being built in Croydon.[6]

In other managerial moves, Mr Deacon of the Sovereign went to be the new manager of the Theatre Royal, Loughborough, a building which had just been leased by the Moorhouse Circuit. His replacement was Mr William H. Clarke, a native of Leicester with experience of the industry.[7] He, in turn, was appointed to an out-of-town cinema in May 1922, and replaced by Mr Richard Rosbottom. He had been for four years at the Electric Cinema in Bournemouth, and he had also seen service in South Wales, Berkshire and Lancashire.[8]

Mr Springett, the manager of the Melbourne for only one year, resigned his post and left Leicester in June 1921. He was succeeded by Mr Arthur Ashley. Before the war, he had been at the White Hall, Derby and the Derby Cinema, but more recently, he had been on the renting side with Wardour Films Ltd and he was well known in the city.[9] All was not well at the Melbourne, for yet another manager was appointed in 1922. The industry as a whole had reported a difficult year, and Mr S. Tait, the new acting manager, attempted to lure more patrons with a small drop in prices to 6d, 9d. and 1/- from 9d, 1/- and 1/3d.

R. Rosbottom, manager at the Sovereign.

The Shaftesbury had two changes of management in as many months. Mr C. Berry resigned in September to start up a motor business in another town. His replacement was Mr Edward Broom, lately at the Stockport Cinema and, before that, at one of Manchester's suburban cinemas. In December, he also resigned through ill-health and returned to his home in Stockport. His replacement, Mr Harry

Barker, was an experienced manager and a welcome addition to the ranks of the Moorhouse circuit. He had had a long professional career in entertainment. For some years, he had been the manager/lecturer for the national tours of the chimpanzee 'Consul the Great' owned by the late Frank C. Bostock. He was also with Fred Ginnett and Wal Pink's 'The Johnstown Flood'. He had managed the Gospel Oak Skating Rink and for several summers he had been producer/manager of Chappel's Promenade Concerts at Great Yarmouth. His cinema experience had been five years management at the Palace, Llanelly.[10]

Prolonged illnesses of managers were usually reported in the trade press, especially if they affected both managerial work and that of the local C.E.A. branch. During 1923, local C.E.A president, Mr Fred Trueman Towers, Snr, had a succession of afflictions that kept him away from both his presidency and the Palace. The secretary, Phillip Joseph, who was assistant manager at the Picture House, was taken seriously ill in March and died some three weeks later. Herbert Gibbon became president and Fred Trueman Towers, Jnr, took over as secretary.

Oliver Rogers, the manager of Imperial Playhouse, High Street, had been reported ill for several months before he vacated his post to go to London. The new manager, Mr Herbert Gibbon, had come from a film promotion job at the Scala, London prior to this appointment. One of his early innovations was the introduction of the 'sun spot novelty', in which a spot light roamed round the audience to a musical accompaniment. A prize was awarded to the member of the audience on whom the spot rested when the music stopped. The Cinema-de-Luxe, in later advertising, claimed to have introduced the idea to Leicester, though it was already a well-known practice at dance-halls.

Fire Hazard Averted

The dire results of a cinema fire were averted by the swift action of the operator at the Cinema-de-Luxe. At twenty-past eight on February 21st 1921, as the third part of the Dorothy Dalton film 'His Wife's Friend' was being shown, yellow smoke was seen to be coming from the top spool housing. 'As quick as lightning', the operator closed the safety shutters and prevented any of the smoke from filtering into the auditorium. He then covered the spool box with a damp blanket and played the chemical extinguisher onto it. The manager informed the fire brigade who, because of the proximity of the fire station, were quickly on the scene. It took twenty minutes to get the programme started again, but all this time, the audience were ignorant of the mishap, whilst being kept amused by the organist. The whole of the third part of the film was destroyed, and the projector, too, was of no further use.[11]

The Hippodrome, Wharf Street

The Empire, Wharf Street had not renewed its cinematograph licence for 1916 and the company that operated it, the New Bioscope Trading Company, had gone into liquidation in 1921. It was re-opened as 'The Hippodrome' on March 13th 1922 by a group of ex-servicemen headed by Mr J.B. Wacks, son of a Leicester clothing manufacturer.[12] There was initial disquiet at the seating plan for 620 as originally presented and concern that viewing from the gallery might affect the eyesight of children.[13] In August 1922 the seating was increased by 130 places. The show was now continuous and there was a programme change twice a week. It was anticipated that variety turns would be introduced later.[14]

The manager was Arnold Graham. He had come from the Majestic, Northampton, but only a month later he is reported as vacating his position, when H.W. Hurst took over as business manager. Mr Hurst had come to Leicester from the Empress, Bromsgrove in March 1921 as a replacement for Mr C. Draycott at the Mere Road Picturedrome. He had also served for eleven years with Bromheads of Manchester. His first acquaintance with Leicester had been with a circus when it visited the Floral Hall in the days before its cinema conversion. He had just lost his position at the Picturedrome, Mere Road where Mr I.P. Wright had became the new proprietor and manager in circumstances that suggested a family rivalry with brother R.M. Wright. His enterprise and style of management quickly brought a change in fortunes at the Empire. But further problems at the Melbourne encouraged the proprietors to seek his expert help and he moved there in November 1922. The management of the Hippodrome was left in the hands of Mr Wacks, the proprietor.

J.B. Wacks, manager at the Hippodrome, Wharf Street.

Cinema Expansion Planned

The editor of the *Mercury* clearly did not feel the time was propitious for cinema expansion. Under the title 'Films and the Film-goer' he sought to give reasons for the 'half-empty cinemas' other than the continued collection of Entertainment Tax. 'Some programmes we have seen of late have not shown the slightest advance or even substantial change from those 10 years ago. Without decrying the many merits of such productions, we see clearly enough the point of view of the cinemagoer who is bored stiff by the constant repetition of ancient stock ideas.'[15]

Even so, four other cinemas were proposed during this period. One was contemplated on a site adjoining the Cinema de Luxe, and amended plans were provisionally approved in December 1919. The proprietor of the Cinema-de-Luxe, Mr T. Jackson, had said that the new cinema would have accommodation for 1,600 as opposed to the present cinema's 950.[16] Nothing more was heard of the project and the Cinema-de-Luxe gave notice of opening a restaurant within the existing building. This was opened in April 1922 with Sid Powell as the catering manager.

Mr Jackson owned three cinemas in Wolverhampton, one each in Kidderminster and West Bromwich and two in Walsall. In May 1922 he attempted to sell his interests in these but none made their reserve price at auction.[17]

Plans were approved for a cinema on the corner of Loughborough Road and Coral Street.[18] No company is listed with the application and the plans do not appear to have survived. Plans were not approved for a cinema in Humberstone Gate.[19] The only other new name in the listings was 'The Scala', an up-market re-naming of 'The King's Hall' from January 14th 1922.[20]

Attempts at Unionisation

Manpower shortages after the war gave strength to many bids for union expansion. The Musician's Union, and the Electrical Trades Union were the main negotiators in the cinema industry on the employees' side and the Cinematograph Exhibitors' Association and the Kinematograph Renters' Society represented the employers. At this time, the National Association of Theatrical Employees increased its activity and the minutes of the Leicester Branch of the C.E.A. reveal a number of attempts to recruit members and to pressure employers. In some parts of London

SCALA PICTURES
and CAFE.
(Late King's Hall) GRANBY STREET
CONTINUOUS PERFORMANCE from 2.
MONDAY, TUESDAY, WEDNESDAY.
DRAG HARLAN
Featuring
WILLIAM FARNUM
Fine Orchestral Music
Cafe Open from 10.30 a.m. to 8.30 p.m.
(Wednesdays and Saturdays 9 p.m.)

The first Scala advertisement January 14th 1922.

in December 1920 the E.T.U. are reported as forcing many cinema managers to sign working agreements by refusing to service their equipment as long as they remained 'black' houses.[21]

Wages were determined by national guidelines and local agreements, but there were many variations linked to staff size and cinema capacity. Though it is not easy to state what rates of pay were in operation in Leicester, the agreement made for Swansea cinemas in January 1920 can serve as a pointer. Chief Operators were paid £5/5/- per week, Assistants £4/4/-, Learners £1. Cashiers in cinemas with one pay box received £3 per week and cashiers in cinemas with two pay boxes, £2/10/-. Cleaners were on a wage of £1/5/-.[22]

Musician's wages were determined very much by the hours of employment and the prestige of the cinema. The basic rate for a twenty-four week negotiated for Nottingham cinemas in May 1920 was: Musical Directors £3/15/- (with 4/- per hour overtime), Other Musicians, £3/10/- (3/6d per hour overtime) and Relief Pianists £2/10/- per week. Larger cinemas with two orchestras paid £5 per week to the main orchestra leader and £4/10/- to the second orchestra leader.[23]

Orchestra poaching was outlawed by a set of rules agreed between the C.E.A. and the Musicians' Union, but Mr Forknall, manager of the Coliseum, complained that an un-named hall had attempted to entice his orchestra away with inducements of greater pay, even though he was paying more than union rates. At the February 1921 C.E.A branch meeting it was agreed that representations should be made to the manager of the hall in question.[24]

The Watch Committee

Several films were submitted to the Watch Committee. In October 1920 no objection was lodged against the presentation of 'Auction of Souls' at the Cinema de Luxe. When it was shown for a week from October 3rd 1920 however it was advertised as 'For Adults Only' and was given four separate bookable performances at increased prices. Billed as 'The Greatest Film of the Age', it was adapted from the book *Ravished Armenia* and starred Aurora Mardiganian.[25] It had been refused a certificate by the British Board of Film Censors. In the same month that this was shown, 'Five Nights' was once again rejected because of 'the undesirability of the subject.'[26]

In May 1922 the Watch Committee saw a film entitled 'Cocaine' prior to its exhibition at the Scala in July. They agreed that it could be shown on condition that two small portions were eliminated, and that the cinema made no advertisement of the fact that the film had been submitted to the Watch Committee. The Scala adhered to this condition but five weeks before the

A scene from 'Auction of Souls'. *Kinematograph Weekly.*

presentation they began their advertising campaign for the film.[27] A correspondent to the *Bioscope* of June 15th, however, did reveal that the film had been passed by the Watch Committee for showing in Leicester.

'Cocaine' was made by Master Films at their Teddington Studios and starred Hilda Bayley, Flora Le Breton and Tony Fraser. The *Bioscope* reported it as an excellent British production and forecast large crowds being drawn. The British Board of Film Censors did not give it a certificate on its first submission in May 1922 but passed it with an 'A' certificate in June after sections had been re-edited, and on condition that its title was changed. It appeared in many parts of the country as 'While London Sleeps' but the Sovereign's presentation in November was under the original title. There is no indication as to which version was shown at either presentation. It played to crowded houses at the Scala, who specially engaged a jazz band to accompany it. 'The band adds much to the enjoyment,' said the *Mercury* critic, 'and the film will be long remembered in Leicester.'[28]

The reputation of the sensuous nature of Eric Von Stroheim's 'Foolish Wives' also required it to be seen by the Watch Committee.[29] They raised no objections and the Scala were able to present it on January 1st 1923 - so successfully that it was retained for a second week. There had been criticism in the national press

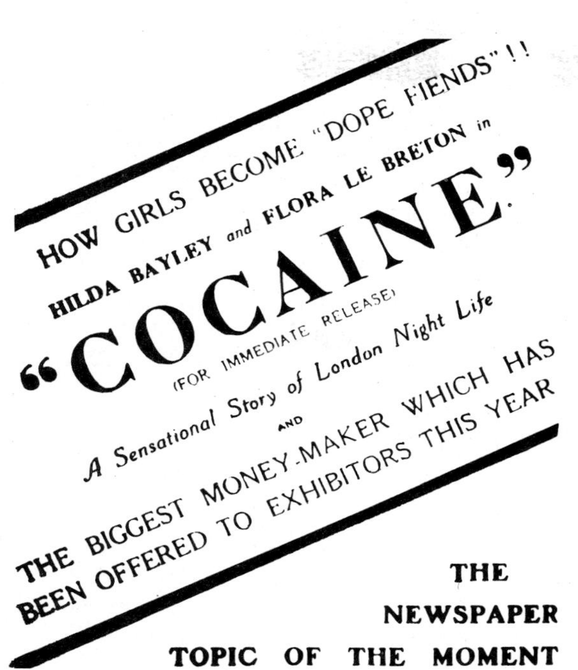

Top: Advertisement for 'Cocaine' in *The Bioscope* May 11th 1922.

Bottom: Trade advertisement for 1922's controversial film.

of the negative nature of the film, and the wisdom of passing it for exhibition; a guarantee for enhanced public interest. In November, Birmingham's Watch Committee had decided against it being shown there. The *Mercury* reviewer found that Stroheim was a 'personality'. 'His trick of wetting his fingers and letting the water drip onto the table cloth, and so deceiving a woman into believing that he was overwhelmed with tears, is extremely realistic.'[30]

The Watch Committee also viewed two somewhat-dated films which the National Council Against Venereal

FLORAL HALL, "THE SUPER CINEMA."
FRIDAY AND SATURDAY, DECEMBER 26th and 27th
ALBERT RAY AND ELINOR FAIR
In a Fox Drama in 5 Acts, entitled,
"WORDS AND MUSIC BY—"
A strong and emotional story, augmented with some fine comedy touches.
LOIS WILSON AND KINGSLEY BENEDICT
In a powerful story of the Jungle,
"MAN AND BEAST"
(FIVE ACTS)
IMPORTANT. LEST YE FORGET!
XMAS HOLIDAYS
Big Attractions and Special Times. XMAS DAY. Open from 3 p.m. till 10 p.m.
BOXING DAY AND SATURDAY, (December 26th and 27th)
Open from 11 a.m. till 10.15 p.m.
ALSO FULL PROGRAMME OF LATEST COMEDIES, TOPICALS, ETC.

PICTUREDROME
MERE ROAD
FRIDAY and SATURDAY.
ELSIE FERGUSON in
UNDER THE GREENWOOD TREE
TAYLOR HOLMES in
RUGGLES OF RED GAP.
'Phone 2580. Matinees: Friday and Saturday

HIGH STREET CINEMA
'Phone 1768 (Imperial Playhouse).
THURSDAY, FRIDAY, SATURDAY,
Dec. 25th, 26th, 27th.
Open at 8 p.m. Xmas Day: 11 a.m. Boxing Day
TWO BIG FEATURE FILMS,
ELSIE FERGUSON,
"HIS PARISIAN WIFE"
In Five reels
and
ALICE BRADY
in
"HER GREAT CHANCE."
Selections by Lombardo and his Band

Leicester Mercury advertisements of 1919 showing Special Programmes for Christmas Day opening.

Disease wished to show. 'Damaged Goods' was based upon a stage play written by the French playwright Eugène Brieux in 1913. The Opera House, Leicester, had staged the play in 1918. A version of it had been made into a film in America in 1915. Samuelson's British version made in 1919 took many liberties with the story and contrived a happy ending. The picture was not passed by the British Board of Film Censors, but the Watch Committee gave permission for it to be shown at various Church Halls when no one under 16 was present.[31]

A 'cinema motor lorry' had been equipped by the National Committee for Combatting Veneral Diseases. It was complete with projector and generator. One showing was at the Junior Training Corps Hall from October 2nd to October 8th, 1922. The second film, 'The End of the Road', was an American film also made in 1919. Originally it was quite sensational in its treatment, but an abridged version was issued later.[32] It had been shown twice before in Leicester, without any apparent interest by the Watch committee.[33]

Once again the cinemas were allowed to be open after 3 o'clock on Good Friday and Christmas Day. There was no Sunday opening except for the occasional approved charity show. On the Election Days of 1923 and 1924 a general extension of the licence was permitted until midnight.[34]

American Films Dominate the Screens

American films still predominated on the local screens, and a number of films that have become classics made their first appearance in the city. Although D.W. Griffith's best known epics, 'Birth of a Nation' and 'Intolerance', were made in 1915 and 1916 they were not given their first showings in Leicester until 1922 and 1921 respectively. The name of Griffith did not really impress

A scene from 'End of the Road'. *Courtesy Kevin Brownlow.*

British audiences until the release of 'Broken Blossoms' in 1920. This was received with great enthusiasm in London and it may well account for the sudden interest in Griffith films during the second half of 1920. In July appeared 'The Greatest Thing in Life' (1919) with Lillian Gish, Elmo Lincoln and Robert Harron; in August and September 'A Romance of Happy Valley' (1919) and 'The Greatest Question' (1920), both with Lillian Gish and Robert Harron. When 'Broken Blossoms' was shown in November at the Cinema-de-Luxe, the *Leicester Pioneer* reported it as 'The most remarkable, and technically the most beautiful film being shown at the present time.'[35] The film was also famous for the playing of Richard Barthelmess who appeared in a November showing of the next Griffith film in Leicester, 'The Idol Dancer'. In December, 1921, the Silver Street Picture House showed Griffith's 'The Love Flower' in the same week that the King's Hall showed 'Intolerance'.

'Way Down East' was shown for two weeks at the Picture House in November 1922. It was announced that 'owing to the enormous cost of this wonderful picture, we have been forced to increase our prices to Stalls 1/6 and Balcony 2/4' [usual prices 1/- and 2/-]. 'Nothing finer has been seen on the screen than the rescue of Anna from the break up of the ice on the river' wrote the *Leicester Mercury* reporter.[36] The two-hour film was shown with a three-minute interval

Dorothy and Lillian Gish in 'Orphans of the Storm'. *Author's collection.*

half-way through. In March 1923 'Orphans of the Storm', starring both Dorothy and Lillian Gish, was shown at the Picture House for two weeks with no increase in prices, although the orchestra was augmented to play a special musical score.

British Productions

British production was picking up after lack of investment during the war. But it always had to struggle against the overwhelming attraction of the expensively-mounted American product. There was a certain sameness about the British offerings brought about, no doubt, by lack of resources. 'The City of Beautiful Nonsense', shown at the Floral Hall in 1920, was typical of the output of the Hepworth Manufacturing Company, inevitably featuring their stock players Chrissie White, Henry Edwards and Stewart Rome. The Samuelson Company relied upon Isobel Elsom, Owen Nares, and Madge Titheradge and featured them in such titles as 'The Edge o' Beyond', 'Gamblers All', 'Sweethearts' and 'Mrs Thompson'. 'Mrs Thompson', which also starred Minna Grey and Bertram Burleigh, was shown on an advertised 'All British' programme with the Master Film 'Darby and Joan' (starring Ivy Close and Derwent Hall Caine) at the Cinema-de-Luxe in November 1920. The Floral Hall was owned by the Stoll Theatres Group who were particularly concerned with the production and exhibition of British films. Each one shown there was accompanied by the words 'A Fine British Production'.

The series film attempted to ensure continuity of attendance without cliff-hanging incompleteness. During 1921 the first series of Stoll's 'The Adventures of Sherlock Holmes' films were shown at the Floral Hall and, a week or two later, at the King's Hall. There were 15 of these two-reel short stories

The advantages of cinema-going in the summer. *The Bioscope* May 18th 1922.

Cards given away at the Floral Hall in October 1923 to promote the British serial 'The Mystery of Dr Fu-Manchu'. *Author's collection.*

starring Eille Norwood and all were directed by the prolific Maurice Elvey. At the same time the Silver Street Cinema was running two American serials: 'The Whirlwind' (Monday to Wednesday) and 'The Vanishing Trail' (Thursday to Saturday) and the Cinema-de-Luxe had 'Son of Tarzan' in weekly instalments. In 1923 the Stoll Company tried again with 'The Mystery of Dr Fu-Manchu', a

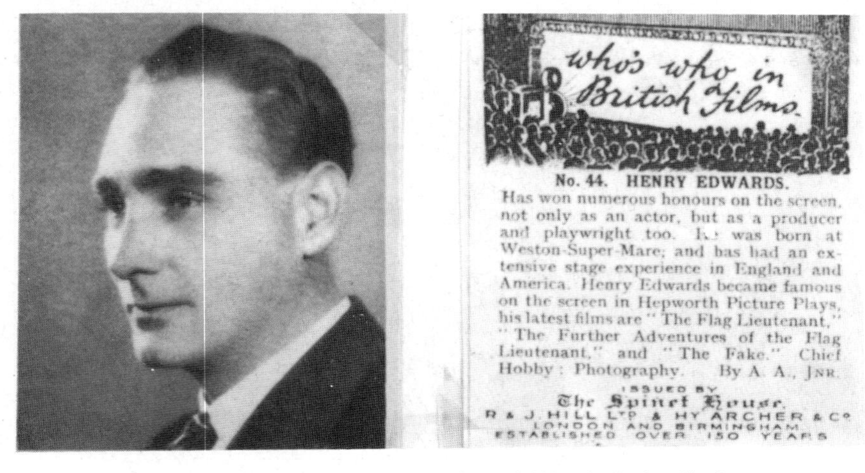

Henry Edwards. From a cigarette card set of 1927. *Author's collection.*

series of 15 two-reelers from the Sax Rohmer stories.[37] The publicity included giving away a picture card of the film to those who attended each week.

In 1922, the *Bioscope* advised exhibitors to give their audiences joy.[38] Comedy features were rare, but the Hepworth 'Alf's Button' starring Leslie Henson (and, inevitably, Alma Taylor and Gerald Ames) was highly successful when it was shown at the Floral Hall on October 20th 1920. Old Charlie Chaplin two-reelers turned up regularly at most of the cinemas often under new names and his new works were always given plenty of prominence.

Another Hepworth film 'Lilly of the Alley' (with Chrissie White and Henry Edwards, of course) was advertised as 'the first no-title film ever produced'. The *Mercury* critic thought that it was a remarkable achievement.[39] It obviously would have pleased the colummnist who wrote the item on the entertainments page of the *Mercury* under the heading 'Have you heard of the Film Story Guide?'. 'This is not an elaborate brochure on 'movie stars', but the man who sits behind you and will keep trying to prophesy the next move in the plot. When tired of this, the same individual imagines that the friend cannot read and forthwith reads every title projected. He is by no means rare.'[40]

Foreign Films

'Foreign' films were shown quite regularly and Leicester audiences were able to enjoy the Italian film 'Things Men Do' with Albert Capozzi and Bianca Belliniconi and Abel Gance's 'J'Accuse' in 1921; the Australian 'The Sentimental Bloke' in 1922; and Jacques Feyder's 'Atlantide' ('the film that made Paris gasp') in 1923.

In 1918, Britain had imposed a ten-year ban on the importing of any German films. This had been dropped in the early 20s, but the Cinematograph Exhibitors' Association did not relent until late in 1922. The first film to be shown in Britain was Fritz Lang's psychological thriller 'Doctor Mabuse'. In all, the film was 17,000 feet long (a showing time of about $3^1/_2$ hours) and it was therefore shown in two parts; part one from Monday to Wednesday, and part two from Thursday to Saturday. The reviewer reported that 'the audience last night were left in a state of mystification'.[41] Small publicity cards had been given away to patrons in the days and weeks before the presentation but the mystification remained.

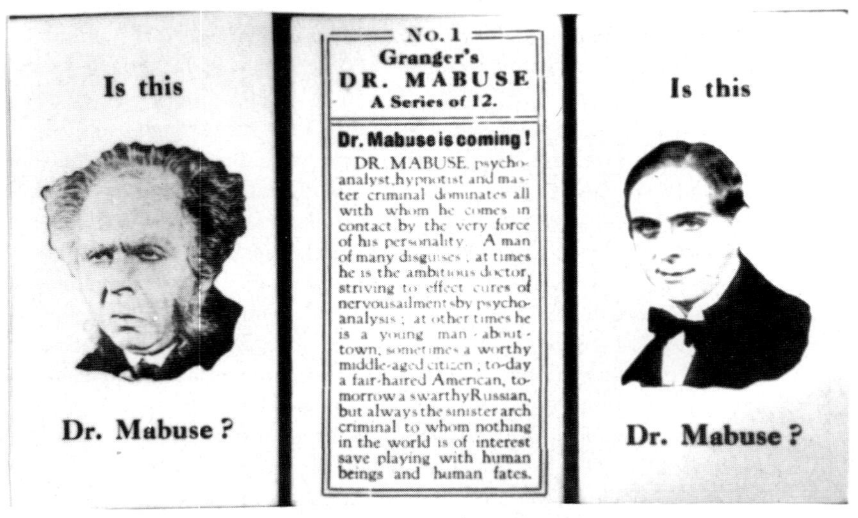

Publicity cards given away at cinemas showing 'Dr Mabuse'. *Author's collection.*

Epics and Stars

The rest of the films were American, and there was little to mystify the public within these. They followed all the tenets of the *Bioscope* article: laughter, adventure, romance and tragedy, but always with a happy ending. The youthful members of the audience were tiring of the helpless bits of innocent femininity that inhabited the film world of D.W. Griffith. Theodosia Goodman helped to bring about the change. With her name suitably changed to Theda Bara, she achieved great success in 'A Fool There Was' in 1914. She made 'Cleopatra' in 1917 but it didn't reach the Cinema-de-Luxe and Leicester until April 1919. The *Leicester Mail* critic reported, with a degree of sarcasm, 'There are over 30,000 people in the show; 80 ships were built in order to be burnt in the battle scenes, and the armies of Rome and Egypt consumed 100,000 lunches - so 'Cleopatra' must be good.'[42]

The star system was well established by this time, and quite often the players' names were printed much larger than the title of the film. Amongst the great stars of this period were Pauline Frederick, Alla Nazimova, George Arliss, Douglas Fairbanks and Richard Barthelmess. Pauline Frederick starred in 'Madame X' billed as 'a great emotional picture' when it was shown at the Floral Hall and the Picture House in April 1921. Nazimova was seen in Ibsen's 'The

Above: Theda Bara as Cleopatra. Shown in Leicester in 1919.
Kinematograph Weekly.
Below: A Will's cigarette card of 1922 showing Margaret Leahy.
Author's collection.

Doll's House' at the Scala in December 1922 and in Oscar Wilde's 'Gorgeously Beautiful and Amazingly Daring "Salome"' at the Cinema-de-Luxe in November 1923.

Douglas Fairbanks had become an established favourite and a partner in the new releasing company, United Artists. In the space of two years he was seen in 'The Habit of Happiness', 'The Mark of Zorro', 'The Half-Breed', 'The Americano' and 'The Three Musketeers'.

Personal appearances by film stars were rare in the provinces but Leicester was graced by the visit of Margaret Leahy in August 1923. She had been met at the Midland Station by the Rev J.T. Coward, chaplain to the Royal Infirmary and had lunch at the Bell Hotel in the company of Mr H.D. Moorhouse, Mr Frank Gray of the Olympia Cinema, Mr Forknall of the Coliseum and Mr Harry Barker of the Shaftesbury. After her visit to the Royal Infirmary she made a tour of the three Moorhouse circuit halls where she had a series of enthusiastic welcomes. At the Shaftesbury, the Leicester Tramways Band greeted her arrival.

London-born Margaret Leahy was the winner from 80,000 hopefuls of the *Daily Sketch* find-

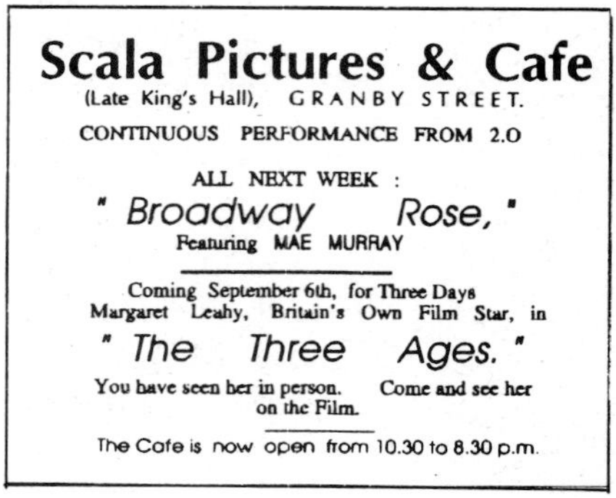

Scala Pictures & Cafe
(Late King's Hall), GRANBY STREET.
CONTINUOUS PERFORMANCE FROM 2.0
ALL NEXT WEEK :
" Broadway Rose, "
Featuring MAE MURRAY
Coming September 6th, for Three Days
Margaret Leahy, Britain's Own Film Star, in
" The Three Ages. "
You have seen her in person. Come and see her on the Film.
The Cafe is now open from 10.30 to 8.30 p.m.

a-film-star competition of 1922. The publicity for the selection and eventual contrywide tour for Margaret Leahy in November 1922 took England by storm. It had originally been intended that she would appear in Norma Talmadge's next film 'Within the Law'. The First National Film Company in Hollywood soon discovered that she had no acting talent and to save face she was cast as the leading lady in Buster Keaton's tripartite comedy 'The Three Ages'. Joseph Schenck, the husband of Norma Talmadge, was chairman of First National, and Natalie Talmadge was married to Buster Keaton. Although picked later in the year as one of Hollywood's most promising newcomers, Margaret Leahy faded from the film scene. When 'The Three Ages' was about to be shown at the Scala in September 1923, the advertisement read 'You have seen her in person. Come and see her on the screen.' [43]

Perhaps the most well-remembered star of the era was Rudolph Valentino. He had appeared in small parts in films since 1918 but he came to world notice in 'The Four Horseman of the Apocalypse'. This film had been given roadshow status on its London release and several more recent films had been shown before its Picture House appearance in April 1923. The advertisement for 'Camille', in which he starred with Nazimova, didn't even mention his name when it was shown at the Scala in October 1922.[44] 'The Sheik', with Agnes Ayres, and 'Blood and Sand' with Nita Naldi were shown at the Picture House in February and April 1923 respectively. In the week before the presentation of 'The Sheik' at the

Alice Terry and Rudolph Valentino in 'The Four Horsemen of the Apocalypse' Of 1921. *Kinematograph Weekly.*

High Street Cinema, Mr Gibbon organised a 'Sheik Ball' at the Queen's Hall. The cinema orchestra provided the dance music.[45]

'The Four Horsemen of the Apocalypse' played for a fortnight at the Picture House from April 30th. All seats were bookable, and there was a price increase once again. There were three performances daily at 2 p.m., 5 p.m. and 8 p.m. A prologue to the film was recited by Mr Harold B. Hill, the manager of the Cinema-de-Luxe, and May Searle sang some vocal sections of the special musical setting. The *Mercury* reviewer remarked on some 'brilliant effects obtained by the augmented orchestra.'[46]

Music and the Cinema

A correspondent to the *Leicester Mercury* on October 14th 1922 had given his own opinion on the sort of 'brilliant effects' the orchestra could produce. 'May I, sir, protest against a hideous practice now in vogue at the local picture houses. At every visit, one's ears are assailed by horrible "appropriate music". When a scene of delicate sentimentality is being shown, the music is of a soft and delicate nature, but as soon as the scene changes character, the conductor taps his baton and a horrible jazz concoction is poured forth. Last evening during a scene depicting a battlefield, the drummer in the orchestra kept up such a din on his big drum that I have suffered a headache ever since.' A likely candidate for his anger that week was Samuelson's first British ten-reeler 'The Game of Life' which included scenes of the Battle of Inkerman. His hate was not shared by another housewife correspondent who said, 'Nothing bothers me, not even the smells or the music.'[47]

The musical accompaniment was clearly valued by the managers as a patron attraction. In considering the prospects for Leicester cinemas in July 1919 the *Bioscope* reviewer stated that the outstanding feature of the majority of them was the music. 'The competition amongst the conductors to secure for their house the reputation of having the best orchestra and playing the highest standard of music is all for the good of the business, and this keenness by the musicians to give of their best should certainly be copied and encouraged in other places.'[48]

W.H. Carter's Orchestra was synonymous with the Picture House. Occasionally, the management would engage a soloist for special musical interludes. Such was the case with the twice-daily performances of violinist Michael Zacharewitsch, engaged for a fortnight in January 1919.

When Mr Frank W. Muston took his leave as leader of the Scala orchestra in March 1922 he was presented with an ebony-mounted walking stick by the staff. He was a third generation member of one of Leicester's most accomplished musical families. After his departure, his successors seemed not to be able to settle. Mr T.G. Kleigh was in charge until Mr Harold Pettes took over in January 1923, and he only lasted until March, when he was replaced by Mr Pares.

E. Gordon Stuart was at the Hippodrome. Mr T.A. Hackett was at the Sovereign with Mrs May Shipton (née Greaves) as pianist. Mr M. Rubenstein was at the Cinema-de-Luxe with Horace Gilbert at the piano. The Melbourne Cinema, sometimes referred to as 'The Five Ways House', had its orchestra conducted by Mr J. Westwood, and the Coliseum orchestra was under the direction of Mr Johnson. The Metropolitan orchestra newly-installed at the High Street Cinema was conducted by Mr M. Offley. In 1922, the Scala employed its 'Celian' orchestra to play at afternoon dances in its large café.

In 1923 the Floral Hall, under the management of Mr W.P. Carter and his assistant, Mr W.S. Travis, completed its post-war improvements with the appointment of a 'Bijoux' orchestra. In March 1919 the cinema had been given a 'face-lift'. The scheme of the decoration was Japanese. Six large bays in the auditorium were painted 'in accordance with true Japanese prints.' Two had scenes from Comedy and Tragedy, and the rest featured bird and fish designs. The artist was Mr Val Prince and the contractor Mr F. Fossett. A carpeted waiting room, described as 'accommodating 300 patrons', was also constructed. So proud of their achievement were the management that they launched the re-opening with a press preview and a banquet at the Grand Hotel attended by the Mayor and Mayoress, the Chairman of the Watch Committee and numerous other council dignitaries. [49]

In the week that Chaplin's 'The Kid' was being shown, alterations to the seating and the balcony were completed at the Olympia. These made it, in the opinion of the *Mercury* reporter, 'one of the best and most comfortable cinemas in the city'.[50]

Harold Hill left the Cinema-de-Luxe in August 1923 to take up an appointment in Birmingham. He was succeeded temporarily by Walter Gay until, in September, Captain Shirley Simpson took up a permanent position. He arrived in Leicester with a reputation for staging impressive promotional activities for his theatre. In October, for the presentation of the film 'The Wandering Jew' (one of the most elaborate British films of the year), he had Mr F.G. Varcoe deliver 'a memorable prologue'.[51]

A New Colour Process

A new colour process was the only technical innovation at this time. Pathécolour was now well established as a colouring process, and both short and

Lady Diana Manners

long films benefitted from its increasing accuracy. Natural colour additive processes such as Kinemacolor in which some form of rotating filter gave intermittent bi-colour or even tri-colour images had proved to be imprecise in registration and uncomfortable to the eyes. Subtractive processes were now developed as a more satisfactory solution. Prizmacolor had been patented by William Van Doren Kelley using orange-red and blue-green separation negatives obtained from a beam-splitting prism.[52] The resulting combined toned image so impressed film producer J. Stuart Blackton that he returned to his native Britain to film 'The Glorious Adventure' using the process. There was heightened local interest in this because the leading role was played by Lady Diana Manners, 'Leicester's Own Film Star'.

Lady Diana, 'a society beauty with no great acting pretentions',[53] was the daughter of the 8th Duke of Rutland and the wife of politician Alfred Duff Cooper. She had appeared as herself, an aristocratic lady doing war-work at an army hospital, in D.W. Griffith's wartime film 'Hearts of the World'. He was so taken with her beauty that he asked her to star in one of his films. Her wedding and, shortly afterwards, a broken leg denied her this opportunity.

FLORAL HALL, PICTURE THEATRE.

ALL NEXT WEEK.

FIRST NATURAL COLOURS DRAMA

J. Stuart Blackton's Epic in Colour—

"THE GLORIOUS ADVENTURE."

FEATURING

LADY DIANA MANNERS and All-Star Cast.

A love romance of the old Cavalier Days. How the fair Lady Beatrice is saved from the hands of the criminal, Bullfinch, by the man she loves, while the Great Fire of London is raging. DON'T MISS IT!

"WELL, I'LL BE —!

Featuring LARRY SEMON.

The King of Mirth as a brave little Sheriff, who gets one of the biggest surprises of his life.
SPECIAL NOTICE.—The Floral Hall will be OPEN ON XMAS DAY from 3 till 10 p.m.
BOXING DAY and WEDNESDAY from 11 a.m. till 10.15 p.m.

Leicester Daily Mercury December 23rd 1922.

Her presence in 'The Glorious

Adventure' and the later Prizma-color costume drama 'The Virgin Queen' had a publicity value well-exploited by the advertising. The film was shown in the last week of December 1922 at the Floral Hall and the Cinema-de-Luxe. 'The colour is realistic and beautiful', said the *Leicester Mercury*. 'There are elaborate settings and gloriously photographed British landscapes.' 'This is a film that will delight everybody - even the anti-cinema critic', declared the advertisement.[54] The *Bioscope* critic was more discerning in his praise when the film was trade-shown in January. 'Though perfection is not yet claimed for the process, its latest stage of development as seen in this production does undoubtedly mark a great technical advance. The reproduction in not always accurate and there is an undue predominance of red in many of the pictures, but against these faults must be set scene after scene of luxurious riches, and dazzling colours.'[55]

During 1923 a weekly series of Prizma-color films were shown both at the Scala and the Floral Hall. Though they were mostly travelogues reference is made to a comedy film 'The Deadly Dagga'. 'Flames of Passion' - a British film made by Herbert Wilcox and Graham Cutts but with an American star, Mae Marsh - had a final sequence in Prizma-colour and a number of specially designed dresses that impressed the writer of the *Mercury's* Women's Corner.[56] This process was not entirely successful, though it did form the basis for the later Cine-color.[57]

The cinema was now firmly established in everyone's consciousness. Most magazines for women had a 'cinema chat' column and featured fashions inspired by the films. Film Star cigarette card sets were very popular with smokers, collectors and tobacco companies alike. There were two rival British film fan magazines for adults, *The Picturegoer* and *Picture Show*. The youngsters had their own magazines: *Girls' Cinema*, *Boys' Cinema* and the comic *Film Fun*. But, most of the publicity and interest was in the lives and the films of the American stars. The British film industry was once again in trouble.

Cigarette cards of Stewart Rome and Theda Bara.
Author's collection.

'Bah! This comes of having a cinema in the district.'
A cartoon by Will Dyson in *The Bioscope* August 26th 1920.

Chapter Six

The cinema in crisis 1924-28

The poor condition of the British film industry was aggravated by the practice of 'block booking'. This meant that a series of programmes was booked at one time; the major film with the minor one; the good with the bad. Bookings and programmes were 'pencilled-in' for months ahead and, because of this, British producers, who could rarely offer packages, often had to wait for as long as two years before their films were given a general release. In 1923, they joined together to create a National Film League. The Prince of Wales spoke at its inaugural luncheon and he asked picturegoers to support British films.

A result of the campaign was the presentation of British Film Weeks. One such was held in February 1924 by the Picture House and the Scala. The offering at the Picture House was 'The School for Scandal' with Queenie Thomas and at the Scala 'The Woman Who Obeyed' with Hilda Bayley and Stewart Rome.[1] Both had been shown to the trade six months previously and were getting their first showings in Leicester. Not all the films shown were of such recent origin, and it became clear for many patrons that the thing to do was to stay away during British Film Weeks. By the end of 1924 all the British studios were temporarily closed.

Entertainment Tax Reduced

A small concession was wrested from the Government in the form of a reduction in the Entertainment Tax. This tax had been created during the war years, and at the end of the war there had been a small reduction in its application. Seats priced under 2d carried no tax, 2d seats carried one-half penny tax, 4d seats carried 1d tax, and seats up to 7d had a tax of 2d added. Considerable activity by the exhibitors to have it removed was only partially successful when, in June 1924, the Labour Government abolished the tax from seats priced up to 6d and reduced it on seats up to 1/3d on the understanding that the reduction would be passed on to the public. This was generally the case, and the *Bioscope* on June 24th reported that in most towns 1/6d seats were reduced to 1/5d, 1/- seats to 10d and 8d seats to 6d.

American Films Draw Crowds

Big American films were drawing the crowds and the accolades. Indeed, American films accounted for 38 per cent of the films shown, and a much larger percentage of the takings.[2] Douglas Fairbanks' 2½ hour spectacular adventure 'Robin Hood' was given its first performance at the Cinema-de-Luxe in front of the Mayor and Mayoress and Sir John and Lady North.[3] A year later 'The Thief of Bagdad' drew the crowds and the Cinema-de-Luxe, at a cost of £50, installed the latest Reflecta screen in time for its presentation. In the same week at the Scala, De Mille's 'The Ten Commandments' was retained for a second week with a specially augmented orchestra and chorus.[4] When the same film was shown at the Hippodrome in October the *Bioscope* reporter praised the quality of the music and effects produced by the resident orchestra led by Cecil Bevan.

Documentaries

The British films that commanded the most enthusiastic audiences were documentaries. Before the 1914-18 war a young man named Harry Bruce Woolfe had been amusing himself in a small hut near Elstree making his 'Secrets of Nature' films. After the war he had the idea of making permanent pictorial records of some of the great battles. With official war footage, newsreels and animated maps, models and diagrams he made the first one, the three-reel 'Battle of Jutland'. Its success as a supporting film led him to tackle a feature length project, 'Armageddon'. This was the story of Allenby's campaign in Syria. No renter would look at it. Undaunted, Bruce Woolfe set about creating his own renting company and he finally managed to get a booking for his film at the Tivoli, in London. Not for the first time, the renters had been wrong. It was an instantaneous success.[5] It was shown in Leicester in February 1924 for two weeks in special matinees at the Palace and when it was shown at the Floral Hall a week later Sergeant Hurcomb 'to whom Jerusalem was surrendered' appeared at each performance.[6] 'Zeebrugge', 'The only film their Majesties went to see in the theatre', was shown at the Cinema-de-Luxe in February 1925,[7] and 'Ypres' was shown at the Picture House in November.[8] 'Mons' was shown at the City Cinema in Armistice week 1926 with a special musical setting, and in the same week the Scala did good business with a revival of 'The Four Horsemen of the Apocalypse'.[9] The culmination of all Bruce Woolfe's work was his 'The Battle of the Coronel and Falkland Islands' shown at the Picture House in Armistice Week 1927. 'As near a reproduction of naval warfare as it could be' said the reviewer.[10]

SCALA.

ALL THIS WEEK.

THE FOUR HORSEMEN OF THE APOCALYPSE

WITH THE LATE

RUDOLPH VALENTINO

THE GREATEST PICTURE EVER MADE.

Approximate Times of Showing:—
1.15, 3.45, 6.0, and 8.20 PROMPT, DAILY.

Prologue by MR. CHARLES HILL
Vocalist: MISS FRANCES KENDALL

Augmented Orchestra under the direction of J. MUSCANT.

Advertisement for Armistice Week 1926.

These early documentary war films had their more peaceful counterparts in travelogues and wild life pictures, often accompanied by the explorers. 'Crossing the Sahara' was shown at the Picture House in October 1924 with a personal appearance by Captain Buchanan and the only two surviving natives.[11] 'The Epic of Everest', the tragic journey of Irvine and Mallory, was shown at the Scala in July 1925 and 'Moana', Robert Flaherty's documentary of life in the South Seas, was a second feature at the Picture House in November 1926.[12]

A wildlife film called 'Chang, Wonderful Chang' was advertised for several weeks prior to its presentation at the Scala in December 1927. It proved to be so popular that it was retained for a second week and the management successfully applied to the Watch Committee for a special extra children's matinee on December 10th. It was especially praised for its close-ups of all types of animals and for the full orchestral and sound effects that were used 'as at the Plaza London'.[13]

Why the Cinema is Popular

Cinema-going was certainly a popular pastime though not necessarily for the reasons given by actor Dennis Eadie, who was appearing at the Royal Opera House in 'Eternal Spring' in the first week in November. In a feature article entitled 'Why the Screen Appeals More Than the Stage'[14]

One of six souvenir cards for 'Crossing the Sahara' when it was shown at the Palace Theatre, London.
Courtesy M. Auborn Collection

Mr Eadie is reported to have said that people go to the cinema because they can go in at anytime, leave at any time and not use their brains in the interval. It is an indication of the mentality of the time, he went on, that they can go in half-way through a story, see it to the end, and pick up the beginning when it comes round to that again.

At the end of the same week, a correspondent who signed himself 'Semper Eadem, Alas' took issue with the theatrical Mr Eadie, whom it was revealed was making his first tour away from London in 20 years. 'The reason that Leicester audiences prefer cinema to the stage,' he wrote, 'is a pure matter of price and accommodation. Cheapness and comfort in the cinema versus exorbitant prices of admission and monumental discomfort in the theatre. For the comparatively small sum of one shilling and sixpence, one can obtain in the cinema a roomy seat with an upholstered fauteuil. For a similar seat at a legitimate theatre, one would have to pay at least four shillings and ninepence.'[15]

The audiences were accommodating enough to make allowances for a complete failure of the electricity in the centre of the city on the afternoon of January 31st 1924. The stoppage lasted half-an-hour during which managers arranged for musical selections to be played.[16]

A Mystery Presentation

In March 1925 armchair travel was central to an enterprising presentation. 'All interested in the unusual on the screen,' wrote the *Mail* reviewer, 'should certainly make a point of visiting the Scala this week, when Ali Ben Aza and his slave present their famous mystery film. Ali-Ben Aza (in person) requests the audience to name any spot in the country where they would like the slave to visit, and, Hey Presto, the trick is done. On the screen, the slave is seen walking through the streets of the place named. Among some of the localities visited besides many streets in Leicester, were the Forth Bridge, the Thames Embankment, Birmingham, and Coventry.'[17] No details of the technical presentation were given, of course. It is possible that the presentation was a combination of a still slide of the location and a superimposed moving image of the 'slave'.

The City Cinema

During this period a number of new cinemas were built, several were extensively re-modelled and two closed their doors. Plans for a cinema in the Market Place had been approved in 1914 but not proceeded with. The *Bioscope Weekly* reported in March 1924 that excellent progress was being made on the site of the City Cinema.[18]

Artist's impression of the City Cinema.
From a report of the opening in *Kinematograph Weekly*.

CITY CINEMA

MARKET PLACE, LEICESTER.

TO-DAY

and All the Week.

J. WARREN KERRIGAN, and LOIS WILSON

in

THE COVERED WAGON

THE GREATEST SCREEN ENTERTAINMENT EVER SEEN

Full Orchestra under the direction of Mr. W. H. CARTER.

Prices of Admission: Stalls 8d. & 1/- Balcony, 1/6 & 2/-

Children Half Price up to 4 o'clock.

The *Illustrated Chronicle* announced that the City Cinema, named to commemorate the new City status conferred on Leicester in 1919, would open on Monday November 3rd with the great film 'The Covered Wagon' and that there would be a full orchestra under the direction of W.H. Carter, formerly of the Picture House.[19] Mr Reginald Lowndes Salmon was recruited as manager. He had been manager of the Picture House, apart from a short break, for the previous eleven years. A new company, the City Cinema Ltd, had been set up to finance the project and the directors were Edmund D. Tyler (chairman), Charles W. Lovesy (managing director), W.H.B. Emson (the owner of the Belgrave Cinema) H.G. Westgate, and S.H. Burdwood; the capital had been subscribed locally. Burdwood and Mitchell, London architects, had good experience in designing cinemas. Rushworth and Dreaper of Liverpool supplied an 'Apollo' organ. The Jury-Metro-Goldwyn projectors were supplied with lenses by Taylor, Taylor and Hobson Ltd of Leicester and the screen was by Walturdaw of London. The chief projectionist was Mr C.L. Collins.

A seating capacity of 2,300 made it the biggest in the city. 'The approach is through the main hall for all

The City cinema in 1991.
Author's photograph.

parts of the house. Spacious waiting rooms within easy reach of both balcony and ground floor accommodate patrons waiting for seats, and two pay boxes with the most modern ticket issuing machine ensure entrance without delay.

'The auditorium has a beautiful scheme of decoration in cream, gold and mauve, the delicate flood lighting from recesses concealed in the walls, the magnificent carpets and furnishings (by Woodfield Bros of Leicester) toning so well with the general scheme, the gorgeous curtains and the great dome.

'The electrical equipment is up-to-date and of the best type. The Neon light sign (the only one in Leicester) on the front of the building catches every eye. The curtains in front of the screen are moved by electric gear, and a stage float is fixed in front to give colour and atmosphere to the screen when required.

'There are seven exits, and, notwithstanding its large seating capacity, the theatre can be cleared in an orderly way in a few moments. A very fine engineering feat has been carried out in the construction of the balcony, which although it has a very wide span, has been built in such a manner that there are no pillars to obstruct the view of those underneath.'[20]

The *Illustrated Chronicle* was very praising of the tasteful decoration, the ventilation and lighting, and the leg-room in between the rows. 'The new cinema will fill a real need in the city, a need so acute, that the other houses will not suffer for they are invariably full to overflowing of an evening.'[21]

Additional information from the *Leicester Mercury* reveals that there were tip-up seats in every part of the cinema upholstered in old gold, and that 'the colour scheme was completed by luxurious carpets of a similar hue studded wiith black. All the lamps were inlaid with Oxford blue.'[22]

The rebuilt Picture House opens

On August 2nd 1925 the Picture House re-opened to a week of packed houses with Buster Keaton's 'The Navigator'. The new manager was Mr John

The Picture House in the week before its rebuilding, May 1924.
The film showing is 'The Cheat' starring Pola Negri. *Courtesy Leicestershire Museums.*

The Picture House, Granby Street. Proposed Town Hall Square elevation. Plans submitted August 28th 1915. *Courtesy Leicestershire Records Office.*

Hamilton Lundy. He had previously been the manager of the Provincial Cinema Theatres House in Northampton and his father was also a P.C.T. manager. His tenure only lasted until November, however, when the licence was transferred to George Henry Luxton.[23] This cinema, too, according to the *Chronicle* article 'satisfies a long-felt want. The present cinema accommodation is woefully lacking in a city the size of Leicester'.[24]

The cinema had been closed since May 5th 1924 for a complete internal rebuild. Plans for this, drawn up by architects Harold Rigg of Regent Street, London, had been approved by the Watch Committee during the war in 1915 but had not been proceeded with because of wartime shortages and restrictions.[25] Unspecified alterations to these plans were approved in September 1923 and on two occasions in January 1925.[26] Seating capacity was increased from 600 to 2,000. The plenum ventilation system, a much-praised feature of the first design,

The Picture House, Granby Street. Proposed Granby Street elevation. Plans submitted August 28th 1915. *Courtesy Leicestershire Records Office.*

was retained, and slightly increased in efficiency. 'No matter where you sit in this enormously long theatre, you get an unobstructed view of the large screen. It is decorated artistically with concealed lighting behind huge silk shades. Around the proscenium arch is a fine canvas painting of a dramatic motif. One is struck by the bold conception of the entrance porch. Film photographs are displayed outside in artistically ornamented panels. The Café is situated so that one does not have to use the mainsteps from the foyer, but one can be transported to it by electric lifts in the vestibule.' [27] Oak-panelling and stucco decorated the café and restaurant. The Savanna Orchestra played there, under the stained glass dome, during lunch, tea and dinner.[28]

The *Kinematograph Weekly* added the information that the contractors for the reconstruction were McLaughlin and Harvey of London, that the projectors were two Kalee No. 6 types, and that the projection throw was 128 feet. The cinema

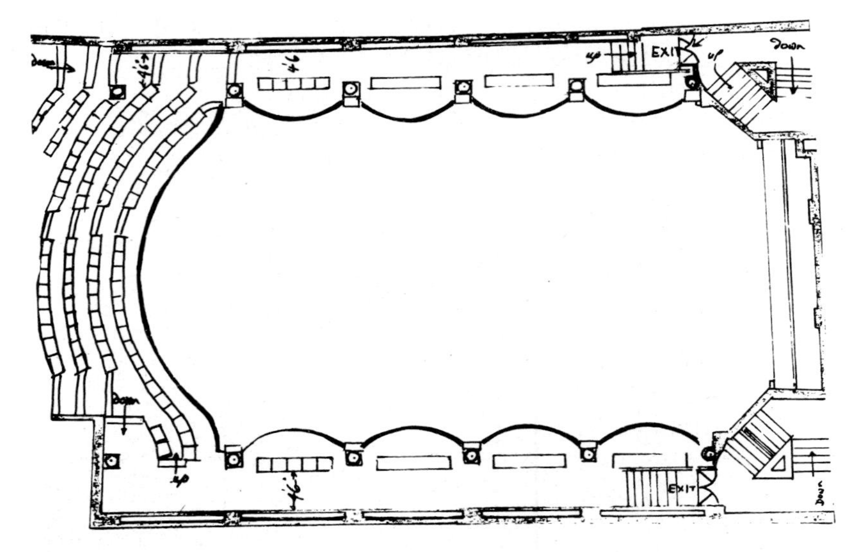

Above: The Picture House, Granby Street. Plan of gallery. Plans by Harold Rigg of Regent Street, London, submitted August 28th 1915. *Courtesy Leicestershire Records Office.*

Right: The Picture House Town Hall Square frontage in 1991. All that remains of 'Leicester's premier cinema'. *Author's photograph.*

had, in fact, been completely turned round so that the projectors were now at the Town Hall Square end of the auditorium.

Mr Alexander Roloff, late of Covent Garden, directed the orchestra. In January 1926 a £6,000 Wurlitzer organ was installed and officially opened by Mr Jack Courtnay, organist at the New Gallery Cinema, London. 'The synchopated music on the organ is rather charming' wrote the Evening Mail. 'It might be held that Mr Courtnay was rather daring in playing 'Faust' in such a manner.'[29] Music was still an important feature at the Picture House and every Friday night there was an extended musical interval for both vocal and instrumental items. During 1925 and 1926 it had advertised itself as 'Leicester's Artistic Centre of Pictures and Music.'[30]

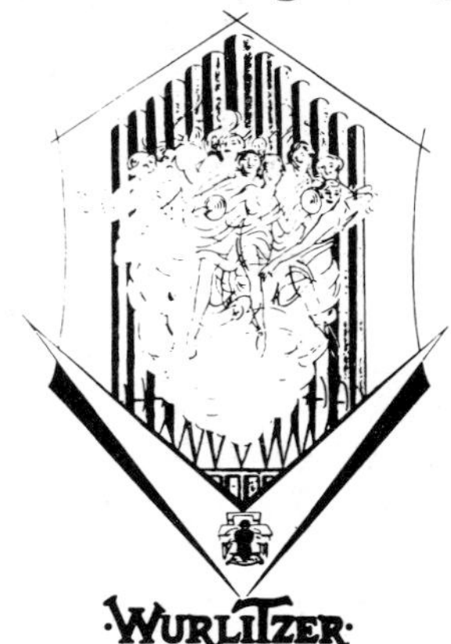

Above and below: Trade advertisements for the famous Wurlitzer organs. *The Bioscope* 1928.

The resident organist, until July 1926 when he left to take up a prestigious position at the West End Cinema, Birmingham, was Charles Willis. In 1926, the *Kinematograph Weekly* claimed that he was one of the the three leading Wurlitzer exponents in the country.[31] The others were listed as Reginald Foort of the New Gallery and Frank Matthew of the Picture House, Sunderland. In a later edition they added the name of Jack Courtnay then at the Plaza, Piccadilly. Born into a musical family, Charles Willis had begun his musical career at the age of 14 as organist in a Kent church. In addition to being an accomplished musician he was described as a 'specialist in trick playing'. Amongst his best imitations were 'crowds cheering, dogs barking, pigs grunting, hens cackling, aeroplanes droning, babies crying and lovers kissing' all of which he produced with the aid of his wonderful Wurlitzer. He was succeeded by Arthur Jenkins.

Charles Willis, cinema organist at the Picture House in 1926. *Kinematograph Weekly.*

Other Cinema Improvements

The Melbourne closed for a few weeks in July 1924 for alterations and re-decoration during which time the manager, Mr Henry Watmough Hurst, took a well-earned holiday. Its August re-opening brought with it 'Melbourne's Melodious Moments', musical interludes with solos by Edith Macalister. A large audience at the re-opening thoroughly appreciated the removal of pillars which had restricted their view of the screen.[32]

The High Street Cinema was closed in 1925 for one month for re-decoration and re-seating. It re-opened on August 3rd, the same day as the rebuilt Picture House. In February 1926 the circle of the Olympia Cinema, still under the management of Mr F.D. Gray, was reconstructed and refurbished with wide tip-up seats. For the re-opening, the orchestra was augmented to five. Further re-decorating took place a year later and a new verandah and outside lighting were added to bring more comfort to those waiting for admittance.[33] The Silver Street Cinema reverted to its previous title of 'The Grand' at the end of 1926 and it was completely re-seated and fitted with a new pay-box and swing doors at the same time.[34]

The improvements at the Coliseum in November 1927 so impressed the *Bioscope* correspondent that he devoted almost the whole of his report to them. 'The interior now presents a warm and cosy appearance, the auditorium being festooned with coloured electric globes. A feature that I have not observed elsewhere is a glass draught screen instead of curtains, which skirts the promenade and effectively excludes draughts from the main entrance. The hall now has comfortable accommodation for 1,560 patrons.'[35]

Managerial Changes

Management of a cinema seemed to be a very precarious appointment. When brothers E. and W. Wallis, owners of seven cinemas in the Coventry area, bought the Silver Street Cinema in March 1924 they provided their own manager, George E. Pankhurst, and their own musical director, Mr Cyril Emms. The previous manager, Mr Fred Trueman Towers jnr, found a position in Rugby. He had been the manager for Midland Electric Theatres Ltd since 1920. The local C.E.A. gave him a parting gift of £10/10/- in recognition of the work he had done for the branch.[36] He returned to Leicestershire in July 1926, managing the re-opening of the Loughborough Playhouse, a cinema controlled by Record Cinemas Ltd.[37]

Harry Goodman had taken over the lease of the Scala in October 1923 and put in his wife, Gladys, as manager. She had a flair for innovative publicity. At a showing of the British Film Week offering 'Bonnie Prince Charlie' she engaged two vocalists dressed as Flora McDonald and Charles Stuart and 'the orchestra's fine interpretation of the bagpipes pleased the audience immensely.' She also added an up-to-date café with special iced drinks from a soda fountain and Cecil Watson's 'Celian' orchestra was in attendance during the day. The cinema orchestra was under the direction of the talented violinist, Mr Anton Tschaikov. He had lately been at the New Scala, Leeds.[38] In January 1925 Redvers R. Smith was appointed manager of the

Mr Fred Trueman Towers jnr pictured with an 'Indian' at the Picture Playhouse, Loughborough, in October 1926. From *The Bioscope.*

Scala, but in July he departed for a post at the Kingsway Cinema, Kingsheath, Birmingham, leaving Mrs Goodman in sole charge again. Another enterprising lady, Barbara Ebbage, is shown to be manageress of the Tudor during 1925.[39]

The displacement of Mr George Taylor as manager at the Scala was something of an embarrassment to the local Branch of the C.E.A., since he was its treasurer. Mr J.B. Wacks was nominated for the now vacant post. A year later, he too, resigned because he was leaving the district to take up the lease of the Wooley Bridge Palace, Glossop.

Mr Hurst resigned his position at the Melbourne and, once again, took up the reins at

Mr Harry Goodman of the Scala.
The Bioscope 1926.

NEXT WEEK:

Monday, Tuesday and Wednesday.	Thursday, Friday and Saturday.
A Wide Open Town	Nibelungs
The Arizona Romeo	Leave it to Jerry
12 Days in Paris (Interest)	Only a Bill Collector (Eddie Lyons Comedy)
Faint Heart (Comedy)	The Lumber Jack
Æsop's	Topical
Topical	Æsop's
Pictorial	Eve's Review

COMING ATTRACTIONS.

IN HIGH GEAR	BEAUTY CONTEST
FOLLY OF VANITY	PAMPERED YOUTH
INNOCENCE	EMPTY SADDLE

Courtesy Mr Leader.

the Hippodrome in November of 1924, replacing the temporary manager Joseph Braham Watts. But his tenure seems only to have lasted until September 30th 1925, when he was replaced by Captain Ernest Ball. He re-introduced variety acts into the cinema, having 'painted some effective backcloth scenes'.[40]

In November 1924, also, Mr E. Nicholls became manager of the Melbourne, but in July 1925 he left and Mr Matthew A. Roberts became temporary manager. Mr Harry James Dacre became the permanent manager in November 1925. He had a long and distinguished career in management with previous posts at the Harehills Picture House and the City Cinema, Boar Lane, Leeds, and most recently at the Coney Street Picture House, York. In 1919 he had also worked as an advertising agent for the distribution company Grainger's Exclusives, in a successful campaign for the film series 'Marvels of the Universe'. His efforts over the next four years turned the cinema into a paying proposition again. His daughter, Margaret, an accomplished singer, also assisted with musical interludes which sometimes lasted as long as twenty minutes.[41]

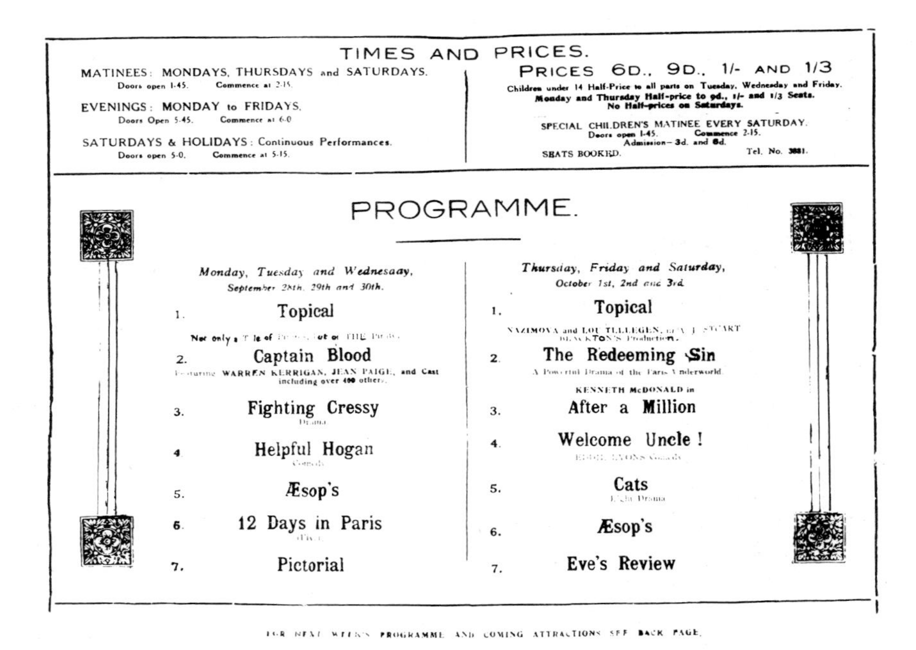

TIMES AND PRICES.

MATINEES: MONDAYS, THURSDAYS and SATURDAYS.
Doors open 1-45. Commence at 2-15.

EVENINGS: MONDAY to FRIDAYS.
Doors Open 5-45. Commence at 6-0

SATURDAYS & HOLIDAYS: Continuous Performances.
Doors open 5-0. Commence at 5-15.

PRICES 6D., 9D., 1/- AND 1/3
Children under 14 Half-Price to all parts on Tuesday, Wednesday and Friday.
Monday and Thursday Half-price to 9d., 1/- and 1/3 Seats.
No Half-prices on Saturdays.

SPECIAL CHILDREN'S MATINEE EVERY SATURDAY.
Doors open 1-45. Commence 2-15.
Admission–3d. and 6d.
SEATS BOOKED. Tel. No. 3881.

PROGRAMME.

Monday, Tuesday and Wednesday,
September 28th, 29th and 30th.

1. Topical
2. Captain Blood
Featuring WARREN KERRIGAN, JEAN PAIGE, and Cast including over 400 others.
3. Fighting Cressy
Drama
4. Helpful Hogan
Comedy
5. Æsop's
6. 12 Days in Paris
7. Pictorial

Thursday, Friday and Saturday,
October 1st, 2nd and 3rd.

1. Topical
NAZIMOVA and LOU TELLEGEN, [illegible]
[illegible] Production.
2. The Redeeming Sin
A Powerful Drama of the Paris Underworld.
KENNETH McDONALD in
3. After a Million
4. Welcome Uncle!
5. Cats
6. Æsop's
7. Eve's Review

FOR NEXT WEEK'S PROGRAMME AND COMING ATTRACTIONS SEE BACK PAGE.

Courtesy Mr Leader.

In October 1924 the three Moorhouse circuit houses experimented with three changes of programme a week: Monday, Wednesday and Friday. They were successful in attracting very good houses for the new arrangement and it stayed in place until early 1925.

The death of Fred Trueman Towers, Snr

Fred Trueman Towers, Snr, had been manager of the Palace Theatre and, by the same token, overseer of the Floral Hall for eleven years. His health had been suspect for some years and various absences and convalescent leaves had been noted both in the minutes of the C.E.A. Branch meetings, at which he had been President, and in the columns of the *Bioscope* and the *Kinematograph Weekly*. After a further three weeks of illness he died in the Leicester Royal Infirmary on November 22nd 1925.

He was 63 and his career had encompassed the general managership of the late George Edwards Theatre Company and Daly's Theatres. For two years he had been manager at the Leicester Opera House for Messrs Bode and Compton before returning to management with George Edwards.

He was a widower with two daughters, Laura and Phyllis, and a son, Fred, who had been, until recently, manager of the Silver Street Cinema. Tragically, he was to have been married that next Saturday to Mrs Martha Louise Hill.[42]

Charity Performances

The Leicester Royal Infirmary was often the recipient of the proceeds of special matinees or Sunday performances. Charitable endeavours of the C.E.A. were edged with the desire to demonstrate to the local licensing authorities that opening cinemas on Sunday was beneficial to the community. The gift from the City Cinema in the week before Mr Trueman Towers' death was of a different order, however. They were celebrating their first anniversary with a charity matinee showing of Jackie Coogan in 'The Rag Man'. A march, 'Anniversary', specially composed by orchestra member Paul Britcher, was received 'with great enthusiasm'.[43]

The Leicester Kinema Carnival at the de Montfort Hall was another charitable enterprise of the local C.E.A. branch. The 1925 event was graced by the personal appearance of two popular British Film stars - Brian Aherne and Queenie Thomas. A profit of £55/12/8d from the Carnival was shared between the Cinematograph Trade Benevolent Fund and the 'Never-seen-the-sea' fund.[44] In 1926 two very minor Stoll Picture 'stars', Joseph Grossman and Sybil Rhoda, were present along with two artists from the current productions at the Opera House and the Palace. The 1927 Carnival was unable to raise a single name of note. A.S. Whittaker, the Chairman for the 1928 Carnival, altered the situation by visiting several British studios in early October and signing up Estelle Brody and Monty Banks as guests. On the night, neither was able to be present, but at very short notice, Carl Brisson and his sister were able to put in an appearance and save the event.

The new manager at the Palace was Mr W.H. Boardman. For the previous 14 years he had been manager of the Brighton Hippodrome, but his stay in Leicester was brief. In April he vacated his position, it was said, 'to go abroad'. His replacement was Mr J.W. Hort who had been assistant manager at the Bristol Hippodrome for some years.[45]

The Westleigh Cinema

The Westleigh Cinema opened its doors for the first time on February 15th 1926. Designs for a theatre with 1,334 seats by W.H. and H.G. Riley had been approved by the Watch Committee on February 27th 1925 and construction of what was then to be called the Regent Picture House began in April.[46] The *Kinematograph Weekly* of February 18th 1926 gave a comprehensive list of the firms that were involved, though it gave the capacity as only 850. The

The Westleigh cinema in the 1950s. *Courtesy Carl Jennings Collection.*

The Westleigh opening announcement.
Leicester Mercury February 13th 1926.

construction was in the hands of W.M. Sharp and Sons of Leicester while F.J. Yates of Leicester had the responsibility for the electrical installations. Turners of Birmingham supplied the seating and Rogers of Leicester the furnishings. Furse of Nottingham supplied the electrically controlled curtains and two Kalee projectors were installed in the operating box.

'The appearance of the building inside suggests roominess and there are no pillars to obstruct the view. The colour scheme is delightful (tangerine and light blue) with large diffused lights hanging from the domed ceiling. The frontage is of a square design, and its Yorkshire stone presents a tasteful appearance. Inside there is a large hall from where two fine staircases, one on each side, lead to the balcony.

'The Kinema, which is owned by the Westleigh Picture House Company, has many interesting points. The main lighting is generated by a Crossley 28 H.P. engine, but gas has also been installed, all the jets being controlled from the operating box, ensuring the supply of light in the event of a failure of the principal supply. It is claimed by the management that generating electricity on the premises is cheaper than taking the corporation supply.' During the time of its building, the *Bioscope* had revealed that the proprietors were connected with those of the Evington.[47]

The opening feature film was 'Little Dorrit', a British film that was already five years old. Also in the inaugural programme was a series of stereoscopic films called 'Plastigrams'. These had been trade-shown in May 1924 and had first appeared in Leicester at the Picture House in October 1925. The publicity poster declared erroneously that 'The actors leave the screen and march straight among the audience causing boundless surprise and no end of amusement'.[48] Red and green glasses did enable the audience to experience some semblance of stereoscopic vision, with objects shooting straight out of the screen, but the *Bioscope* reviewer was not very impressed.

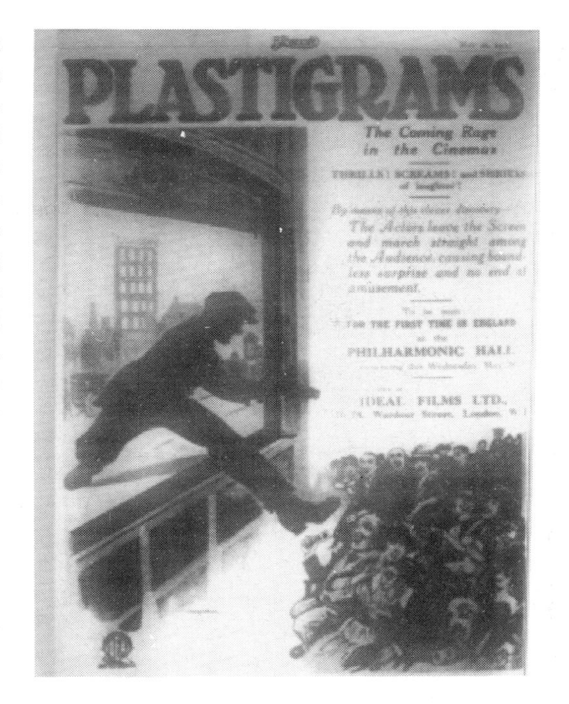

'Plastigrams', a stereoscopic film in the opening programme at the Westleigh.

The manager was Mr Arthur A. Griffin and the orchestra was under the direction of Harold E. Gilbert (Horace Gilbert's brother). His violin solos are well remembered by local patrons. 'Mr Gilbert would walk up and down the aisle at the children's matinees playing for the community singing that preceded the show. The matinees of other cinemas were considered to be a bit rough, but it was a case of music soothing the savage breast at the Westleigh'.[49] There was one house nightly beginning at 6.30 p.m. with matinees and programme changes on Monday and Thursday. A singing and music licence had been granted from noon until 11 p.m. This was the first such extension in the city and most of the other cinemas were quick to apply for a similar licence.

Cinemas and the General Strike

The Crossley engine at the Westleigh would certainly have been useful two months later when the General Strike was called by the T.U.C. in support of the miners. One of the first acts of the Government on May 6th was to order a 50 per

An animated comment on the General Strike.
The Bioscope May 27th 1926.

cent reduction in electricity usage.

Mr W.N. Blake, the National President of the C.E.A. was in Leicester that day to address an evening meeting of the Leicester Branch. Instead, he immediately motored to London to persuade the Electricity Commissioners to countermand the order. A 50 per cent reduction in lighting and power would have meant that cinemas could not maintain two houses daily. They would, thus, be forced to operate at a loss or close. On learning that the order had been given by the Minister of Mines, Mr Blake switched his attention to him, or at least to one of his secretaries. By 3.15 p.m. he had got his answer. Within half-an-hour, he had telegraphed all the Branch Secretaries that the Minister was more desirous to see the citizens of the country entertained in cinemas than to see them on the streets. The restriction was lifted on the understanding that cinema houses should cut down lighting to an absolute minimum.[50]

To circumvent carriage problems, the Film Transport Service had been established at about the time of the 1919 rail strike. When being transported, the highly inflammable cinema films were required to be sealed in heavy metal containers. They could not be sent by normal postal delivery nor carried on public transport, except in separate baggage vans. In the *Kinematograph Year Books*, all cinemas are listed with their nearest railway station from which each cinema collected its films.

During the General Strike 'dumps' were centred on the offices of regional film distribution companies. These were used as clearing houses for the films already in the area. The local exhibitors needed to arrange their own transport to deliver and pick up their films.[51]

Leicester's 'dump' was at Birmingham and even rival cinemas assisted each other in transporting films to and fro. In their first two return trips to the 'dumps' the Film Transport Service moved 6,600 reels of films.[52]

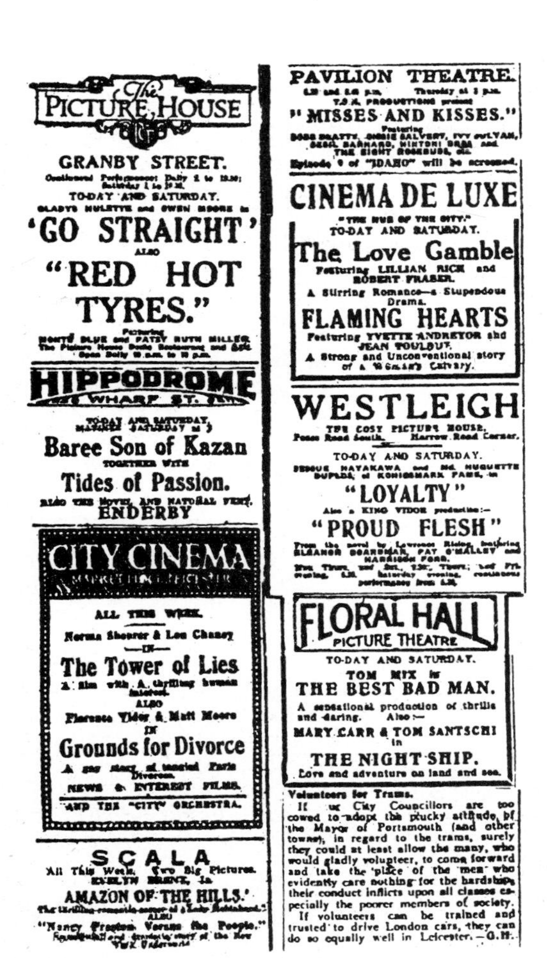

Volunteers for Trams.

If our City Councillors are too cowed to adopt the plucky attitude of the Mayor of Portsmouth (and other towns), in regard to the trams, surely they could at least allow the many, who would gladly volunteer, to come forward and take the place of the men who evidently care nothing for the hardships their conduct inflicts upon all classes especially the poorer members of society.

If volunteers can be trained and trusted to drive London cars, they can do so equally well in Leicester.—G.H.

Cinema advertising during the General Strike.
Leicester Mercury May 7th 1926.

The emergency issues of the *Leicester Mercury* during the strike all contain the usual number of cinema advertisements and no actual mention of cancelled programmes. Some cinema employees were members of the E.T.U. and it is most likely that they would have been called out. It is, however, ominous that one item in a *Bioscope* chat page suggests that managers should look carefully at the terms of the contracts of their employees in relation to stoppages.

The post-strike meeting of the Leicester C.E.A. branch indicated that there was little disruption to programmes during the dispute, and that a more pressing topic of debate was the non-payment by some members of the £1 levy requested to pay for the temporary increase in transport costs. The emergency transport system had been very effective. There had been little harassment of the F.T.S. lorries armed, as they were, with special letters from the President of the Board of Trade indicating the purpose of their deliveries.[53]

The Aylestone Cinema

'The Aylestone Cinema' opened on October 4th 1926. Since the demise of the Lyric, there had been no screen entertainment in the suburban region of south-east Leicester. The opening ceremony was performed by one of the directors, Mr Evan Barlow, and three local councillors were in attendance with a full house of patrons.

AYLESTONE CINEMA
GRACE ROAD (CORNER OF MILLIGAN ROAD)
MONDAY NEXT OCTOBER 4th.
(MATINEE 2.30 p.m.)
All Star Programme, Special Musical Item:-
Madame LETTIE NOURISH (Contralto)
MONDAY, TUESDAY and WEDNESDAY
Programme includes:
When the Door Opened
Featuring
JACQUELINE LOGAN & WALTER McGRAIL.
THE LOVE THIEF.
Featuring Norman Kerry and Greta Nissen.
COMEDY, Etc.
Evenings 6 to 10 p.m. Continuous (except Sat.)
Saturday 6 to 8, 8 to 10.15 p.m.
Mat. Mon & Thurs, at 2.15, Children's Mat.
Sat. at 2. Price 3d. and 6d.

The Aylestone cinema building in 1991. *Author's photograph.*

The decorating scheme inside the large hall was blue and old gold with curtains and carpets to match; the seating (variously reported as 'over 1300' and '1206') was all tip-up supplied by Turners of Birmingham. The projectors were Kalees; the motorised screen curtains, by Furse of Nottingham, concealed the 12 by 16 foot screen, and the fan ventilation was by English Electric. The manager, Fred Stafford, was the son of one of the directors, Frank Stafford. He came to Aylestone after some years at the Picture House, Shepshed, and he had recently been married to Miss Mabel Bamford at the St Bartholomew's Church, Leicester. The third director was Bert Cole, the builder.

The opening film, starring Jacqueline Logan and Walter McGrail, was appropriately named 'When the Door Opened'. The supporting film was 'The Love Thief' with Norman Kerry and Greta Nissen and Madame Lettie Nourish sang several songs. Matinees were on Monday and Thursday at 2.15 p.m.. The continuous evening performance began at 6.00 p.m. in mid-week. On Saturday there was a special children's matinee at 2.p.m and there were two separate evening performances: 6 p.m. to 8 p.m. and from 8 p.m. to 10.15 p.m..[54]

More Managerial Changes

On Tuesday November 9th 1926 Mr Herbert Gibbon, the manager of the High Street Cinema, collapsed at work and died shortly afterwards at his home. He had been manager for four years but during 1926 he had been in failing health. Under the professional name of Nelson Barry, he had had a previous career in the music halls (some of the C.E.A. reports referred to him as Barry Gibbon). He had also managed the artistic foyer settings for the spectacular films 'Intolerance' and 'Birth of a Nation' in London and the Provinces. He was 61 and he was survived by two daughters and a son.[55]

A.S. Whittaker. Chairman of the Leicester C.E.A. Branch and General Manager of the City Cinema. *Kinematograph Weekly.*

In December 1926 Mr Albert Smith Whittaker replaced Mr

Lowndes Salmon at the City Cinema. He came to the new post with a reputation for showmanship and flair. He had been in management since 1913, when he took over the Miners' Welfare Hall cinema at Seven Sisters, Glamorgan. Subsequently, he became the manager of the Theatre Royal, Swansea, before moving to Hackney. After military service in India he returned to Wales as the assistant manager of the Cardiff Empire. He was successively manager of the Cardiff Olympia (1,850 seats) and the Capitol (2,600 seats) before taking up the post as general manager of film distribution group, United International Corporation Ltd in March 1925.[56] His plans for the City included opening a café on the second floor of the cinema and the introduction of special musical settings and variety acts into the programmes.[57] His assistant manager was Mr Cecil P.J. Churton, a Huntingdonshire man new to the business.[58]

At this time Mr W.P. Carter was manager of the Floral Hall; Mr Rosbottom was at the Sovereign; Mr I.P. Wright at the Picturedrome, Mere Road; Mr Harry Barker at the Shaftesbury; and Mrs Edith Black at the Belgrave.

In 1926 Mr Roland Wright sold his interest in both the Imperial, Green Lane Road, and the Star to his partner Mr Alfred Mynard.[59] Probably as a consequence of this arrangement, Mr H.W. Hurst was appointed manager of the Star and Mr W.H. Tyers became manager of the Imperial, now referred to as 'cinemas of the Mynard Circuit' by the *Bioscope*.[60] Roland Wright continued in the trade in 1927 as manager of the High Street Cinema.[61]

The Cinema-de-Luxe Changes Hands

A publicity stunt for the western 'Pioneer Trials' when shown at the Cinema de Luxe in 1924. *Kinematograph Weekly.*

The Cinema-de-Luxe came under the ownership of Midland Counties Cinemas Ltd in April 1925. They already had several cinemas in the Wolverhampton, Kidderminster and West Bromwich areas. It would seem that these were all formerly the cinemas of the immediate past owner, Mr Thomas Jackson. His firm Jackson Allen Cinema Consolidation Co. Ltd went into liquidation during the year.[62] Mr Shirley Reginald Simpson, who had been manager of the theatre for almost two years, was retained. According to the *Bioscope* he had been innovative with his effective and novel advertising campaigns and had 'introduced nightly musical interludes with suitable lighting effects and the use of coloured lights.' Mr Simpson had been a captain in the Indian Army before becoming manager of the Provincial Cinematograph Theatres' Queen's Theatre in Wolverhampton and from thence to Leicester's Cinema-de-Luxe.[63] He had acquired his flair for effective advertising and presentation at the Manchester College of Art. In April 1924 'Pioneer Trails', a run-of-the-mill Vitagraph western, had played to full houses because of some well-organised publicity. An eye-catching pictorial display and some local 'Red Indians' did the trick.

The musical director, Mr Clare Speight, had only just recently replaced Michael Rubenstein who, it was reported had gone to take up an important appointment at the Bank of England.[64] Mr Speight was a remarkable violinist. He had toured the country as a soloist when only ten years old and he was conducting an orchestra at the age of 18. Three years later he was musical adviser for Sir Walter de Frece's Theatrical Circuit. He had been also been the conductor at Stoll's Middlesex Theatre. This was his first appointment as director of a cinema orchestra.[65]

Music and Showmanship

In 1925 E. Gordon Stuart, who had been musical director at the Hippodrome since its re-opening in 1921, was presented with 'a beautiful umbrella suitably inscribed, as a token of the appreciation of the manager, Mr H.W. Hurst and his staff'. He was leaving to take up a new position at the Palace, West Bromwich. The new director was to be Charles

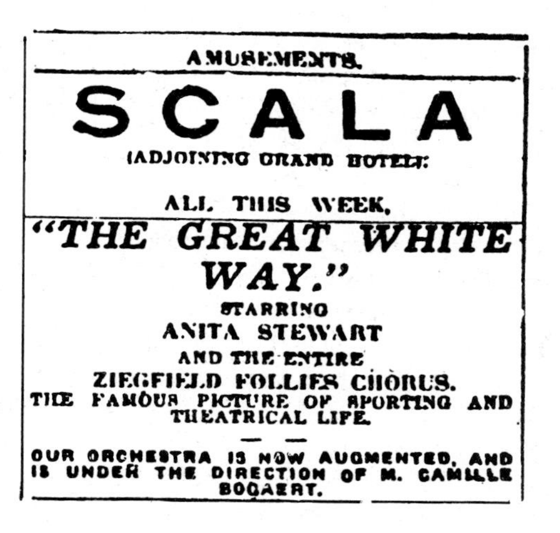
AMUSEMENTS.

SCALA

(ADJOINING GRAND HOTEL)

ALL THIS WEEK,

"THE GREAT WHITE WAY."

STARRING

ANITA STEWART

AND THE ENTIRE

ZIEGFIELD FOLLIES CHORUS.

THE FAMOUS PICTURE OF SPORTING AND THEATRICAL LIFE.

OUR ORCHESTRA IS NOW AUGMENTED, AND IS UNDER THE DIRECTION OF M. CAMILLE BOGAERT.

Leicester Mercury October 1924

Harrison, son of the well-known Harrison Bros comedians. He had recently been conductor of the revue 'Brilliants'.[66]

Several musical innovations were made during this period. Special musical arrangements and special scores were much more frequent, but they were still commented upon as luxuries.[67] The Herbert Wilcox film 'Chu Chin Chow' starring Betty Blythe and Herbert Langley was shown with four separate performances daily at the Scala with an augmented orchestra and vocalists.[68] 'I Pagliacci' at the Cinema-de-Luxe had a sung prologue by Mr Harold Deacon,[69] and 'The Niebelungs', also at the Scala, was shown at three separate performances daily with special music conducted by guest conductor, Monsieur Camille Bogaert. He was normally musical director of the Capitol, Hanley.[70]

Lesser films also had their special musical items. Harold Lloyd's 'Girl Shy' at the Cinema-de-Luxe had a prologue sung by Reg Ewen. The Richard Talmadge film 'Smiling Through' contained vocal solos by Madame May Fewkes for the title song and 'Parted'. The British film 'Reveille', starring Betty Balfour, was shown at the Sovereign with songs rendered by Connie Papes.[71]

Showmanship was ever present in the industry and when, in October 1925, the Picture House projected 'The Dancers', the foyer was festooned with streamers and balloons, and up-to-date jazz numbers accompanied the film.[72] In January 1927 the Scala attempted to bring some authenticity to the musical accompaniment of Cecil B. de Mille's 'Volga Boatmen' by engaging Feodor Kesloff and the Original Russian Quartet. In May the Scala, as befits its title, had an Opera Week with Hugette Duflos as Sophia in 'Der Rosenkavalier'. On-stage voices were provided by Miss Phyllis Wolfe and Mr Fred Bennett. Although continuous performances were still presented the cinema asked patrons to try to 'see the film from its commencement'. In June a new orchestra, the 'Chordeans', was reported to have been engaged at the Scala. The Fred Bennett Orpheus Choir (actually a quartet consisting of Eleanor Stokes (soprano), Doris Lorton (contralto), Clifford Fulwood (tenor) and Fred

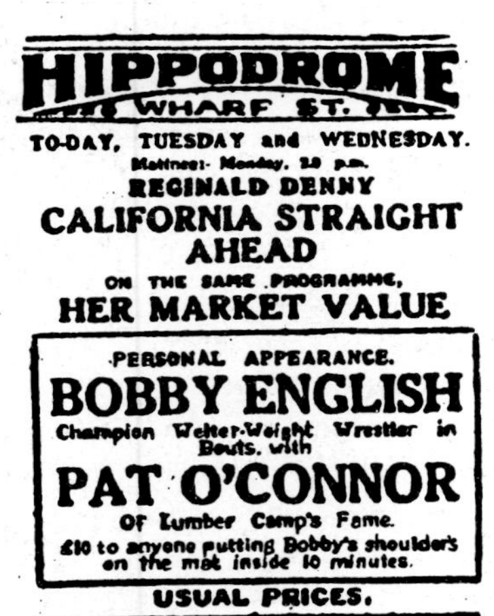

Films and 'Live Action' at the Hippodrome in October 1926.

Bennett (baritone) provided a prologue to the film 'In A Monastery Garden' at the City in July 1928.

In March 1928 J. Arthur Warburton had taken over from Eric Roloff as the musical director at the Picture House Cinema. He came from the Deansgate Picture House, Manchester with a reputation for quality. He had been a violinist with the Hallé Orchestra for some years. Praise was soon heaped on him in his new post. The *Bioscope* reviewer in April declared that it was the music and musical effects that had brought about good business for 'The Ghost Train' [73]

Such was the competition for increased audiences that double features, variety acts and special musical engagements abounded. Monsieur Mercado, the violinist, became musical director of the Scala in August 1927, and Hilda Ward's Bijou Band livened up their café. She was followed in September by Mr Rueby Shunshine and his Band. Tommy Sandilands (boy tenor) was at the Picture House in September 1927 and again in July 1928. The Wigston Temperance Band under the direction of Charles Moore played for musical interludes at the City Cinema in October. The Westleigh engaged Al Stevens and his Drigos Seranaders Dance Band in the week that they showed 'The Rosencavalier' and 'The Merry Cavalier' and a week later staged a mannequin parade provided by the Morgan Squires store.

British Week at the City Cinema in May 1927 saw the special presentation of Maurice Elvey's box office success 'Madamoiselle from Armentieres'. Eric Stanley provided vocal items and the orchestra was augmented with sound effects to bring noisy accuracy to the scenes of wartime combat. The film had already had a seven day presentation at the Picture House in April, in the same week that Eric Stanley was providing a voice commentary to the film 'The True Life Story of John Lee' at the Cinema de Luxe.

Betty Blythe, the star of 'Queen of Sheba' and 'She', made a personal appearance at the

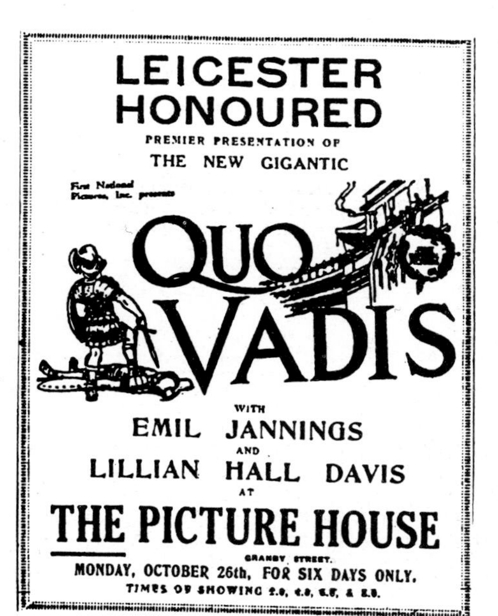

Leicester Mercury October 24th 1925.

Tuesday and Thursday matinees at Floral Hall in the week of January 4th 1926. She was at the Palace in a variety act entitled 'Story and Song'.

But the outstanding musical experiment was the presentation of what the advance publicity called 'The Musical Comedy of the Screen'. 'The Prince and the Maid' was shown at the Picture House in October 1925. Travelling with the film was a company of leading singers. 'This,' said the *Mercury* report, 'is the first successful attempt to put something more than pictures on the screen.' To ensure perfect synchronisation, the music of the vocal score was superimposed on the foot of the screen where it could be seen by the conductor and the singers. The film also contained a ballet sequence danced to the music of the orchestra.[74] The film originated in Germany and starred Ada Svedin and Charles H. Cay. Hans Ailbout composed the music to lyrics by Adrian Ross. The *Kinematogaph Weekly* critic commented that the film would have been more effective if the words had been sung in English.[75] It is surprising that the local reviewer did not mention this.

Later in the week an article entitled 'The Passing of the Silent Screen' contained another review of the film and a prediction that 'this latest system does much to bring nearer the date when silent pictures will be things of the past.'[76]

A single local vocalist, Mr Fred Bucknell, accompanied a similar experimental film later in the year at the Scala. Billed as 'The Perfect Song Film' the Innovation Productions 'Memories' was a one-reel novelty. A couple recall the death of their son in the war while the on-stage singer renders 'Tommy

A trade advertisement in *The Bioscope* 1925.

Publicity for 'Quo Vadis'.

Lad', 'Just a Song at Twilight' and 'Land of Hope and Glory'.[77] A number of companies produced illustrated song series and a later group of British-made films called 'Synchopated Melodies' showed pictures of the well-known bands of Jack Hylton, Jack Payne and Sydney Firman, with which the cinema orchestra had to synchronise.[78] The Westleigh engaged Mr P. Cruikshank to accompany what they billed as 'Film Songs' in October 1926.

A correspondent to the *Mercury* in March 1928 was critical of some of the musical intrusions. 'I went to see a most excellent film in Leicester. It was wonderfully well acted, and held the attention except in the scenes where it should have gripped most. And why did it fail there? Simply because, for no apparent reason whatever, a woman sang. This spoiled the whole scene; it jarred. It was so incongruous to have a woman singing in the middle of a love scene. Yet some folks in the audience clapped.'[79] The film in question was 'Seventh Heaven' starring Janet Gaynor and Charles Farrell.

Spectacular Films

'Don Juan', the Warner Brothers' Vitaphone sound synchronised experiment, was shown at the Picture House in 1927 without any special comment and no special score. There had been insufficient Vitaphone installations world-wide for it to be shown with its recorded music at its première in London. The interest at that time was in the presentation of 'Ben Hur'. Spectacle films were popular with Leicester audiences. In 1925 the Picture House had staged the British première of 'Quo Vadis', the last of the Italian super-productions. The foyer had been decorated to resemble a Roman vestibule whilst Roman soldiers stood at either side of the entrance. 'It is not often that we have the chance to see a film first', said the *Evening*

Publicity postcard showing the Roman triremes in 'Ben Hur'. *Author's collection.*

Mail reporter.[80] The *Mercury* critic was less accommodating and complained that too much attention was paid to the spectacle and not enough to the story.[81]

The *Illustrated Chronicle* reporter was just as dismissive about 'Ben Hur'. 'It is interesting to note that 100,000 extras were used, but we have seen crowds on the screen before. It might be a crowd of 1,000 or 1 million, the mind does not grasp the immensity. Similarly, the now-famous chariot race is simply a prolonged thrill of the variety so much beloved of film producers.' He reserved his praise for the sub-plot. 'It is in the sub-title of the Life of Christ that one finds the film's true greatness.'[82] Notwithstanding this criticism, the film's two-week run at the Picture House broke all records and the occasional police presence was necessary to control the waiting crowds along Granby Street.

Many of the Life of Christ scenes were in two-colour Technicolor, a process that was being increasingly used for prestige extracts. When Douglas Fairbanks' film 'The Black Pirate' was shown in January 1927 the *Illustrated Chronicle* critic thought that, since it was entirely in colour, it was 'a landmark in the history of the movies'. The film contained the first underwater Technicolor shots but another all-Technicolor film 'Wanderer of the Wasteland' had been shown in Leicester at the City Cinema in April 1925. The *Leicester Mercury* observed that 'The Black Pirate' was in a new colour process but the *Evening Mail* made no mention of the colour at all.

The new Technicolor system was not without its problems, however, and Mr Massey, manager of the Coliseum in 1956, recalled that the double-emulsion colour film could come apart during projection and on re-winding. Its increased thickness could also give problems in the projector 'gate' and it was difficult to avoid excessive scratching.[83]

Pathécolour was still the most colourful process to be seen, though its complicated processing meant that feature films were few and far between. 'Cyrano de Bergerac' was shown at the City Cinema in February 1925 and 'Konigsmark', starring Huguette Duflos, was shown at the same cinema in April.

A British firm, Spectrum Films, persisted with an additive system using red-orange and blue-green rotating filters and a short film using this process, 'Paris Fashions in Advance', was shown at the Floral Hall in November 1924. The film ran at 24 frames per second and the requirement of a special projector mechanism limited its widespread use.[84]

Children and the Cinema

The social aspects of cinema-going were discussed at a meeting of head teachers in Leicester in June 1926. One of the speakers had suggested that the atmosphere of the cinema was wrong. The Rev W. Gater, headmaster of the City Boys' School, said that he had noticed no ill effects due to the picture houses. Miss Davies of Alderman Newton Girls' School agreed and advocated special cinemas for school children. An un-named manager, who had been invited to speak at the conference, thought that the censorship of films had left very few that were harmful to children. A social worker believed that the cinema provided children with a brighter world than they could experience in their own drab surroundings.[85]

At one of the local Cinematograph Exhibitors' meetings, the managers had debated the problem of children in the cinema, from a slightly different angle.[86] Mr Gray, manager of the Olympia, said that it had been agreed some years ago that childen in arms should not be paid for. 'The difficulty was that the child could walk to the cinema, but when it got there it was picked up and became a child in arms.' Mr Gibbon, manager of the High Street Cinema, said that he had had a party of six go to his house the other day with one child. 'He told them that they must pay for the child. They told him that they had not done so before, and could get into other places without paying. They went away, and he saw them go into another kinema without paying.' He went on to say that he had had as many as a dozen perambulators in his vestibule. He had now got rid of them. 'Children,' he went on, 'were a nuisance to other people, and the attendants had to be continually speaking to them'. Mr Leopold Wacks, proprietor of the Hippodrome, Wharf Street, thought that individual managers had to take these decisions. 'It is a domestic matter, and depends on the class of patrons of the house. If they took certain areas and said that parents had to leave their children at home, they might as well close down at once.'

Mr Wright said that the debate was not about excluding children but about deciding whether all children should be paid for. He wanted a notice exhibited outside the cinemas which said that all children over 12 months old had to be paid for. Mr Wacks said that his house was a working class house and that he was against the notice. He thought that only children occupying seats should be paid for. Mrs Goodman of the Scala thought that all children should be paid for. Eventually, it was agreed by ten votes to two that children over twelve months should be paid for.

Cinema Poster Ban

Youthful escapades gave the Watch Committee some concern in 1925. On September 18th the *Evening Mail* reported that a poster outside the Cinema de Luxe for the film 'The Wings of Youth' had been banned by the Chief Fire Officer. 'The picture represents an artist's palette, upon which reclined three amorous couples, while underneath, Mephistopheles inserted a paintbrush through the handle of the palette, apparently with the intention of upsetting it. There was nothing in the attitudes of the figures to give offence and altogether it struck one as quite ordinary.' The Watch Committee had said that the film itself was inoffensive, but the poster was misleading and 'it was an appeal to the prurient mind to induce them in to see what was not being shown.' The film was described as 'a poignant tale of erring daughters. A mother's love and sacrifice rescues the girls from a whirlpool of jazz'. It was a minor Fox film starring Madge Bellamy, Ethel Clyton and Freeman Wood and it had an 'A' certificate. It was not considered worthy of special advertising space in the *Kinematograph Weekly* or the *Bioscope*.

By the next day, the *Evening Mail* had changed its stance and in an editorial under the title 'Indecent Posters' declared, 'We are somewhat concerned about the banned poster which was exhibited outside the Cinema-de-Luxe, and which was yesterday ordered down.' In fact, the Watch Committee sent down the Fire Officer to announce to the management that unless the poster was covered over in 10 minutes the cinema would be closed for the evening. The poster was quickly covered over with another bearing in red 'THIS HAS BEEN BANNED'. 'Indecent posters ought to be rigorously supressed,' continued the editor, 'for the whole tendency seems to be to get as near to the indecent as possible.'[87] The Bill Posters' Association had already objected to the poster.

The legal page of the *Bioscope,* in the edition of October 1st, included a wordy condemnation of the Watch Committee's attitude and rightness. It would appear that their threat of closure had also included a threat of licence withdrawal. The *Bioscope* thought that they did not actually have the power to do this on this pretext and that they had acted in a high-handed manner.

As a result of the censure, Captain Shirley Simpson felt obliged to resign his post, and also to leave Leicester.[88] The local branch of the C.E.A. presented him with a cheque for 10 guineas (£10.50p) 'as a token of their fellowship'. Later in the month he was reported to have taken up the position of manager of the Savoy Cinema, Grimsby. The incident clearly did not affect his standing in the Cinema world since, in July 1928, he is reported as being appointed to the management of the new Regal super-cinema at London's Marble Arch. Mr George Taylor was appointed as his replacement at the Cinema-de-Luxe.[89]

Cinema Closures and Plans for Others

The Cinema-de-Luxe was placed on the market for auction on October 27th 1926 but it failed to find a buyer. The *Bioscope*, reporting with regret that such a large hall should be taken off the list of cinemas, said that it was likely the hall would be taken over by the Salvation Army and used for their own purposes.[90] In the event, the management of the Scala looked after its affairs for a further six months. It finally closed on Easter Saturday, April 23rd 1927.[91] George Taylor, the manager, was not unemployed for long. He obtained a position as manager of the Capitol Cinema, St Austell, Cornwall in July 1927.[92]

When the Grand Hotel changed hands in March 1928 it heralded the end for the Scala Cinema. The lease was due to expire in September and the new owners of the hotel had indicated that they wished to carry out alterations which included converting the cinema hall to its original use as a banqueting hall. The Scala did good business during the summer months but it had to close on September 8th 1928.[93]

Only one week later the *Bioscope* announced that the Pavilion was about to close to make room for road

CINEMA DE LUXE.
TO-DAY.
The American Venus
A PARAMOUNT PICTURE.
STARRING ESTHER RALSTON & ALL-STAR WELL-KNOWN CAST.
AND BIG SUPPORTING PROGRAM.

The last advertisement for the Cinema de Luxe.
Leicester Mercury Saturday April 23rd 1927.

improvements. It gave good details of the venue's history from its origins as an entertainment hall for a public house to its current Palace of Varieties status. The report was premature, however, since the local council granted a short term tenure to a local company to run the hall until it was needed for demolition.[94]

Sir Oswald Stoll surprised the annual shareholders meeting of the Leicester Palace with the announcement that the Floral Hall was to be demolished and replaced by a new cinema on an extended site. He said that the present cinema was making substantial profits, and they would be ready to make a start on the new building at an early date.[95]

A proposal to site a new cinema on the corner of Mayfield Road and London Road had been presented before the Watch Committee in June 1927. Rumours in the trade press concerning the possible building of a super-cinema had been circulating since March and the *Bioscope* reported in May that land had been purchased for the erection of a cinema on the London Road.[96] The plans were rejected at the July meeting of the Watch Committee, on the grounds that the proposed cinema would be next to a petrol filling station. There was a well-founded fear of a cinema conflagration. Even as late as March 1928, however, there were reports that the site was being developed for a cinema.

Proposals for significant alterations at the Hippodrome were approved by the Watch Committee early in July 1927. The whole of the ground floor was to be re-designed, the stage to be removed and the screen relocated. The projection room and the re-winding room would be rebuilt on the second floor. The building work necessitated the closure of the cinema from June 30th until Bank Holiday Monday August 1st. The re-opening programme had a double feature of Dorothy Gish in 'Nell Gwynne' and Pola Negri in 'Good and Naughty'.[97]

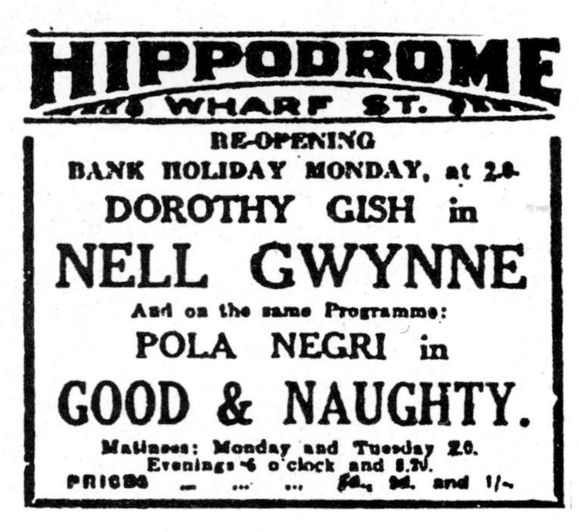

Re-opening of the Hippodrome.
Leicester Mercury July 30th 1927.

Construction of an outside verandah, to protect waiting patrons in bad weather, was completed in October in the same week that the manager Captain Ball announced his resignation from the Hippodrome and the film trade. The new manager was Mr John Brown from Leeds but in June 1928 the licence was further transferred to Robert W. Marchbanks.[98]

Another important managerial change took place in January 1927, when George Luxton left the Picture House to become managing director of the Tower Cinema, Peckham. His replacement George Basil Grantham only stayed until January 1928, when Philip Gorton took over. For seven years he had been at the Scala, Birmingham and had recently filled an appointment for the P.C.T. in Walsall.[99] As befits a new manager, he made a few changes to his theatre. The café was jazzed up somewhat with a new blue and gold colour scheme and the replacement of the old chairs with 200 new Lloyd Loom ones. An up-to-date 'His Master's Voice record reproducer' was set up in the Dome restaurant to provide popular orchestral and operatic selections.

In January 1928 the H.D. Moorhouse circuit acquired the Sovereign Picture House and installed a new manager, Mr Percy Swanwick. He was transferred from the Criterion Picture House, Walkden, a Lancashire HDM house.[100] Mr H.W. Hurst is reported to be returning to Leicester in October 1928 but there is no indication of his new post. He had left employment at the Star only a year previously to take up management of the Oldfield Park Picture House in Bath.[101]

Watch Committee and Controversial Films

The Watch Committee viewed two films during this period. 'Dawn', directed by Herbert Wilcox and starring Sybil Thorndike, was the story of Nurse Edith Cavell, executed by the German High Command as a spy in the 1914-18 war. Many people felt that opening up old wounds would endanger attempts at reconciliation. In February 1928 the British Board of Film Censors would not give it a certificate. It is now known

Dame Sybil Thorndike and Maurice Braddell in 'Dawn'. *Author's collection.*

'The King of Kings'. H.B. Warner as Jesus. *Pathé.*

that the Foreign Secretary, Sir Austen Chamberlain, had indicated both to Herbert Wilcox and T.P. O'Connor, President of the Board, his repugnance to its production. The Leicester Watch Committee saw no reason to deny it a showing, although there was one un-named dissentient. According to *The Bioscope* report, he protested on the grounds that 'it reflected on the Germans.' The Mayor remarked that the film was sentimental rather than anti-German, and he saw no reason why the citizens of Leicester should not see it.[102]

De Mille's 'King of Kings' was not submitted to the British Board of Film Censors because it had long been their policy not to allow the materialised figure of Christ to be portrayed on the screen. The Watch Committee had no objection to it being shown at the Evington Cinema when they viewed it on July 24th 1928. There had been some well publicised disagreements reported in the press. The Sheffield Watch Committee had first of all banned it, then reconsidered and suggested that it should be shown only when the cinema management had declared that there would be no applause or smoking during its performance. Sheffield Council had then overturned their decision. A Junior Imperial League debate on the subject in Leicester, also reported in the press, decided in favour of it being shown.[103] The Evington had record attendances at its October showing and the one week booking was extended by an extra three days.[104]

Leicester's Film Tastes?

In 1926 a survey in the *Illustrated Chronicle* attempted to discover 'Leicester's Film Tastes'.[105] In a masterpiece of generalisation, the article assured readers that Sheffield liked picturesque and sentimental films; that Birmingham and Cardiff liked films that lend themselves to musical accompaniment, and that Newcastle liked night-club scenes and bathing beauties. The information was said to be from a survey by Sidney Morgan of the British Film Producers' Society. In Rachel Low's *History of the British Film*, Sidney Morgan is shown to be secretary of the British Association of Film Directors.[106]

The reporter's own follow-up elicited the somewhat bland view that Leicester people do not care whether a film is a comedy or a drama as long as it is a good one but the musical accompaniment was important. The manager of the Picture House said that the comedy features of Harold Lloyd, Buster Keaton and Charlie Chaplin were a great attraction. The City Cinema manager re-iterated the statement that the audience had no particular preference apart from quality. The Floral Hall manager thought that his audience had no particular preferences and this dictated the wide variety of films that he showed.

British Films and the Quota Act

The Cinematograph Films Act of 1927, which came into force on January 1st 1928 for an intial period of ten years, was usually referred to as the Quota Act. Its twin aims were to restrict blind and advanced booking and to provide for an initial quota of 7% of British films for the renter and 5% for the exhibitor. It did not have the universal approval of the industry and its eventual vague application only marginally improved the condition of the British film industry. The 'Quality' pictures that were produced were off-set by a larger number of 'Quota Quickies'.

Film programmes in the city centre cinemas were now all double features except when there were special programmes or when the feature was of an unusual length. An animated cartoon, an interest film and a newsreel might also be included. With mid-week programme changes in many cinemas, there was an enormous choice of films to be had each night in the city and its suburbs. In 1927 the response to a cinemagoers' questionnaire organised by Sydney Bernstein[107] revealed that 33 per cent of them went once a week, and 47 per cent went twice a week. Despite the depression, cinema-going retained its popularity.

Chapter Seven

O.K. for Sound 1929-31

By the time Leicester heard its first 'Talkie' of the new era the debate about the success or failure of this addition to cinema was over. In November 1928 the *Leicester Mercury* had printed a statement by film star Pola Negri that 'Talkies would not last long', but few could doubt that it was prompted more by vested interest than common sense. During the next two years every cinema in Leicester was converted to sound. Some, indeed, went through the process twice as rival sound systems replaced each other.

Orchestras dismissed

The new technology produced unemployment and redundancy amongst the cinema musicians in an era of deep recession. Some, used to playing classic compositions both as part of the film programme and during the intervals, had already decided to leave when special musical scores were sent with the films. 'They were not prepared to lower their standards to play such drivel'.[1]. Mr Massey recalls that some of the orchestras would only play for the feature films and not the shorts. They were accomplished musicians and strong members of the Musicians' Union.[2] When the first sackings occurred, local musicians made representations to the City Council for the formation of a municipal orchestra.[3] Some followed this with the circulation of pamphlets urging the public to boycott cinemas where musicians had been sacked.[4] Neither action had any effect.

W.H. Carter managed to keep his orchestra together for a short time after his displacement. They gave a series of concerts on Sunday evenings at the Corn Exchange from October 1930.[5] The viability of the orchestra away from the cinema had already been established with a well-attended municipal concert at the de Montfort Hall in May 1929.[6]

Eric Roloff, the brilliant violinist and leader of the Picture House Orchestra, was eventually a founder member of Thomas Beecham's London Philharmonic

Orchestra when it was formed in 1932 and he played in that orchestra's first concert at the de Montfort Hall on March 30th 1933.[7]

Conditions of Employment

With four thousand cinemas across the country, the number of employees on the exhibition side of the film industry amounted to around 20,000. Less than one-third of these belonged to the National Association of Theatrical Employees (N.A.T.E.) and only 1,000 projectionists belonged to the Electrical Trades Union (E.T.U.). Their employment conditions were not to be envied. Projectionists in the Manchester area worked between 60 and 75 hours per week for wages between £1/4/- (£1.20) and £2, depending upon the capacity of the cinema. An attempt to make a local agreement for a 48 hour week, paid overtime and one week's holiday each six months was opposed by the national committee of the Cinematograph Employers' Association. The Birmingham branch of the E.T.U. claimed that their conditions were bad also. Chief operators were getting only £2/5/- (£2.25) per week. Nationally negotiated rates of pay were not achieved until late in the decade.[8]

The New Sound Systems

The technology of sound-on-film had been developing since 1906 with the experiments of Eugene Lauste in Britain and those of Lee de Forest in America and Britain from 1924; yet Warner Brothers chose the less-than-reliable synchronised disc approach for their Vitaphone process. The 16-inch records, playing at $33\frac{1}{3}$ revolutions per minute from the centre outwards, were placed on the turntable of the combined projector and gramophone player. A 'Start' frame on the film was placed in the projector gate, and the needle arm was placed in the central groove next to a marked arrow. When the switch was thrown, the projector and the disc started simultaneously and remained in synchronisation throughout the reel. If frames were lost from the film, through damage or reel-joining, they had to be replaced by blank frames. Excessive vibration and shaking of the projector due to faulty mounting could cause the needle to jump a groove and lose synchronisation. Records could be lost or broken in transit, so usually two sets accompanied each film. Moreover, the transit cost of film and discs was almost doubled. The advantage with the disc system was in better amplification and sound reproduction, if the disc surface had not been mis-used.

Fox films put their reliance on the Movietone sound-on-film process developed from the work of Lee de Forest and Thomas Case. This

A Western Electric projector fitted with a Kalee Indomitable No.8 capable of playing sound-on-film or sound-on-disc.
Courtesy Cinematograph Theatre Association Bulletin.

variable-density system made by the Western Electric Company was at first incompatible with the Radio Corporation of America's (RCA) variable-area sound-on-film process. In 1928. the two companies collaborated on removing the incompatible components and sounded the death-knell for disc systems.[9] But neither system was perfect and poor quality printing from a duplicate negative could result in hissy and indistinct sound while a poorly set exciter-lamp could cause reduced volume.

By the time Leicester cinemas were negotiating for the purchase, hire purchase or rental of 'talkie' equipment there were a number of attachments and whole projectors which were compatible with both sound-on-film and sound-on-disc presentations. Outright purchase of the machine without the associated amplifier and wiring of the cinema was around £600. Cinemas could lease/purchase on a one-, two- or three-year basis but added to this there were maintenance and service charges. Some of the smaller Leicester cinemas had a turnover of less than £100 per week and the switch to sound represented a significant financial burden coupled with the increased rental percentages that the distributors required for sound films. Most cinemas needed considerable constructional change in order to accommodate the loudspeakers behind the screen.

1929 began with some ominous rumblings of things to come. Advertising for the Aylestone cleverly announced that this was its third year of sound programming and the prospective patrons were invited to 'Hear Bert Johnson's orchestra and see . . . the current film'. The City Cinema also emphasised the quality of its live music with 'Meet the Boys' evenings, in which individual members of the orchestra performed solos. The Picture House Café had now dispensed with its pianist and was advertising music from 'The Wonderful His Master's Voice Electrical reproducer, playing daily'.

'The Jazz Singer'

When 'The Jazz Singer' eventually arrived in Leicester it was shown as a silent film. In fact, apart from the songs and two small sections of unscripted conversation, 'The Jazz Singer' was very much a silent film with a synchronised music track. The *Leicester Mercury* reviewer was disappointed. '"The Jazz Singer" in which Al Jolson makes his bow before a Leicester audience at the "City", fails to come up to expectations because it is incomplete. In the early stages of

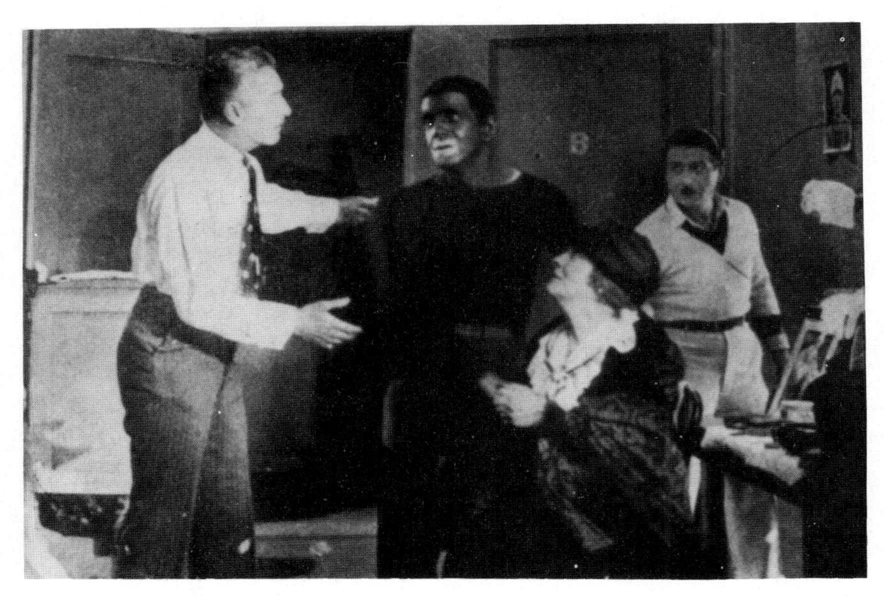

'The Jazz Singer'. *Courtesy Warner Brothers.*

the picture, one has a feeling that there is something vital missing, and later on one realises what this factor is. It is Al Jolson's voice. This film was obviously filmed as a "talkie" - the whole story hinges on "the voice with a tear in it", - and because it is silent, it loses a great deal of its effect. There are long close-ups of Jolson's facial contortions. It was a "talkie" when it was shown in London, but we in the provinces must wait for this mechanical addition. The film is one to enjoy, but we would have liked to have heard the voice.'[10]

Still attempting to hold the musical high ground, the City Cinema resurrected de Mille's 1926 film 'The Volga Boatmen' with a special musical score and a prologue by the Volga singers devised by the manager, Mr A.S. Whittaker.[11] The Picture House showed the spectacular wartime flying film 'Wings' with special music and effects by J. Arthur Warburton and the orchestra and musical interludes by George L. Simpson on the Mighty Wurlitzer organ.[12] Their resident organist, Mr Sidney T. Wallbank, had left to take up an appointment at the Regent Cinema, Dudley and he was succeeded by Mr A. Bevan.[13]

'Talkies' in Loughborough

In April the Victory Cinema in Loughborough stole a march on Leicester by advertising 'The Talkies, and British too', but the Leicester newspaper reports do not reveal what the films were.[14] The *Loughborough Echo* is also lacking in detail. 'The very latest attraction in the cinema world, the sound and speech films, otherwise known as 'The Talkies', will be featured in each programme commencing Monday next and onwards. For the first few weeks, the management have decided to present short films only, two in every programme. These short attractions will consist of musical, singing and instrumental, and all talk films.'[15] A cautionary note is struck by a denial that the orchestra would be disposed of. As it turned out, the talkies did not actually materialise as advertised. They could not be shown until the following Monday because all the wiring had not been completed.[16]

Tracing the British origin of the films shown in Loughborough also has its problems. The first British feature film to be released was Alfred Hitchcock's 'Blackmail' (trade shown in June 1929), but British Talking Pictures, a company formed in 1928 to exploit de Forest's Phonofilms system, had arranged to convert cinemas to sound for £300 and to guarantee a 3,000 feet programme of items weekly at a rental of £16/10/- a week. Only short subject films were available by April 1929, though a part-talkie feature 'The Crimson Circle' had been trade shown using a disc system in March.[17]

Several other companies using sound-on-disc systems also produced short

The opening announcement for the first 'talkie' in Leicester. The top right panel gave details of the sound apparatus to be used.

musical, instrumental and comedy films during 1928 and 1929. British Acoustic Films had shown some talkie political films by means of a cinema van in Hinckley and South Wigston in November 1928. This sound-on-film system used a separate synchronised machine for the sound playback. Any of these systems could have been the one used at the 'Victory' talkies. At the end of the year, when the cinema did show its first feature film, it was Columbia's sound-on-film 'The Donovan Affair'. The accompanying film was the twelve-minute 'Chelsea Nights' starring Carl Brisson and Mimi Crawford. The orchestra was transferred to augment the orchestra of the sister cinema 'The Empire', which in the same week was showing Abel Gance's 'Napoleon'.[18]

'The Singing Fool' at the Palace

Competition for the first talkie to be shown in Leicester was hotting up. On June 10th the Picture House gave advance notice of its approaching presentation of 'Showboat' and, on June 18th, the Palace placed a huge advertisement in the *Mercury* announcing its presentation of 'The Singing Fool' with sound on June 20th.

The local branch of the Cinematograph Exhibitors' Association did not seem perturbed that a 'Variety' house was about to 'steal a march' on the local cinemas. Mr Whittaker of the City had raised the issue at the June 25th meeting, but the new chairman, Roland Wright, said there was no use 'crying about it' since the variety theatres had not objected to cinema houses having variety acts. In that very week the City had included two 'turns' in its programme! Indeed, Mr Whittaker was the prime showman of 'stage presentations'. The stage at the City was only 5 feet 6 inches deep and it had no wings, yet the performances were well presented. In April, 1929 a spectacular musical prologue to the silent film 'Rose Marie' gave the cinema one of its most successful weeks. Eleanor Stokes sang the 'Love Call' with 'real colour and expression' in front of a Canadian Rockies set. For the Saturday evening performance there was a queue 300 yards long outside the cinema.[19] . In September 1928 Mr Whittaker had been elected to the Cinema Select Circle a group of only 100 top managers.

Sir Oswald Stoll had announced in April that the whole

Sir Oswald Stoll, proprietor of the Leicester Palace and Floral Hall. Drawn in 1926.

Above: Eleanor Stokes sings the prologue to 'Rose Marie' at the City Cinema in April 1929.
Kinematograph Weekly.
Below: A cartoon in the *Leicester Mail* June 20th 1929.

of his cinema circuit was to change over to talkies as soon as possible, both for feature films and shorts, and that the inclusion of 'talkie' short films in the variety programme would sacrifice at least three 'turns'.[20] The City Cinema tried counter-measures by greatly increasing the size of its advertising space and including a stage show with its two feature films. The Floral Hall had a cameraman roaming the city streets. Then it attempted to lure patrons into the cinema so that they could see themselves on the screen. It also added to its advertising the slogan, 'Our programmes are not Talkie, yet

powerful enough to speak for themselves'.[21]

The Palace pulled all the stops out for the afternoon opening of 'The Singing Fool'. The projector was one which could handle both the Vitaphone sound-on disc system and the Movietone sound-on-film system. Sir Oswald and Lady Stoll, owners of the theatre circuit, were in attendance. The *Mercury* was full of praise. 'A Leicester audience had its first experience of the Talkies yesterday. Technically, the opening performance was an immense success. Speech was for the most part clearly audible in all parts of the house, and the orchestral accompaniment which is so important a feature of 'The Singing Fool' was quite indistinguishable from the real thing. It was remarked by the critical, however, that it slurs some of the vowel sounds and is variable in its consonants. These details could be noticed in the topical film representing Mr MacDonald introducing the new cabinet. Nevertheless, the familiar accent of the Prime Minister's voice was easily recognisable.'[22] Ramsay McDonald had at one time been a Leicester M.P., so his voice was well-known. His radio broadcasts were now quite commonplace, too.

All seats were bookable at theatre prices. Boxes (for four persons) were 9/4 (47p) and 7/4 (36p), stalls and fauteilles 2/4 (12p), fauteuilles (first four rows) 1/10 (9p), circle 2/4, balcony 1/- (5p) and gallery 6d (2p).

The new equipment was not without its problems. The *Bioscope* reported that during the second week there was an unfortunate breakdown in the 'talkie' apparatus and the concluding half-hour of the 'Singing Fool' had to be played through silent. 'The house was crowded, but the *contre-temps* was accepted philosophically except on the part of some 'galleryites' who thought that they had been done out of their money. The necessary adjustments were made in a few minutes after the house had been cleared.[23] 'The Singing Fool' remained at the Palace until July 13th when it was succeeded by 'On Trial', 'a sensational murder mystery talkie' that suffered from a poorly-recorded sound-track and wooden diction.[24]

The Danger of Cinema Fires

Cinema fires were mercifully quite rare, despite the high inflammability of cellulose nitrate film stock. One much publicised tragedy took place at a special 1929 Christmas showing at the Glen Cinema, Paisley, when a fire in the projection room caused a panic for the exits. Seventy children were suffocated or crushed to death. A projection room fire at the Picturedrome Mere Road on August 2nd thankfully occurred before patrons arrived. Electrical apparatus and a number of complete films were destroyed.[25] In October 1930 the fusing of an electric wire on the stage of the City Cinema during a performance caused some alarm. Swift action by the manager gave reassurance to the audience and there was no interruption to the programme.[26]

Mishaps for cinema employees did not all take place on the premises. Leslie Mansfield, the leader of the City Cinema orchestra, was due to be married at St Peter's Church on June 29th. At first there was no clergyman present to conduct the ceremony. He had had a lapse of memory about the time of the service. Fortunately another cleric came to the rescue and relieved everyone's anxiety.[27]

Mr G.H. Scarborough, who besides being a director of the Evington Cinema was chairman of the local C.E.A., had a serious car accident in June 1931 and was in a critical condition for several days. He was able to resume his duties after six months convalescence.[28]

'Showboat' at the Picture House

The Picture House installed the Western Electric sound-on-film system to present Universal's 'Showboat' beginning on Monday June 24th 1929.[29] The manager, Mr Philip Gorton, created some excellent publicity by employing a touring 'Showboat' mounted on a five-ton Dennis chassis. 'Darkie attendants grouped round a pneumatic Calliope organ taken from a genuine Mississippi Show boat.'[30]

There was no increase in their house prices at circle 2/-, balcony 1/6 and stalls 1/-. The review of the film was placed under the title 'Have Talkies Come to Stay?'.[31] 'There has been so much said in advance of 'Showboat' that everyone has been prepared for a good thing. The film at the Picture House is of that order. There is more a treat for the ear than the eye, but this is not a disparagement of 'talkies', since in their infancy they promise to make good. So much of the first portion of the film is silent that there is justification for thinking

The trailer used in the Midlands to publicize 'Showboat'. *Kinematograph Weekly.*

that there is an unnecessary bashfulness in introducing the human voice. Its absence is helpful in the final summing up as to the respective merits of Silent and Talkie. It is now possible to make comparison with a 'talkie' at another theatre, and the general opinion is that talkies have come to stay. To miss 'The Singing Fool' is to miss a piece of cinema history, and more important to miss something good. As far as one can see from first impressions, the talkies will dye the screen a deeper American.' The *Mercury* reported that the whole programme was to be in sound, 'even the trailers announcing forthcoming attractions'.[32]

The second talkie at the Picture House on July 4th was Columbia's first sound film, 'The Donavan Affair', an all-dialogue comedy-thriller. There was also a silent second feature 'Love's Sacrifice'. Musical accompaniment on the Wurlitzer organ was provided by Miss Frances Ross, the only musician retained at the cinema.

The City Cinema defiantly advertised Alice Terry and Ramon Novarro in the re-issue of the six year-old 'Scaramouche', 'a 100% Silent Film: Stage and Screen Show at Normal Prices'.[33]

MONDAY NEXT
FOR ONE WEEK ONLY.

CONTINUOUS PERFORMANCE
12.30 — 10.30 p.m.

SEE AND HEAR
LAURA LA PLANTE
IN
SHOW BOAT
DAILY AT
12.45, 3.20, 6.0, 8.35 p.m.

PRECEDED BY MOVIE-TONE VARIETY ACT AND COMEDY.

NO INCREASE IN PRICES.
CIRCLE - - 2/-
BALCONY 1/6
STALLS - - 1/-
Including Tax

NO INCREASE IN PRICES.

PICTURE HOUSE CAFES
OPEN DAILY 11 a.m.—10 p.m.

American Slang at the the Cinema

The unfamiliar vocabulary of the talkies prompted the writer of the Filmland column in the *Illustrated Chronicle* to print a glossary.[34]

Weenies, Janes, Dames, Broads . . . . Girls
A dim bulb, a banana, a sap, an oil can . . . . a fool
Dope, snow, coke . . . . cocaine
A gat, a rod . . . . a gun
In hock . . . . in pawn
Sugar daddies . . . . men who 'protect' girls.

In September the *Mercury* critic in reviewing 'The Follies of 1929' said that the harsh Americanisms were more marked than ever.[35] He described the latest method of American love-making. 'Y' got wan?' ' Sure' 'Waal, gimme wan'. Then follows a close-up of kissing. It got very monotonous after we had heard it several times.'

Romance of a sort was the subject of an amusing letter to the *Leicester Mercury* on September 19th 1929. Under the title 'Courting Couples in the Cinema' the correspondent, signing himself 'Flicker', described how the 'lolling lovers, before, behind, to the left, and to the right, seem to have little discretion. One sits among young people who seem there merely to cuddle and talk drivel. If people want to canoodle, which is only natural, I suppose - why should they make a public exhibition of their pastime? After all, some people go to the cinema with the serious intent of enjoying the pciture, and to be surrounded by a lot of dreamy youngsters bent on emulating the silly close-ups on the screen is, to say the least, repulsive.' 'Give level headed cinema-goers a chance,' he concluded.

The Palace advertised a 'Double sound bill' from July 29th with 'In Old Arizona' and 'Old Kentucky Homes'. The latter film may only have been a synchronised sound short for the theatre had also engaged the services of 'The Kentucky Jubilee Choir', almost certainly consisting of 'black-faced' minstrels. On Monday August 5th the Palace returned to live entertainment though it continued to show Movietone news, comedy shorts and Mickey Mouse and other cartoons with the occasional special 'talkie'.

Some films originally conceived and produced as silent films had synchronised sound tracks added. These were usually advertised as such by the cinema. The United Artist's film 'The Rescue', starring Ronald Colman and Lili Damita in her first American film, had a musical track and some ritual choral items in the Javanese location. It was presented at the Picture House with a supporting silent film.[36]

Sound Films in the Suburbs

The Olympia Cinema closed during July and August for structural alterations, re-decoration and the installation of British Talking Picture sound equipment. It re-opened on September 9th with the Vitaphone film 'On Trial'. Its second talkie was 'The Singing Fool'. Evening performances were continuous from 6.40 p.m. and there were matinees on Monday and Thursday at 2.45 p.m. Prices of admission were circle 1/-, side circle 9d, and stalls 6d. The Sovereign, Shaftesbury and Coliseum, the other H.D.M. Circuit cinemas, are also reported to have put in B.T.P. sound systems in September, but their first advertised sound films do not appear until December.[37]

Carl Brisson visited the City Cinema on the evening of September 9th on a promotional tour with Alfred Hitchcock's last silent film 'The Manxman'. 'Frantic flappers left their seats last night and mobbed Carl Brisson after the smiling film star had appeared on stage. Mr. Brisson had made the tactical error of kissing one admirer, and there was no stemming the feminine tide after that.' Also present in the audience was Mary

Carl Brisson and Anny Ondra in 'The Manxman'.
Author's collection.

We can keep
Silent no longer!
The City adopts a sound
policy—
After carefully investigating all
the various systems of Talkies
we have decided to instal the finest
equipment available and will
soon be presenting to you the finest
and best
TALKIES & SOUND PICTURES
Wait—
SEE IT & HEAR IT
AT
The CITY
You will be Glad!

Marshall, the winner of the *Leicester Mercury* film competition. Her prize had been an opportunity to take part in the production at Elstree studios. It was the first time she had seen the film since its completion.[38] She is also reported as having been in the films 'Paradise' with Betty Balfour and 'My Wife's Husband' with Monty Banks, both for British International Pictures.[39]

'The Unwritten Law', advertised as a '100% British Talking Picture', was shown at the Picture House in the week of September 19th. This three-reel mini-feature had been trade-shown on the same day as 'Blackmail'. It was made by British Sound Film Producers using the R.C.A. system. The British producers showed little interest in disc sound and either used Western Electric or R.C.A. to record the sound. 'Blackmail' was presented at the Picture House in November and advertised as a British all-talking film directed by Alfred Hitchcock. 'The best yet' said the reviewer.

Talkies at 'The City'

On September 23rd the City Cinema showed its first talkie, the musical 'Broadway Melody'. Manager A.S. Whittaker returned from his holiday in Brighton to hasten the preparations.[40] There was no increase in admission prices but all seats were bookable and there were 4 separate performances each day. This was M.G.M.'s first full talkie and Leicester was one of the first provincial cities to hear its original musical score and see its celebrated Technicolor sequences.

A week later the Picture House gave Universal's 'Broadway' its Midlands' première. This was a backstage musical with huge sets, geometrical dancing sequences that anticipated Busby Berkeley and a Technicolor night club sequence.

In November the Gaumont-Provincial Cinematograph Theatre circuit acquired the City Cinema.[41] The immediate effect was an announcement that 'We can stay silent no longer. The City adopts a sound policy and we are now installing the finest equipment available to show M.G.M.'s 'The Trial of Mary Dugan'.[42] This was the first talkie for Norma Shearer. According to the Leicester Mercury, 17 tons of sound equipment had been installed in record time.[43] The Western Electric system installed could show both sound-on-film and sound-on-disc presentations.

A British Movietone news item with a local flavour was shown at the Palace on November 4th. 'At one point,' said the reviewer, 'Lord Blandford, at the Quorn Hunt meet, laughingly calls out "Be careful what you say, the talkies are here!"'.[44]

The Palace presented a new aspect of cinema exhibition beginning in November 1929. On Saturday mornings, for a uniform rate of sixpence, an audience of young people could sit in any part of the house to view a series of instructional films. The Lord Mayor and leaders of education in the city were present at the initial programme when films depicting botany, zoology, travel and history were shown.[45]

The Picture House had their annual Christmas Eve treat for youngsters and the City Cinema showed Buster Keaton's 'The Cameraman' to an audience of 2,000 poor children on New Year's Day.

The 'Imperial' Sound System

During 1929 the Star and the Imperial installed their own 'Imperial' sound system developed by the owner, Alfred Mynard. This sound-on-film system was used fairly widely in the Midlands and the Potteries because of its advantageous purchase and leasing system.[46]

The following year began with extremely good attendances. There was an unprecedented demand at the Picture House to see Warner Brothers' 'The Desert Song', the part-Technicolor operetta starring John Boles and Carlotta King. An extra performance was arranged at 11.30 on the Saturday morning and the cinema was again packed to capacity.[47]

Silent Films Still Please the Critics

For their first film of 1930 the Floral Hall showed an old form of 'talkie', when Ratcliffe Holmes presented his own film 'Interviewing Wild Animals'. The

City Cinema showed the silent film 'The Cossacks' with John Gilbert and Renée Adorée. The *Mercury* reviewer, ignoring the modernism of the talkies, boldly declared that 'The art of silent narrative is lavishly developed in this film.'[48] In February his allegiance was further displayed: 'That the silent film can hold its own even in the present day is proved by the support accorded to The Evington. Mr West holds the fort there, and so long as he presents good pictures allied to good music (Mr Horace Gilbert), and under the best conditions, the theatre will remain a popular rendezvous.'[49] In May he was clearly beginning to tire of indifferent sound reproduction. 'Silent pictures make a welcome change in a present day programme. There is a first class production as a supporting feature, and it is positively soothing to sit back and let the story percolate into the mind instead of having to remain in a state of continuous concentration.'[50] By the end of the year he was quite oppositional. 'The talkies manage to get a song and dance in somehow. In many cases, the effects are incongruous. To judge by recent productions, the producers have deliberately put in a musical interlude because they think the public want it. Really, it is about time the new conventions were ruthlessly broken down. They have become more fixed and more foolish than the worst we expected when silent films held their own.'[51]

The Prince's Cinema

A new name appeared on Monday January 27th 1930 when 'The Prince's Theatre' opened its doors. The Cinema-de-luxe building had not had a cinematograph licence since April 23rd 1927.[52] The McNaughton Music Hall Syndicate had considered purchase in view of the impending demolition of the Pavilion in September 1928 but the Pavilion was given a short term reprieve and they abandoned the idea.[53] A local syndicate bought it two months later, with a view to equipping it as a live theatre which could stage London productions. Two of the purchasers were Harry Westgate and Edmund Tyler, already directors of the City Cinema. The third was a Mr J.A. Hartop. To facilitate their intentions, they formed a company, the Prince's Theatre Co. (Leicester) Ltd. [54] It was this group that now leased it to Associated British Cinemas Ltd.

Although the exterior still retained the appearance of the Temperance Hall the interior had undergone major reconstruction. The architect for this was Arthur Hall of St Martins, Leicester, and the main contractor was Sharp and Sons. The new balcony was built supported on steel and concrete with girders from the Leicester firm of R.C. Searle and Co. Ltd. New seating for 1,170 people was supplied by the Theatre Equipment Co. Ltd of London. Initially, the projectors were the two silent Kalees already installed.

The Prince's cinema, Granby Street, *circa* 1931. *Courtesy C.E. John Aston collection.*

The electrical equipment was installed by F. Webb and Sons and the cinema was the only one in Leicester to use a three-phase supply. Moreover, it was the only one not to have its D.C. generator in the basement. It was placed on a bed of concrete and cork in its own thickly padded and sound-proofed room beside the projection room.

All the doors of the theatre were made of teak. The stairs were steel and the walls of the auditorium were hung with steel sheeting decorated, at the lower level, with an embossed design in bronze and gold. In each of the recesses in the upper walls a panel of trees had been painted. The balconies were gilded and the ceiling was panelled in cream and gold.

Carpeting for the floor of the auditorium and the balcony was rich rose-coloured Wilton with felt under-padding

PRINCES THEATRE,

GRANBY STREET.

TO-DAY AND ALL THE WEEK.

The 100 per cent. All Talking, Singing, Dancing and Colour Picture.

GOLD DIGGERS OF BROADWAY.

IT'S STUPENDOUS.

APPROXIMATE TIMES OF SHOWING:

2-15 4-8 5-45 7-29 9-6

PRICES AS USUAL.

Leicester Mercury February 26th 1930.

supplied by R. Morley and Sons of Leicester. They also supplied the rose-coloured marbled rubber on the entrance steps. Outside the front canopy was decorated with art metal work by the Dryad Company of Leicester. The new manager, Mr Wally Roberts, had been with the ABC organisation at the Newton Picture House, Birmingham.[55]

Above: The Temperance Hall as the Essoldo in the 1950s - but little changed from its days as the Prince's.
Courtesy Carl Jennings Collection.
Left: Leicester Mercury January 25th 1930.

PRINCES
THEATRE
GRANBY STREET.

GRAND OPENING
ON
MONDAY NEXT
JANUARY 27th.
WITH
"WOULD YOU BELIEVE IT"
WITH AN ALL-STAR CAST
AND
MILTON SILLS in
"THE CRASH"

Special Musical Presentations
by
CARTER
and the
PRINCES ORCHESTRA

PRICES 1/- 1/6 2/
Doors open 2.0. Cont. 2.30 to 10.30.
LEICESTER'S NEW LUXURY CINEMA
"THE PRINCES"

The re-opening was attended by the Lord Mayor and Corporation but the films presented were silent, and not of very recent origin. The main film 'Would You Believe It?' was a British comedy directed by and starring Walter Forde. It had been released six months earlier and re-released in October 1929 with a sound track. The supporting film, 'The Crash' starring Milton Sills and Thelma Todd was a somewhat creaky 1928 melodrama from First National, only enlivened in the last reel by a spectacular train wreck.

W.H. Carter and his orchestra left the City Cinema to conduct the Prince's Orchestra. Their last performance at the City had been in the week of January 15th. Leslie James remained at the City to play their newly installed Wurlitzer organ, while George Hunt became the organist at the Prince's.

Their first sound presentation, four weeks later, was 'The Gold-diggers of Broadway'. Since the theatre had been wired for sound with Western Electric from the outset, it is difficult to understand why they didn't re-open with this. It was so popular that its original two-week booking was extended to four weeks, a record for the city. The new sound projectors must have been dual-system, since 'Gold-diggers of Broadway', a lavish Warner Brothers musical in two-colour Technicolor, was presented on Vitaphone discs.

Managerial Changes

Also in January, Mr A.S. Whittaker, the manager of the City Cinema, left Leicester to become manager of the Pavilion, Shepherd's Bush, another P.C.T cinema. He was succeeded by Mr Vernon F. Hill, who came to Leicester from the New Savoy in Grimsby. Mr Hill had joined the Royal Naval Air Service and become a Flying Officer. He had also been connected with the Transatlantic flight of the R34 airship. Away from his duties, he had arranged film shows for the troops. He had also been manager at the Grand, Nottingham. His stay in Leicester was quite brief for, in July, he was appointed to be manager of the new super cinema, the Windsor, being built at Bearwood, Smethwick. His successor at the City was Mr E.D. Hainge.[56]

Wally Roberts' tenure at the Prince's was similarly short. In June he returned to 'the hardware city' to resume his managerial duties at the Bordesley Palace, Birmingham, but two months later, he resigned from the A.B.C. circuit to take up the management of the Tudor Cinema back in Leicester.[57]

More Suburban 'Talkies'

The Tudor Cinema featured its first 'All Talking Week' beginning on February 22nd. The film was United Artists' 'Bulldog Drummond'. From the record books of the cinema that have been deposited in the Leicestershire Record Office, it is possible to see that there were more patrons (1,453) on the Saturday night for the last silent film, Alan Dwan's 'The Far Call', than for the first Saturday of talkies (1,253). In the week as a whole, however, 'Bulldog Drummond' was seen by 6,471 patrons as against 4,800 for the split week of Garbo's 'The Mysterious Lady' and 'The Far Call'.

A lobby card for the first talkie at the Tudor in February 1930. *United Artists.*

In February, too, the Evington had a double bill of the British films 'The Silent House' and 'Noisy Neighbours' - inspired programming for the times! In April it installed Western Electric equipment for showing Bill Boyd in 'The Flying Fool' and a short comedy talkie 'Big-time Charley'. Also included in the programme was John Grierson's silent British documentary 'Drifters'. The reviewer thought that 'the acoustic properties of the Evington were well suited for talkies'.[58] In the same week, Mr F. Griffin, the manager of the Westleigh, also took charge of Western Electric sound equipment. The first talkie, Columbia's social comedy 'The Fall of Eve', was supported by a silent film 'Melody Master'.[59] Mrs Florence Tomlinson, who as Florence Parker was relief pianist at the Westleigh, remembers that the orchestra leader, Horace Gilbert, emigrated to India to lead the Governor of Bombay's orchestra.

Also in April, a special committee was appointed by the City Council to look into the possibility of cinema entertainment at the de Montfort Hall. It was considered that too many alterations to the interior would need to be made and the idea was dropped.[60]

'The Pavilion' Closes

The Pavilion Variety Theatre had changed to showing feature film programmes during its last eighteen months of operation. Its cinematograph licence expired on May 24th 1930 and the theatre closed completely on November 29th 1930. Street improvements in Belgrave Gate necessitated the demolition of the building and George Gray, who had been its manager for twenty five years, became manager of a local public house.[61]

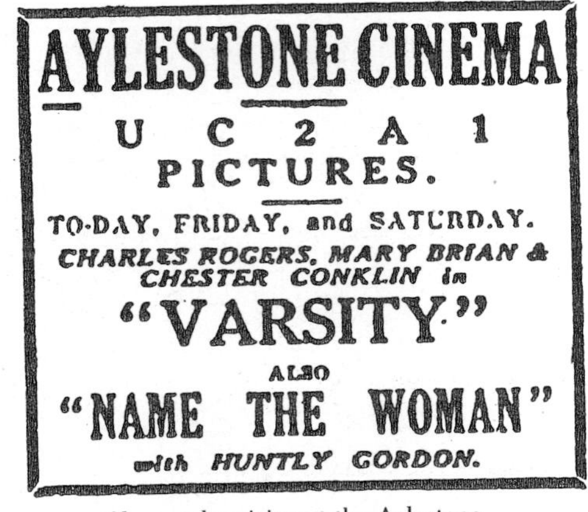

Clever advertising at the Aylestone September 19th 1929.

The Last Outposts of Silence

The Aylestone had not yet converted to sound. Fred Stafford's clever advertising included the line 'Say it Silently - UC2A1 pictures'. In November, it installed British Thompson Houston sound equipment and a new larger screen for showing its first 'talkie' - Vitaphone's 'Paris'.[62] This part-coloured film was the sound debut for Jack Buchanan.

On December 8th the Floral Hall - 'Leicester's Premier Silent House' - capitulated and installed the Picturetone sound system to show a double bill of Warner Brothers talkies. The main feature was 'The Furies', a stagey drama starring H.B. Warner and Lois Wilson, and the second feature had Dorothy Mackail and Basil Rathbone in 'The Flirting Widow'.

'The City of Leicester Official Film' was shown at the Picture House during Christmas week. The *Leicester Mercury* for December 23rd reported that the film gave 'a useful idea of the civic importance of the city and the extent of its chief industries.' It was made for the City Council but no copy appears to have survived.

The Silver Street Cinema Closes

The Silver Street Cinema closed at the end of 1930 owing to the expiry of the lease. It was anticipated that it would be sold to be converted into business premises. The sale took place on March 18th 1931 but no details were given of the purchaser.[63] In later years, the building appears to have been a used as a dance hall.

The Hippodrome installed B.T.H. sound equipment at about this time and the High Street cinema was now the only city centre cinema without sound. Its advertising carried the slogan 'This House is still silent'. Pride was taken n employing sound effects and a synchronised musical score, especially when they replayed classics such as the Lon Chaney version of 'The Phantom of the Opera'.[64]

The special season of silent classics continued with Buster Keaton's 'The General' and 'Steamboat Bill Junior' and Valentino's 'Son of the Sheik'. In March 1931 it closed for redecoration and the installation of Western Electric sound equipment. Mr R.M. Wright, who was also the proprietor of the Picturedrome, Mere Road, had obtained a ten-year lease on the building. The re-opening on 14th May featured the R.K.O. wartime spy film 'Inside the Lines' starring Betty Compson and Ralph Forbes. Shortly afterwards the cinema was renamed 'The Arcadia'.[65]

Mr Wright, a keen and vocal member of the local C.E.A. committee, had been campaigning for several years for the legal banning of 'stink bombs' in cinemas. He had caused several young offenders to be arrested by the police but, since there was no appropriate bye-law, prosecutions did not follow. In January 1931 the City Council passed the required bye-law that made the use of stink bombs in cinemas an indictable offence, carrying a £5 penalty.[66]

The *Bioscope* reported that 1931 had opened 'under rather trying circumstances with trade only moderate and little spare money floating around.' It was sufficient to keep the local cinemas 'marking time' and several of the down town cinemas were drawing full houses.[67]

'The Palace' becomes a cinema

Sir Oswald Stoll had decided that the Palace would cease to be a Variety Theatre and convert entirely to film performances. The manager, Mr J. Lort, gave the musicians a fortnight's notice and a new Western Electric sound projector was installed. Throughout 1930 the Palace had been regularly showing films in the afternoon and live variety in the evening. There had been earlier speculation that the Stoll circuit were planning to build a super cinema in Leicester. This proposition had now been abandoned.[68]

The Palace with the projection box in the upper circle. *Courtesy Leicester Mercury.*

Sydney Parsons, manager of the Prince's, Granby Street, in 1931.
Courtesy Mrs L. Hall.

The Prince's Cinema celebrated its first anniversary with the presentation of 'All Quiet on the Western Front.' The manager of six months, Mr Sydney Parsons, had made a great success of the cinema for A.B.C.. He was a Leicester man returning after sixteen years. He had been one of Leicester's first Boy Scouts. In the war he had served in Belgium with a Leicester battery of the Artillery, the 147th. He had considerable experience as an actor, a singer and a musical comedy producer. Most recently, he had been, for five years, the leasee and general manager of the Lyric Theatre, Limerick. Whilst in Ireland, he had also done some successful exploitation work for Universal Pictures. Later in the year, with Mr Parsons as area supervisor, the ABC circuit negotiated the control of the Melbourne. Mr Gilbert Boddy, who had taken over from Mr Dacre in March 1930, remained as manager. A Turner sound screen and a new Western Electric sound system replaced the previous fitments.[69]

The H.D.M. circuit made some administrative changes. Mr Harry Barker, a hard working member of the local C.E.A., left the Shaftesbury to go to the Tower Cinema at Broughton, Manchester. He was succeeded by Mr L. Wynne of Manchester. Mr Charles Meads of the Sovereign and Mr A.A. Forknall of the Coliseum changed places.[70]

Watch Committee pass banned Russian Film

The silent Russian Film 'Mother' had been refused a certificate by the B.B.F.C. on the grounds that 'its scene was Russia, that its action concerned a strike, and that forces of order were depicted firing on a mob'. After many protests the censor's personal view was somewhat amended but he still refused to pass the film. The reviewer in the *Bioscope* clearly recognised the Governmental

A poster for the original London screening of 'Mother'.
Courtesy National Film Archive.

pressures. He wrote: 'Though it has been banned by the censor on political grounds, it failed to evoke in me a desire to rush out and burn Regent Street.'[71] On 27th June 1930, after viewing the film, the Leicester Watch Committee passed it for showing as an 'A' film at the Floral Hall.

The difficulties encountered in the showing of 'foreign' films, especially those from the Soviet block, had encouraged the founding of the Film Society Movement. First indications of a film society in Leicester occurred during 1929. The Society was founded on April 28th 1931 and the first season began in the Vaughan Working Men's College on October 10th.[72]

A foreign language had given the Watch Committee a problem in January 1931. Maurice Chevalier was booked to appear at the de Montfort Hall for one matinee and one evening performance, but permission had been refused for certain of his songs to be sung in French. 1,000 people had turned up for the matinee but no amount of persuasion by the promoters would induce the Chief Constable to go against the ruling of the Watch Committee. Both performances were abandoned.[73]

A New Era

The cinema industry had reached another transitional stage. It had developed from a scientific curiosity to a major popular art form. In its new mode it would once again devise its own conventions. Silent cinema would be mourned briefly, but acoustic improvements would soon banish all opposition. Three-colour Technicolor would brighten the screen and defeat all rivals for more than a decade and new cinemas would serve the city well for the next thirty years.

The 1930 census had revealed that Leicester had a population of 239,111. With 20 cinemas this worked out at approximately 1 cinema per 12,000 persons. According to the *Bioscope* reviewer, this meant that there was room for another two cinemas.[74] These would shortly be forthcoming. A site had been secured and plans were being prepared by G.H. Scarborough for a cinema at Wigston Road, Clarendon Park to be called 'The Knighton Kinema'. It would eventually open in 1934. Messrs. R.M. Wright and C.E. West were also named in the proposals.[75]

The Trocadero

Plans for a new style of cinema, just beyond the tram terminus at the junction of Scraptoft Lane and Uppingham Road, had been approved in 1930.[76] It was to have a seating capacity of 2,000 and a stage that could be used for variety acts and small theatrical productions. Adjoining the cinema would be a café and a large ballroom with accommodation for 500 people. There would also be a free car park with room for 500 cars. This entertainment complex would occupy three acres and was expected to cost £45,000 to complete (later reports put the cost between £60,000 and £70,000). The enterprise was being promoted and constructed by the builder Bert Cole to the plans prepared by Herbert Langham F.R.I.B.A. of Manchester. Mr Cole was also managing director of the Aylestone Cinema.[77]

Trevor Jones, manager of the Trocadero.
Kinematograph Weekly.

Trevor M. Jones was appointed manager. He had previously been at the Super in Oxford for six and half years. He had started in the industry as a 'rewind-boy' and worked his way to the top.[78] He was also an accomplished musician and he had wide experience as a stage manager.

The opening of the Trocadero on October 1st 1931 was a sensation. The Lord Mayor, Councillor H. Carver, J.P., was in attendance. It had originally been announced that Jessie Matthews and Sonnie Hale would be present too but instead there was a personal appearance by 'the attractive British Film Star, Dodo Watts', who

The Trocadero in 1963. *Courtesy Leicester Mercury.*

had just appeared in the Maurice Elvey colour film 'The School for Scandal' and who was under contract to British International Pictures. She, it seems, almost missed the occasion by going to Victoria Station instead of St Pancras for the Leicester train.

Miss Dodo Watts in the grounds of Scraptoft Hall before the opening of the Trocadero. *Courtesy Leicester Mercury.*

Over 1,000 patrons, including many with complementary tickets, could not gain admission. The *Leicester Mail* reported that crowds began to gather long before the opening time and that when the cinema was full those left outside attempted to push their way in. The police were powerless to control them and in his own attempts at control, Bert Cole 'was divested of his gold watch and chain'. Fortunately, these were returned to him the next day.

Inside the theatre every seat was taken and there was a loud cheer when the Lord Mayor made his appearance. Miss Dodo Watts received a rousing reception when she was introduced and she congratulated Mr Cole upon the beauty of the cinema. The Lord Mayor, in declaring the cinema open, said that Mr Cole had shown courage and enterprise in providing the people of Humberstone and district with one of the most beautiful cinemas in the city. The Lady Mayoress and Miss Watts were presented with a bouquet each by the children of Mrs Myhill and with a basket of flowers by Mr Cole's daughter Gwen.

The *Mercury* described the cinema as 'a spacious-looking red-brick building, and not at all out of tone with the neighbourhood. Alpine gardens surround it,

and provide a dash of colour against the red-brick work. The gardens themselves are worth seeing.' The report goes on to describe the new ventilating system which could either cool or warm the air whilst it was being filtered.

The interior decor was very colourful as the ceilings and roof had been painted to create a sunset effect. There was ample room between the rows of seats. Carpeting the auditorium alone cost £1,000. The entrance hall resembled the lounge of an expensive hotel with a marble terrazzo floor set with a large star.[79]

The opening film was 'Toast of the Legion', the Technicolor Musical comedy starring Bernice Claire and Walter Pidgeon. It was made by Warner Brothers under the title of 'Kiss Me Again' and it was based upon the Victor Herbert operetta 'Madamoiselle Modiste'. On the stage there was Georges Durante in a 'sensational wire act' and entertainers, the Haden-Herbert Four. Jimmy Campbell and his band provided the music.

Prices of admission were 2/- (10p), 1/6d ($7^1/_2$p), 9d (4p) and 6d ($2^1/_2$p). In the first nine days, 35,000 patrons paid for admission.[80] The cinema was open from 2.30 p.m. until 10.30 p.m. A change of programme was normal on Thursdays with the variety acts booked for the whole week.

The second week's offering was a double feature of Victor McLaglen in 'Three Rogues', the British title for the film 'Not Exactly Gentlemen', and Joan Bennett in 'Doctors' Wives'. Thursday's programme change included the British farce 'Plunder' starring Tom Walls and Ralph Lynn.

December 31st 1931

Although there were 21 cinemas in Leicester on the last day of 1931, only 13 of them advertised their programmes in the *Leicester Mercury*. The offered fare of these provides an interestign reflection on the cinema industry. Of the fifteen films listed, eleven were American and four British. Only two cinemas, both in the city centre, were showing a double feature. The Palace had a film programme supplemented by the performances of Miss Elsa Groocock's ballet school. Three of the city centre cinemas were showing their programmes for the whole week, a factor linked to the festive season rather than the strength of the programme.

With the opening of the Trocadero, the modern super cinema had arrived in Leicester. The thirties would see a profusion of grand palaces; The New Coliseum, The Carlton, The Fosse, The Knighton, The Roxy, The Regal, The Savoy and The Odeon. Their story covers the second era of cinema in Leicester and requires another volume and another teller.

PRINCES'
ALL THIS WEEK
Douglas Fairbanks
and BEBE DANIELS in
REACHING FOR THE MOON
'The Flying Fool'
KINEMA CARNIVAL JANUARY

AYLESTONE CINEMA
TO-DAY, FRIDAY, and SATURDAY
EVELYN LAYE and JOHN BOLES
in
'One Heavenly Night'

WESTLEIGH
"CIMARRON"
A GREAT PICTURE

LITTLE THEATRE
THIS WEEK
An Original Christmas Entertainment for Children & Grown-ups.

EVINGTON
TO DAY.
THE SPECKLED BAND
By Sir Arthur Conan Doyle.
Nancy Price, Lyn Harding, Angela Baddeley and Raymond Massey.
Free Car Park

CINEMA BALLROOM CAR PARK CAFE
MEET ME AT THE
TROCADERO
TO DAY, FRIDAY, and SATURDAY.
RICHARD BARTHELMESS
'THE FINGER POINTS'
ON VARIETY STAGE
4 DANCING MIDDIES,
'LES BEAUCAIRES.'
JIMMY CAMPBELL and HIS BAND

FLORAL HALL
PICTURE THEATRE
CLIVE BROOK BUDDY ROGERS RICHARD ARLEN and FAY WRAY
in
"THE LAWYER'S SECRET."
Also
"I TAKE THIS WOMAN."
GARY COOPER and CAROLE LOMBARD
PARAMOUNT SOUND NEWS

BOULEVARD PALACE
SKATING —TWICE DAILY— —2.30 and 7.30—
CARNIVAL NIGHT, TO-NIGHT. — 7.30 till 12.30. —
FANCY HATS, STREAMERS, NOVEL-

OLYMPIA
THURSDAY, FRIDAY, SATURDAY.
GEORGE ARLISS in
"THE MILLIONAIRE,"

SHAFTESBURY, Overton Rd
THURSDAY, FRIDAY, SATURDAY.
GEORGE ARLISS in
"THE MILLIONAIRE."

SOVEREIGN CINEMA,
THURSDAY, FRIDAY, SATURDAY.
"LET'S LOVE & LAUGH."

COLISEUM THEATRE
THURSDAY, FRIDAY, SATURDAY.
"ADVENTURES IN AFRICA"
"THE RINGER."

PICTURE HOUSE
GRANBY STREET
ALL THIS WEEK
'SKIPPY,'
with Jackie Cooper & Robert Coogan.
COMEDY, INTEREST, and CARTOON.
Next Week: "DADDY LONG LEGS."

The PLAYHOUSE EAST ST LEICESTER
LEICESTER'S REPERTORY THEATRE.
7.30 TO-NIGHT. 7.30

CITY CINEMA
A Stupendous Holiday Programme!
SYDNEY HOWARD — JOAN WYNDHAM
'UP FOR THE CUP.'
ALSO
HELEN TWELVETREES in 'A WOMAN OF EXPERIENCE.'
Soon. "DADDY LONG LEGS"

ARCADIA
HIGH STREET
TO-DAY, FRIDAY, and SATURDAY
'The Criminal Code'

LEICESTER PALACE
'RANGO,'
LAUREL & HARDY
'Stout Hearts and Willing Hands.'
GROOCOCK

OPERA HOUSE
TWICE DAILY.

Leicester Mercury December 31st 1931

Reference Guide to Some Leicester Cinemas

Some opening and closing dates are approximate.

'*': Building still remains in part or whole.

More than one figure may be given for seats as, at various times, the seating capacity was changed by rebuilding and by re-seating.

Cinema	Opening Date	Closing Date	Seats	
*Aylestone	21.8.26	27.7.68	1206	
Belgrave	19.3.13	30.4.60	720	760
*Belvoir Picture Playhouse	17.12.12	1915	207	
*Boulevard		30.7.10	1917	600
*Carlton, Gypsy Lane	5.8.34	25.5.68	1304	
*City	3.11.24	11.4.64	2000+	2023
reopened as Odeon	12.10.64	1967		
rebuilt for Cinerama	1967	31.5.75	772	
*New Coliseum	4.11.33	1968	1000	
*Old Coliseum	c.19.3.12	2.11.33	1900	
*Empire, Wharf Street	20.6.08	1915	1000	
*Empress, Belvoir Street	16.6.10	10.1910	207	
Empress, Mere Road	19.4.10	10.1910	420	
*Evington	16.10.16	28.4.79	978	
Floral Hall	26.12.10	2.1959	722	900
*Fosse	28.9.36	8.81	998	
*High Street (Electric)	26.8.10	21.8.15	700	
Imperial Playhouse	21.8.15	1922		
High Street (again)	1922	1931		
Arcadia	1931	1940s	780	
Cameo (Continental)	1949	1968		
Classic/Cameo	1968	c.1975	608	
*Hippodrome, Wharf Street	13.3.22	1940s	750	850
*Imperial, Green Lane Road	5.12.12	10.6.61	460	700
(re-opened as an Asian Cinema until 1982)				
*King's Hall	29.7.15	31.12.21	700	
as The Scala	1.1.22	8.9.28		
Knighton Kinema	1937	30.11.63	1291	
*Lyric, Knighton	13.2.13	1916	500	

*Melbourne	4.5.20	1970(?)	944	941
(as an Asian Cinema)	1979	1980		
*Odeon	29.7.38	Still open	2182	
Olympia	6.3.13	1959	1504	800
Palace (Variety Theatre)	17.6.01	1931	1089	
(Cinema)	1931	1937	1883	
	1938	1946	1568	
	Closed altogether 21.2.59			
Pavilion	1.1.10	24.5.30		
Picturedrome, Mere Road	1.1.12	?1942	420	700
Picture House	22.12.10	5.5.24	700	950
rebuilt	2.8.24	4.1973	1626	
*Regal	16.11.36	30.5.59	1080	
*Roxy	3.8.36	10.8.68	1800	
*Savoy	1937	Still open as Cannon		
*Shaftesbury	8.10.14	13.8.62	830	
Silver Street Cinema	19.7.10	late 1930	650	1000
(The Grand Electric Palace)				
*Sovereign	22.12.19	14.1.61	900	
Star	6.8.14.	1958	800	960
Temperance Hall (shows)	1.1.10	1911		
(Metropolitan Pictures)	1.1.13	1914	1000	
(Cinema de Luxe	1.9.15	23.4.27		
(Princes)	2.1.31	1950s	1170	
(Essoldo)	1950s	2.7.60		
Trocadero	1.10.31	1963	2131	
*Tudor	21.4.14	12.7.58	975	1250
*West's, Cank St.	12.1907	4.1909		
Westleigh	15.2.26	9.5.64	1334	

Notes to Chapter One.
The beginnings. Pages 1 - 28

1. Wood (1947) page 89.
2. Wood (1947) page 89.
3. Barnes (1976) page 86.
4. Wood (1947) page 96.
5. Wood (1947) page 101.
6. The handbill was described in the *Leicester Mercury* Nov 8th 1924 but, sadly, not illustrated.
7. Barnes (1976) page 146 and illustration.
8. Barnes (1976) appendix 1.
9. Barnes (1976) page 101. Paul's Theatrograph was also known as the Animatographe, under which name it was advertised at the Opera House, Leicester.
10. *Leicester Daily Post* Dec 25th 1896
11. *Leicester Daily Post* Dec 29th 1896.
12. Barnes (1988) page 219 and *Leicester Mercury* Nov 4th 1924.
13. *Leicester Daily Post* Feb 2nd 1897 and *Leicester Daily Mercury* Feb 2nd 1897.
14. Barnes (1988) page 218.
15. *Leicester Daily Post* Feb 2nd 1897.
16. *Leicester Daily Post* Feb 2nd 1897.
17. *Leicester Journal* Mar 19th 1897; the Catalogue of Leicester Commemorative Exhibition, 1897 page 106 and Barnes (1976) page 12.
18. *Leicester Daily Post* Sept 7th 1897.
19. Barnes (1983) page 49.
20. *Leicester Daily Post* Dec 24th 1897.
21. Barnes (1983) page 229 and R.W. Paul's *Catalogue 1898* [National Film Archive]. 'The Clock Tower, Leicester' 40 ft; 'London Road, Leicester' 40 ft. (It is quite possible that this is actually the Granby Street item, wrongly titled by Paul, but recognised correctly by the local reviewer.); 'Pantomime Rehearsal' 40 ft.; 'Shovelling Snow at Leicester' 20 ft.
22. *Leicester Daily Post* Jan 3rd 1898.
23. *Leicester Daily Post* Aug 23rd 1898.
24. *Leicester Daily Post* July 3rd 1900.
25. *Leicester Daily Post* Oct 1st 1900.
26. *Leicester Daily Post* Apr 12th 1898.
27. *Leicester Daily Post* Apr 12th 1898.
28. Barnes (1983) page 143.
29. *Leicester Daily Post* Apr 19th 1898.
30. Barnes (1983) page 144.
31. *Leicester Daily Post* Apr 19th 1899.
32. *Leicester Daily Post* Oct 2nd 1900.
33. Barnes (1976) page 172.
34. *Leicester Daily Post* May 7th 1901.
35. Barnes (1983) pages 28-33.
36. *Leicester Daily Post* Apr 2nd 1901.
37. *Leicester Daily Post* June 25th 1901.
38. Barnes (1988) page 80.
39. *Leicester Daily Post* Aug 6th 1901.
40. Barnes (1983) page 155.
41. *Leicester Daily Post* June 25th 1901.
42. *Leicester Daily Post* Dec 31st 1901.
43. *Leicester Daily Post* Feb 18th 1902.
44. Gifford (1986).
45. *Leicester Daily Post* Mar 11th 1902.
46. *Leicester Daily Post* Mar 18th 1902.
47. *Leicester Daily Post* June 30th 1902.
48. *Leicester Daily Post* Apr 1st 1902.
49. John Barnes in letter to author, Feb 1992.
50. *Leicester Daily Post* Aug 19th 1902.
51. Gifford (1986) ref.00520.
52. *Leicester Daily Post* Oct 28th 1902.
53. *Leicester Daily Post* Dec 6th 1902.
54. *Leicester Daily Post* Jan 26th 1903 (An R.W. Paul Film).
55. *Leicester Daily Post* July 7th 1903.
56. *Leicester Daily Post* Oct 12th 1903.
57. Gifford (1986) ref.00705.
58. Mellor (1971) page 21.
59. *Leicester Daily Post* Apr 5th 1904.
60. Mellor (1971) page 23.
61. *Leicester Daily Post* Dec 12th 1904.
62. *Leicester Daily Post* Apr 19th 1904.
63. Coe (1981) page 112.
64. *Leicester Daily Post* Sep 14th 1905.
65. *Leicester Daily Post* Nov 28th 1905.
66. Low and Manvell (1948) page 109.
67. Low and Manvell (1948) page 108.
68. *Leicester Daily Post* Sep 25th 1906.
69. Mellor (1971) page 18 and Anderson (1983) pages 16 and 32.

70. Low (1948) page 265.
71. *Leicester Daily Post* May 22nd 1906.
72. Gifford (1986) ref. 01387 and 01422.
73. *Leicester Daily Post* Apr 2nd 1907.
74. Coe (1981) page 94.
75. *The Kinematograph and Lantern Weekly* Aug 8th 1907.
76. *Leicester Daily Post* May 14th 1907.
77. *Leicester Daily Post* Aug 6th 1907.
78. *Leicester Daily Post* Dec 31st 1907.
79. *Leicester Daily Post* Oct 29th 1907 and Gifford (1986) ref. 01697.
80. *Leicester Pioneer* Oct 28th 1907.
81. Coe (1981) page 95.
82. *Leicester Daily Post* Jan 5th 1909.
83. *Leicester Daily Post* Dec 19th 1904.

Chapter Two.

Finding a home. Pages 29 - 67.

1. Author's interview with Mr Charles E. West at the Evington Cinema on March 5th 1956. He is also known to have given the date as December 1906. There is no documentary evidence concerning the opening date. The earliest trade reference to 'West's Pictures' is in the *Bioscope* December 30th 1909. Mr West was not able to show me any memorabilia although during this interview he made the small sketch of the appearance of the front of the premises.
2. Leicester Daily Post Feb 3rd 1908 and Gifford (1986) ref. 01405.
3. *Leicester Daily Post* June 20th 1908
4. *Leicester Daily Post* Oct 10th 1908
5. *The Bioscope* Nov 25th 1909.
6. *The Bioscope* May 20th 1909
7. *Leicester Daily Post* Sep 15th 1908
8. *Leicester Daily Post* May 12th 1908. A review of the Palace programme
9. *Leicester Daily Post* Sep 18th 1909.
10. Mr C. West, interview 1956.
11. Leicester Watch Committee minutes 1910, paras. 255, 516 & 517.
12. *Kinematograph and Lantern Weekly* Mar 24th and 31st 1910.
13. Leicester Watch Committee minutes 3 May 1910; *Kinematograph and Lantern Weekly* Apr 28th 1910; *Leicester Pioneer* Apr 23rd 1910
14. Mr C. West, interview 1956.
15. Leicestershire Record Office plans 15511.
16. *The Bioscope* Oct 6th 1910.
17. *Leicester Pioneer* Apr 23rd 1910.
18. *Kinematograph and Lantern Weekly* Apr 7th and 14th 1910.
19. Leicester Watch Committee minutes June 18th 1910.
20. Leicestershire Record Office plan 15360, Mar 1910.
21. *Kinematograph and Lantern Weekly* June 23rd 1910.
22. *The Bioscope* Oct 6th 1910.
23. *Kinematograph and Lantern Weekly* June 23rd and *The Bioscope* June 30th 1910.
24. *Leicester Pioneer* June 25th 1910.
25. Author's interview with Mr Gilbert, Roxy Cinema, 1956.
26. *The Bioscope* Oct 6th 1910.
27. *Kinematograph and Lantern Weekly* Feb 2nd and 16th and Mar 30th 1911.
28. *The Bioscope* May 4th 1911.
29. Leicester Watch Committee minutes July 4th 1910.
30. Leicester Watch Committee minutes July 19th 1910.
31. *Leicester Pioneer* June 25th 1910.
32. Thomas (1969) page 31.
33. *Leicester Daily Post* June 21st 1910.
34. Author's interview with Mr Gilbert, Roxy Cinema, 1956.
35. Leicestershire Record Office plans 15534 1.4.1910.
36. *Leicester Daily Mercury* July 26th 1910.
37. *Leicester Daily Mercury* July 29th 1910.
38. *Kinematograph and Lantern Weekly* Aug 18th 1910.
39. Thomas (1969) page 18.
40. Low (1948) page 101.
41. *Kinematograph and Lantern Weekly* Aug 4th and 18th 1910.
42. *Leicester Pioneer* Apr 8th and 15th 1911

43. Leicestershire Record Office plan 15464 1.3.1910; Leicester Watch Committee minutes July 19th 1910.
44. *Leicester Daily Mercury* July 29th 1910.
45. *Leicester Daily Mercury* July 30th 1910.
46. *Leicester Pioneer* Aug 20th 1910.
47. *Leicester Pioneer* Aug 27th 1910.
48. *The Bioscope* Aug 26th 1910.
49. *Leicester Daily Mercury* July 5th 1910.
50. Leicestershire Record Office plan 15515 1.4.10.
51. *Kinematograph and Lantern Weekly* Dec 1st 1910.
52. *The Bioscope* Aug 26th 1910.
53. *The Bioscope* Mar 18th and Oct 14th 1909.
54. *Leicester Pioneer* Aug 27th 1910.
55. *Leicester Daily Post* May 10th 1910. On its letterhead, it is called The Provincial Cinematograph Theatres Ltd., but in many local reports and in the trade press it is also referred to as the Provincial Cinematograph Company.
56. *Kinematograph and Lantern Weekly* June 9th 1910.
57. *Kinematograph and Lantern Weekly* July 7th 1910.
58. *Leicester Daily Post* Dec 23rd 1910
59. The wife of Sir William Bass, the chairman of the company.
60. Caryatids are draped female supporting figures.
61. *Leicester Daily Post* Dec 23rd 1910.
62. *Leicester Daily Post* Dec 15th 1910.
63. *Kinematograph and Lantern Weekly* Oct 6th and Dec 22nd 1910.
64. There is no record in the Watch Committee minutes minutes of the granting of a licence to the Floral Hall for December 1910 but the twelve month licence was renewed on December 26th 1911.
65. *Leicester Daily Post* Jan 1st 1911 and *Kinematograph and Lantern Weekly* Jan 5th 1911.
66. *The Bioscope* Jan 5th 1911 and *Kinematograph and Lantern Weekly* Jan 5th 1911.
67. *Kinematograph and Lantern Weekly* Feb 11th 1909.

Chapter Three. Finding an audience. Pages 68 - 89.

1. *Leicester Daily Post* Jan 31st 1911 and *The Bioscope* Jan 26th 1911.
2. *Leicester Daily Post* May 6th and July 19th 1911.
3. *Kinematograph and Lantern Weekly* Jan 5th 1911.
4. *Leicester Daily Post* June 21st and June 23rd 1911.
5. *Leicester Daily Post* June 23rd 1911 and *Kinematograph and Lantern Weekly* Jan 5th 1911.
6. *The Bioscope* Feb 16th 1911.
7. Leicester Watch Committee minutes Dec 16th 1913.
8. *Leicester Daily Post* Dec 23rd 1911.
9. Leicester Watch Committee minutes Sep 19th 1911, Feb 6th 1912 and Mar 19th 1912.
10. Brian Hornsey's research established the transition from Belgrave Skating Rink to Coliseum Cinema. Letter to author 1992.
11. *The Bioscope* Dec 19th 1912 .
12. *The Bioscope* Dec 19th 1912.
13. *The Bioscope* May 1st 1913.
14. *The Bioscope* Jan 9th 1913.
15. *Kinematograph and Lantern Weekly* July 7th 1910 .and *The Bioscope* Jan 4th 1912.
16. *Leicester Daily Post* Jan 23rd 1912.
17. *Leicester Daily Post* Mar 5th 1912.
18. *Leicester Daily Post* June 11th 1912.
19. *Leicester Daily Post* June 18th 1912.
20. *Leicester Daily Post* June 19th 1912.
21. *Leicester Daily Post* Aug 15th 1912.
22. Leicestershire Record Office plans 17491, 20.9.1912; Leicester Watch Committee minutes Dec 3rd 1912; *The Bioscope* Dec 19th 1912.
23. *The Bioscope* Jan 30th 1913.

24. Leicester Watch Committee minutes Dec 17th 1912; *The Bioscope* Jan 30th and July 3rd 1913.
25. Low (1948) page 115.
26. *Leicester Pioneer* Dec 28th 1912.
27. Leicestershire Record Office plans 17851 28.1.1913.
28. Leicester Watch Committee minutes Aug 26th 1910 and Feb 14th 1913.
29. *The Bioscope* Feb 20th 1913.
30. *The Bioscope* Feb 20th and Mar 6th 1913.
31. *The Bioscope* July 24th 1913.
32. Leicester Watch Committee minutes Sep 28th 1912; *The Bioscope* Oct 17th 1912.
33. Leicestershire Record Office plans 17585 28.10.1912.
34. *The Bioscope* Mar 13th 1913.
35. *The Bioscope* Oct 16th 1913.
36. *Leicester Daily Post* Dec 21st 1912.
37. *The Bioscope* July 10th, Aug 21st and Sep 11th and 25th 1913.
38. *Leicester Daily Post* Jan 1st 1913.
39. *The Bioscope* Oct 9th 1913.
40. An actual programme at the Picture House in March 1913. All films shown were released on March 20th 1913.
41. *Leicester Daily Post* Jan 17th 1913.
42. *Leicester Daily Post* Mar 10th 1913.
43. *The Bioscope* Oct 2nd 1913.
44. Leicester Watch Committee minutes Mar 19th 1912.
45. Leicester Watch Committee minutes Dec 11th 1912.
46. *Leicester Daily Post* Aug 31st 1912.
47. *Leicester Daily Post* Aug 12th 1913.
48. *Leicester Daily Post* Sep 16th 1913.
49. e.g. *Leicester Daily Post* Sep 30th 1913.
50. Leicester Watch Committee minutes Dec 18th 1912 and Apr 21st 1914.
51. Leicestershire Record Office plans 17819, 14.2.1913; copy of plans 27.2.12.
52. Leicester Watch Committee minutes July 1st 1913, June 15th 1914 and July 7th 1914.

Chapter Four.

The war years. Pages 90 - 129.

1. *The Bioscope* Aug 7th 1912, Jan 1st and 8th and May 28th 1914.
2. Leicester Watch Committee minutes April 21st, 1914. Leicestershire Record Office plan 17819, 14.2.1913.
3. *The Bioscope* Jan 29th 1914.
4. Leicester Watch Committee minutes Jan 28th 1914. Leicestershire Record Office plan 18647, 1.1.1914; *The Bioscope* Jan 13th 1916.
5. Leicester Watch Committee minutes Oct 6th 1914. Leicestershire Record Office plan 19003 18.5.1914.
6. *The Bioscope* Oct 15th 1914.
7. *Leicester Daily Post* Jan 1st 1914.
8. *Leicester Daily Post* July 20th 1915 and *The Bioscope* June 10th 1915.
9. *The Bioscope* Mar 26th and June 18th 1914.
10. *Leicester Daily Post* Feb 17th and Mar 2nd 1914.
11. *Leicester Daily Post* Mar 16th 1914.
12. *Leicester Daily Mercury* Apr 28th 1914.
13. Low (1948) page 104
14. *Leicester Daily Mercury* May 5th 1914.
15. Gifford (1986) ref.04632 and *The Bioscope* May 7th 1914.
16. *The Bioscope* Apr 9th 1914 and Gifford (1986) ref.03559.
17. *The Bioscope* Oct 1st 1914.
18. *The Bioscope* Mar 5th 1914. Shown as Dennis Godwin in *Leicester Daily Mercury* Sep 21st 1915.
19. *The Bioscope* Feb 19th 1914.
20. *The Bioscope* Apr 9th 1914.
21. *Leicester Daily Post* Apr 11th 1914.
22. *The Bioscope* Oct 15th 1914.
23. *Leicester Daily Post* Aug 4th 1914.
24. *The Bioscope* Aug 20th 1914.
25. *The Bioscope* Aug 27th 1914.
26. *The Bioscope* Sep 3rd 1914.
27. *Leicester Daily Post* Dec 22nd 1914.
28. *The Bioscope* Sep 24th and Dec 3rd 1914.
29. *The Bioscope* Oct 1st 1914.

30. *The Bioscope* Feb 4th 1915.
31. *Leicester Daily Mercury* Sep 21st 1915 and Leicester Watch Committee minutes Dec 14th 1914, Mar 16th and Sep 1st 1915.
32. *The Bioscope* Nov 5th 1914.
33. *The Bioscope* Feb 4th 1915.
34. *The Bioscope* May 20th 1915.
35. *The Bioscope* June 10th 1915.
36. *Leicester Daily Post* Feb 23rd 1915 and *The Bioscope* Feb 25th 1915.
37. *Leicester Daily Post* May 11th and July 27th 1915, both at the Floral Hall.
38. *Leicester Daily Post* Jan 26th 1915.
39. *Leicester Daily Post* Feb 9th and Apr 10th 1915.
40. *Leicester Daily Post* June 29th 1915.
41. *Leicester Daily Mercury* Sep 29th 1915.
42. *Kinematograph and Lantern Weekly* Dec 5th 1918.
43. *Leicester Daily Post* May 25th 1915.
44. *The Bioscope* Sep 9th and 23rd 1915.
45. *Leicester Daily Mercury* Sep 30th 1915.
46. *Leicester Daily Mercury* July 29th 1915
47. *Leicester Daily Mercury* Sep 7th 1915.
48. Leicester Watch Committee minutes Jan 1916.
49. Leicester Watch Committee minutes Dec 16th 1913.
50. Leicester Watch Committee minutes Sep 1st 1915.
51. *The Bioscope* Jan 14th 1915.
52. *The Bioscope* July 1st 1915.
53. *The Bioscope* Jan 13th and Oct 6th 1916.
54. *The Bioscope* Mar 18th 1915.
55. *The Bioscope* Feb 4th 1915.
56. Low (1950) page 128.
57. *Leicester Daily Post* Oct 9th and 11th 1915.
58. *Leicester Mercury* Oct 12th 1915 and *Leicester Evening Mail* Oct 12th 1915.
59. *Leicester Evening Mail* Oct 13th 1915 and Low (1950) page 128.
60. Leicester Watch Committee minutes, June 1916.
61. *Leicester Daily Post* Oct 20th 1914.
62. *Kinematograph and Lantern Weekly* Jan 2nd 1918.
63. *Leicester Daily Post* Apr 20th 1915.
64. *Evington Echo* No. 66 Sep 1989, Stanley Goddard.
65. *Leicester Mercury* Oct 17th 1916.
66. *Kinematograph and Lantern Weekly* Oct 27th 1916.
67. *Evington Echo op. cit.*
68. *Kinematograph and Lantern Weekly* Dec 12th 1918.
69. *Evington Echo op. cit.*
70. *Kinematograph and Lantern Weekly* Jan 3rd and 17th 1918.
71. *Kinematograph and Lantern Weekly* Dec 5th 1918 and *The Bioscope* July 3rd 1919.
72. *Leicester Daily Post* Mar 16th 1915.
73. *Leicester Daily Post* Sep 4th 1916.
74. Leicester Watch Committee minutes Feb 28th 1917.
75. The Floral Hall advertised its opening.
76. *Kinematograph and Lantern Weekly* Dec 19th 1918.
77. *Kinematograph and Lantern Weekly* Feb 28th 1918
78. *Kinematograph and Lantern Weekly* Nov 7th 1918.
79. *Kinematograph and Lantern Weekly* Nov 14th 1918.
80. *Leicester Daily Post* Feb 8th 1916.
81. *Leicester Daily Post* Feb 11th 1918.
82. *Leicester Daily Post* Aug 20th 1918.
83. *Leicester Daily Post* Jan 23rd 1917.

Chapter Five. Post-war period. Pages 130 - 157.

1. *The Bioscope* July 3rd 1919.
2. Leicester Watch Committee minutes Apr 1st and Oct 1st 1919.
3. Leicester Watch Committee minutes May 4th 1920.
4. Leicestershire Record Office plan 20374 7.7.1916.
5. Author's interview in 1956 at the Coliseum Cinema when Mr Trueman Towers was area supervisor for the H.D. Moorehouse Circuit.

6. *The Bioscope* July 3rd 1919 and Dec 16th 1920.
7. *The Bioscope* Dec 29th 1920 and Jan 27th 1921.
8. *The Bioscope* May 26th 1927.
9. *The Bioscope* June 9th and July 21st 1921.
10. *The Bioscope* Dec 1st 1921.
11. *The Bioscope* Mar 3rd 1921.
12. Leicester Watch Committee minutes Mar 7th 1922.
13. Leicester Watch Committee minutes Jan 4th 1922.
14. *Leicester Mercury* Mar 14th 1922 and *The Bioscope* Mar 23rd 1922.
15. *Leicester Mercury* Feb 7th 1922.
16. Leicester Watch Committee minutes Oct 1st 1919 and Dec 2nd 1920 and *The Bioscope* Jan 8th 1920.
17. *The Bioscope* May 11th and June 8th 1922.
18. Leicester Watch Committee minutes July 30th 1919.
19. Leicester Watch Committee minutes Dec 21st 1920 and Jan 26th 1921.
20. Leicester Watch Committee minutes Dec 6th 1921 and *Leicester Mercury* Jan 14th 1922
21. *The Bioscope* Dec 3rd 1920.
22. *The Bioscope* Jan 29th 1920.
23. *The Bioscope* May 13th 1920.
24. *The Bioscope* Feb 10th 1921.
25. Leicester Watch Committee minutes Oct 1st 1920 and *Leicester Pioneer* Oct 4th 1920.
26. Leicester Watch Committee minutes Oct 12th 1920.
27. *Leicester Mercury* June 13th 1922.
28. *Leicester Mercury* July 18th 1922.
29. Leicester Watch Committee minutes Dec 21st 1922.
30. *Leicester Mercury* Jan 1st 1923 and *The Bioscope* Nov 2nd and 9th 1922.
31. Leicester Watch Committee minutes Sept 8th 1922.
32. Brownlow (1990), pages 58-69, discusses both these films in detail.
33. The presentation at the Association Hall on Apr 11th 1921 is prefaced with 'a return visit'.
34. Leicester Watch Committee minutes Dec 6th 1923 and Oct 29th 1924.
35. *Leicester Pioneer* Nov 29th 1920.
36. *Leicester Mercury* Nov 28th 1922
37. *Leicester Mercury* Oct 24th 1923.
38. *The Bioscope* Feb 9th 1922.
39. *Leicester Mercury* July 7th 1923.
40. *Leicester Mercury* Apr 12th 1921.
41. *Leicester Mercury* Apr 23rd 1923.
42. *Leicester Evening Mail* Apr 14th 1919 and McKernan (1992).
43. *The Bioscope* Aug 23rd 1923 and *Leicester Mercury* Aug 25th 1923.
44. *Leicester Mercury* Oct 2nd 1922.
45. *The Bioscope* Apr 5th 1923.
46. *Leicester Mercury* Apr 30th 1923.
47. *Leicester Mercury* Jan 31st 1922.
48. *The Bioscope* July 3rd 1919
49. *Leicester Daily Mail* Mar 15th 1919; *Leicester Mercury* Jan 26th 1923; *The Bioscope* Jan 18th and Mar 8th 1923; and *Kinematograph Weekly* Mar 13th 1919.
50. *Leicester Mercury* Oct 11th 1921.
51. *The Bioscope* Aug 23rd and Sep 13th 1923.
52. Low (1971) page 281.
53. Low (1971) page 126; Cooper (1987) page 76.
54. *Leicester Mercury* Dec 27th 1922.
55. *The Bioscope* Jan 12th 1922.
56. *Leicester Mercury* Dec 11th 1922.
57. Thomas (1969) page 38

Chapter Six. The cinema in crisis 1924-28. Pages158 - 195.

1. *Illustrated Leicester Chronicle* Feb 25th 1924.
2. Low (1971) page 72.
3. *Illustrated Leicester Chronicle* May 10th 1924.
4. *Leicester Mercury* Jan 19th 1925.
5. Low (1971) - see references to Bruce-Woolfe.

6. *Leicester Mercury* Feb 14th and 23rd 1924.
7. *Leicester Mercury* Feb 23rd 1925.
8. *Leicester Evening Mail* Nov 23rd 1925.
9. *Illustrated Leicester Chronicle* Nov 6th 1926.
10. *Illustrated Leicester Chronicle* Nov 30th 1927.
11. *Leicester Mercury* Oct 18th 1924.
12. *Illustrated Leicester Chronicle* Nov 27th 1926.
13. *Illustrated Leicester Chronicle* Dec 6th 1927.
14. *Leicester Mercury* Nov 3rd 1924.
15. *Leicester Mercury* Nov 7th 1924.
16. *The Bioscope* Feb 7th 1924.
17. *Leicester Evening Mail* Mar 3st 1925.
18. *The Bioscope* Mar 6th 1924.
19. *Illustrated Leicester Chronicle* Nov 1st 1924.
20. *Kinematograph Weekly* Nov 6th 1924.
21. *Illustrated Leicester Chronicle* Nov 8th 1924.
22. *Leicester Mercury* Nov 4th 1924.
23. Leicester Watch Committee minutes July 29th and Nov 10th 1925 and *Kinematograph Weekly* July 30th 1925.
24. *Illustrated Leicester Chronicle* Aug 3rd 1921.
25. Leicester Watch Committee minutes Sep 1st 1915.
26. Leicester Watch Committee minutes Sep 28th 1923, Jan 7th and 28th 1925.
27. *Kinematograph Weekly* July 30th 1925.
28 *The Bioscope* Aug 6th 1825
29. *Leicester Evening Mail* Jan 11th 1926.
30. *Leicester Evening Mail* July 31st 1925.
31. *Kinematograph Weekly* July 15th 1926.
32. *The Bioscope* July 3rd and Aug 7th 1924.
33. *Leicester Evening Mail* Feb 22nd 1926, *The Bioscope* Feb 25th 1926 and Sep 8th 1927.
34. Leicester Watch Committee minutes Dec 7th 1926 and *The Bioscope* Dec 30th 1926.
35. *The Bioscope* Nov 24th 1927.
36. *The Bioscope* Mar 6th 1924 and Oct 30th 1924; author's interview with Fred Trueman Towers at The Coliseum Cinema in 1956.
37. *Kinematograph Weekly* Aug 5th 1926.
38. *The Bioscope* July 27th 1922; *Kinematograph Weekly* May 8th 1924; *The Bioscope* May 22nd 1924.
39. *The Bioscope* Feb 12th 1925.
40. Leicester Watch Committee minutes Sep 30th 1925 and *The Bioscope* Feb 4th 1926.
41. *The Bioscope* July 17th 1919, Oct 7th 1926 and Mar 5th 1930.
42. *The Bioscope* Nov 26th 1925.
43. *The Bioscope* Nov 12th 1925.
44. *The Bioscope* Jan 14th 1926.
45. *The Bioscope* Feb 4th and Apr 1st 1926.
46. *The Bioscope* Apr 23rd 1925.
47. *The Bioscope* Aug 30th 1925.
48. *The Bioscope* May 29th 1924.
49. Author's interview with Mr H. Bates, Leicester, 1958.
50. *The Bioscope* May 13th and 27th 1926.
51. *The Bioscope* May 6th 1926 (Emergency Issue).
52. *The Bioscope Ibid.*
53. *The Bioscope* May 13th 1926 (2nd Emergency Issue).
54. Leicester Watch Committee minutes Oct 28th 1925 & Sep 21st 1926; *The Bioscope* Oct 14th 1926.
55. *The Bioscope* Nov 18th 1926.
56. *The Bioscope* Mar 12th 1927.
57. *The Bioscope* Dec 23rd 1926.
58. *The Bioscope* Feb 4th 1926.
59. *The Bioscope* June 26th 1929 and June 16th 1931.
60. *The Bioscope* Dec 23rd 1926.
61. *The Bioscope* Sep 8th 1927.
62. *The Bioscope* Apr 23rd 1925.
63. *The Bioscope* Mar 13th 1924.
64. *The Bioscope* Jan 1st 1925.
65. *The Bioscope* Mar 19th 1925.
66. *The Bioscope* Apr 23rd 1925.
67. *Leicester Mercury* May 24th 1924.
68. *Leicester Mercury* Jan 18th 1924.
69. *Leicester Mercury* May 1st 1924.

70. *Leicester Mercury* Dec 12th 1924 and *The Bioscope* July 8th 1926.
71. *The Bioscope* Mar 19th 1925.
72. *Leicester Mercury* Oct 12th 1925.
73. *The Bioscope* Mar 20th and Apr 26th 1928. This was 'The Ghost Train' made by Gainsborough for Michael Balcon in Germany with a British cast.
74. *Leicester Mercury* Oct 18th 1925.
75. *Kinematograph Weekly* Aug 20th 1925.
76. *Leicester Mercury* Oct 20th 1925.
77. *Leicester Daily Mail* Dec 12th 1925.
78. Gifford (1986) ref.8207.
79. *Leicester Mercury* Mar 12th 1928.
80. *Leicester Daily Mail* Oct 31st 1925.
81. *Leicester Mercury* Oct 31st 1925.
82. *Illustrated Leicester Chronicle* Oct 24th 1927. The reporter noted the sub-title wrongly. It says 'A Tale of Christ'.
83. Author's interview with Mr Massey, 1956, concerning his time as projectionist at the Belgrave, Shaftesbury and Sovereign cinemas.
84. Low (1971) page 281.
85. *Illustrated Leicester Chronicle* June 19th 1926.
86. *The Bioscope* June 12th 1924.
87. *Leicester Daily Mail* Sep 19th 1925.
88. Leicester Watch Committee minutes Sep 30th 1925.
89. *The Bioscope* Oct 22nd 1925.
90. *The Bioscope* Nov 11th 1926.
91. *The Bioscope* Apr 28th 1927 and Leicester Watch Committee minutes Feb 15th 1927.
92. *The Bioscope* July 7th 1927.
93. *The Bioscope* Apr 5th and Sep 12th 1928.
94. *The Bioscope* Sep 19th and 26th 1928.
95. *The Bioscope* Mar 22nd 1928.
96. *The Bioscope* Mar 17th, Apr 7th and May 19th 1927.
97. Leicester Watch Committee minutes June 16th and July 27th 1927 and *Leicester Mercury* July 30th 1927.
98. *The Bioscope* Oct 27th 1927 and Leicester Watch Committee minutes June 19th 1928.
99. *The Bioscope* Jan 13th 1927 and Jan 12th 1928; Leicester Watch Committe minutes Jan 28th 1928.
100. *The Bioscope* Jan 12th 1928. In the Watch Committee minutes he is recorded as Leonard Swanwick.
101. *The Bioscope* Oct 31st 1928.
102. Leicester Watch Committee minutes Apr 17th 1928; Low (1971) page 66; *The Bioscope* Apr 26th 1928.
103. *The Bioscope* Apr 5th 1928.
104. *The Bioscope* Oct 17th 1928.
105. *Illustrated Leicester Chronicle* Jan 23rd 1926.
106. Low (1971) page 91.
107. *The Bioscope* Aug 4th 1927.

Chapter Seven. O.K. For sound. Pages 196 - 225.

1. Author's interview with Mr Horace Gilbert, Roxy Cinema, 1956.
2. Author's interview with Mr Massey, manager of the Coliseum, 1956.
3. *The Bioscope* Sep 18th 1929.
4. *The Bioscope* Oct 9th 1919.
5. *The Bioscope* Sep 3rd, 1930 .
6. *The Bioscope* May 8th 1929.
7. Letter by Geoffrey B.Hollings, *Leicester Mercury* June 24th 1956.
8. Low (1988) pages 17-19
9. Coe (1981) pages 99 and 105.
10. *Leicester Mercury* Feb 11th 1929.
11. *Leicester Mercury* Mar 9th 1929.
12. *Leicester Mercury* Apr 13th 1929.
13. *The Bioscope* May 1st 1929.
14. *Leicester Mercury* Apr 29th 1929.
15. *Loughborough Echo* Apr 19th 1929.
16. *Loughborough Echo* Apr 26th 1929.
17. Low (1971) pages 203-205.
18. *Loughborough Echo* Nov 29th 1929.
19. *Kinematograph Weekly* Apr 2nd and 11th 1929.
20. *Leicester Mercury* June 22nd 1929.
21. *The Bioscope* Apr 10th 1929.
22. *Leicester Mercury* June 21st 1929.
23. *The Bioscope* July 3rd 1929.

24. Hirschhorn (1979) page 65.
25. *The Bioscope* Aug 7th 1929.
26. *The Bioscope* Oct 22nd 1930.
27. *The Bioscope* July 10th 1929.
28. *The Bioscope* June 10th 1931.
29. *The Bioscope* May 1st 1929.
30. *The Bioscope* June 26th 1929.
31. *Leicester Mercury* June 25th 1929.
32. *Leicester Mercury* June 22 1929.
33. *Illustrated Leicester Chronicle* July 4th 1929.
34. *Illustrated Leicester Chronicle* June 29th 1929.
35. *Leicester Mercury* Sep 3rd 1929.
36. *Illustrated Leicester Chronicle* Aug 10th 1929.
37. *The Bioscope* July 10th, Sep 4th and 11th 1929. The Coliseum, 'The Canning Murders Case'; the Sovereign and the Shaftesbury, 'The Wolf of Wall Street', all in the week beginning Dec 16th 1929.
38. *The Bioscope* Sep 11th 1929 and *Leicester Mercury* Sep 10th 1929.
39. *The Bioscope* July 25th 1928. The latter film was released under the title 'Weekend Wives'.
40. *The Bioscope* Sep 4th 1929.
41. *The Bioscope* Nov 13th 1929.
42. *Leicester Mercury* Nov 26th 1929.
43. *Leicester Mercury* Nov 23rd 1929.
44. *Leicester Mercury* Nov 4th 1929.
45. *The Bioscope* Nov 20th 1929.
46. Brian Hornsey's conversations with Mr A. Maynard jnr, reported in letter to author.
47. *The Bioscope* Jan 15th 1930.
48. *Leicester Mercury* Jan 7th 1930.
49. *Leicester Mercury* Feb 4th 1930.
50. *Leicester Mercury* May 6th 1930.
51. *Leicester Mercury* Dec 2nd 1930.
52. Leicester Watch Committee minutes Feb 15th 1927.
53. *The Bioscope* Nov 7th 1928.
54. *The Bioscope* Nov 14th 1928.
55. *The Bioscope* Jan 29th 1930 and *Kinematograph Weekly* Jan 30th 1930.
56. *The Bioscope* July 30th and Sept 24th 1930.
57. *The Bioscope* July 30th 1930.
58. *Leicester Mercury* Apr 22nd 1930.
59. *The Bioscope* Apr 2nd and 23rd 1930
60. *The Bioscope* Apr 9th 1930.
61. *The Bioscope* May 21st 1930.
62. *The Bioscope* Nov 5th 1930.
63. *The Bioscope* Mar 25th 1931.
64. *Leicester Mercury* Nov 3rd 1930.
65. *Leicester Mercury* May 14th 1931 and *The Bioscope* May 20th 1931.
66. *The Bioscope* Feb 4th 1931.
67. *The Bioscope* Jan 8th 1931.
68. *The Bioscope* June 19th 1929 and Jan 8th 1931.
69. *The Bioscope* Sep 30th and Nov 11th 1931 and *Kinematograph Weekly* Feb 27th 1930.
70. *The Bioscope* Sep 23rd 1931.
71. Low (1971) page 67.
72. Leicester Film Society 100th programme notes Feb 3rd 1951.
73. *The Bioscope* Jan 8th 1931.
74. *The Bioscope* July 15th 1931.
75. *Kinematograph Weekly* Oct 1st 1931.
76. *The Bioscope* June 11th 1930.
77. *Kinematograph Weekly* Oct 8th 1931.
78. *The Bioscope* Sep 16th 1931.
79. *The Bioscope* Oct 7th 1931 and *Leicester Mercury* and *Leicester Evening Mail* Oct 1st 1931.
80. *The Bioscope* Oct 21st 1931.

Bibliography

PRIMARY SOURCES:

Newspapers

Illustrated Leicester Chronicle
Leicester Daily Post
Leicester Evening Mail
Leicester Daily Mercury
(later *Leicester Mercury*)
Leicester Pioneer
Evington Echo

Periodicals

The Bioscope 1908-1932
The Kinematograph and Lantern Weekly 1907-1919
The Kinematograph Weekly 1919-1932.

Yearbooks

Kelly's Directories for Leicester.
Kinematograph Yearbook 1915.

Catalogues

The Leicester Commemorative Exhibition catalogue 1897
R.W. Paul's Catalogue 1898
Gaumont Catalogue 1906
The Edison Kinetogram 1910-13

Official Documents

The Minutes of the Leicester Watch Committee (in Leicestershire Record Office).
Deposited cinema plans (in Leicestershire Record Office).

Author's interviews with managers and projectionists 1955-56

Mr Gick, retired projectionist
Mr Horace Gilbert, manager of the Roxy
Mr Massey, manager of the New Colisuem
Mr Fred Trueman Towers, supervisor for H.D.M. Circuit
Mr Charles E. West, manager of the Evington and partner in the West Scarborough Circuit.

SECONDARY SOURCES

Anderson, Charles, *A City and its Cinemas* , Radcliffe Press, 1983.
Barnes, John *The Beginnings of Cinema in England',* David and Charles, 1976.
Barnes, John *The Rise of the Cinema in Great Britain* Bishopsgate Press, 1983.
Barnes, John *Pioneers of the British Film* Bishopsgate Press, 1988.
Barnes, John *Filming the Boer War* Bishopgate Press, 1992.
Bergan, Ronald *The United Artists Story* Octopus, 1986.
Bird, John H. *Cinema Parade* Cornish Bros., Birmingham. no date.
Blum, Daniel *A Pictorial History of the Silent Screen* Hamlyn, 1953.
Brownlow, Kevin *Behind the Mask of Innocence* Cape, 1990.
Coe, Brian *The History of Movie Photography*, Ash and Grant, 1981
Cooper, Artemis, *The Diana Cooper Scrapbook 1892-1986* Hamish Hamilton, 1987.
Eames, John Douglas *The MGM Story* Octopus Books, 1975.
Eames, John Douglas *The Paramount Story* Octopus Books, 1985.
Gifford, Denis, *The British Film Catalogue 1895-1985*, David and Charles, 1986.
Hirschhorn, Clive *The Universal Story* Octopus Books, 1983.
Hirschhorn, Clive *The Columbia Story* Pyramid Books, 1989.
Hirschhorn, Clive *The Warner Bros. Story* Octopus Books, 1979.
Hunnings, Neville, M. *Film Censors and the Law* Allen and Unwin, 1967.
Leacroft, Helen and Richard *The Theatre in Leicestershire*, Leicestershire Libraries Service, 1986.
Low, Rachel and Roger Manvell *The History of the British Film 1896-1906* Allen and Unwin, 1948.
Low, Rachel *The History of the British Film 1906-1914* Allen and Unwin, 1948.
Low, Rachel *The History of the British Film 1914-1918* Allen and Unwin, 1950.

Low, Rachel *The History of the British Film 1918-1929* Allen and Unwin, 1971.
Low, Rachel *Film making in the 1930s Britain* Allen and Unwin, 1985.
McKernan, Luke *Topical budget* BFI Publishing, 1992.
Mellor, George *Picture Pioneers* Frank Graham, 1971.
Thomas, D.B. *The First Colour Motion Pictures* HMSO, 1969.
Walker, Alexander *The Shattered Silents* Elm Tree Books, 1978.
Wood, Lesley *The Miracle of the Movies* Burke, 1947.

A typical two-projector box of 1913.

Index

David Richard Williams B.A.(Hons) was born in Leicester in 1932. He attended Caldecote Road Junior School, Braunstone, and he was a regular Saturday matinee patron of the Roxy Cinema, Fulhurst Avenue. He was further educated at Alderman Newton Boys' School until 1950. After National Service in the R.A.S.C., he trained as a teacher of History and English at Borough Road College, Isleworth. He became a member of the British Film Institute at this time. He returned to Leicester as a teacher, first at Montrose Junior School and then at Caldecote Road School. He was an active member of the Leicester Film Society and eventually, in 1962, its Secretary. He left Leicester in 1964 to take up a post in Lecturer in Education at Bede College, Durham. In 1966 he was appointed Senior Lecturer in Film and Television at the same college, a post he held until the closure of the College in 1979. He lectured briefly in the School of Education of Durham University and then returned to teaching with mentally handicapped young people. He is married with two grown-up children.